Library of
Davidson College

XLII

AMERICAN COMMERCE

AMERICAN COMMERCE

AS AFFECTED BY THE WARS OF THE FRENCH REVOLUTION AND NAPOLEON

1793-1812

BY

ANNA C. CLAUDER

[1932]

AUGUSTUS M. KELLEY • PUBLISHERS
CLIFTON 1972

First Edition 1932
(*Philadelphia*: Privately Printed, 1932)

Reprinted 1972 by
AUGUSTUS M. KELLEY PUBLISHERS
Reprints of Economic Classics
Clifton New Jersey 07012

I S B N 0 678 00905 8
L C N 68-55509

PRINTED IN THE UNITED STATES OF AMERICA
by SENTRY PRESS, NEW YORK, N. Y. 10013

AMERICAN COMMERCE AS AFFECTED BY THE WARS OF THE FRENCH REVOLUTION AND NAPOLEON, 1793-1812

A THESIS

IN HISTORY

PRESENTED TO THE FACULTY OF THE GRADUATE SCHOOL OF THE
UNIVERSITY OF PENNSYLVANIA IN PARTIAL FULFILLMENT
OF THE REQUIREMENTS FOR THE DEGREE
OF DOCTOR OF PHILOSOPHY

ANNA CORNELIA CLAUDER

PHILADELPHIA
1932

To
My Mother

PREFACE

The political and diplomatic phase of the relations of the United States with England and France during the wars of the French Revolution and Napoleon has often been told—notably by McMaster and Channing, and for the latter part of the period, most completely by Henry Adams.

It seemed worth while, however, to undertake a study of the period from the commercial side, to try to find out just how the American shippers fared, under the bewildering succession of the orders and decrees of the belligerents, which aimed to limit their activities.

For the commercial side of the story, there are five main bodies of material; merchants' letters, court decisions, state papers, customs records and newspapers. The great body of the merchants' letters of the period is found in the historical collections of the New England coast cities, such as Salem and Newport. The county of Essex, Massachusetts, containing the ports of Salem, Newburyport, Marblehead and Beverly, has an especially valuable collection of records. Here we find the fascinating accounts of those romantic early voyages to the far east, and to the northwest coast of North America by the youthful Derbys, Silsbees, and Crowninshields. The cream of these accounts have found their way into print in the publications of the Essex Institute, in the pages of Hunt's Merchant's Magazine, and later in the books of Morison, Peabody, Paine and others. In his Maritime History of Massachusetts, Morison gives a remarkably rich bibliography of lives and voyages of shippers and merchants, a good portion of which fall within our period. Many of these books and monographs are difficult to procure, being out of print, or privately published. I was able to examine nearly all of them, however, which are found in the Library fo Congress. There are still valuable unpublished records in private hands, and Morison laments that many such are probably being destroyed each year as worthless, by otherwise intelligent people. The Newport Historical Society has collections of merchants' letters for the period, some of which have been published by the

Massachusetts Historical Society. Newburyport has published a history of her Marine Society.

In contrast to the voluminous records proudly treasured in New England ports, New York, Philadelphia and the southern cities seem to have had little interest of appreciation for their own beginnings in the far eastern trade. Philadelphia possesses an unrivalled collection (covering trade to Europe and the West Indies, as well as to the East) in the manuscripts of her great merchant, Stephen Girard. Since the publication of Professor McMaster's authoritative life of Girard, access to this collection has unfortunately, by the decision of the Board of City (Philadelphia) Trusts, been closed even to historical students. Through the kindness of Professor McMaster, I was able to examine an abstract of some of this manuscript material.

The merchants' letters still in manuscript, which I have been able to examine are: (1) the collections in the manuscript division of the New York Public Library, including the Jumel and Desobrey Letter Book, the Leroy Bayard and McEwen papers, and the Lawrason and Fowle Correspondence; (2) In the manuscript division of the Library of Congress, I have examined the extensive Ellis-Allan collection, the Taylor-Bourne papers, and the Collins collection; (3) Of the disjecta membra of the Champlin Papers, I have been able to examine three collections; in Newport, letters, books of the firm of Champlin and Robinson, of that city, for the years 1805–1809; in Providence business correspondence of the same firm, and in Boston, still other of the Champlin papers, known as the Wetmore Collection. At Newport, I also went through the extensive correspondence of (4) the firm of Gibbs and Channing for the years 1805–1809, and at Salem, I examined (5) the Derby Family manuscript and Commercial Papers, 1804–1815.

Court decisions, contain excellent and pertinent material on shipping matters. The famous Robinson Reports of the decision of the High Admiralty court in London is, of course, familiar to all students of the period. But the American legal sources have not, I believe, hitherto been extensively tapped. I have used Cranch's Reports for cases in the Federal courts, and have also found much data in the records of cases appealed to the Supreme Courts of the states, notably those of Massachusetts, New York, and Pennsylvania.

These legal records are not altogether satisfactory as sources. They are often provokingly silent as to material facts, such as the exact beginning and termination of a voyage, and the precise restriction of the belligerent government, in the case of seizure, which interfered with its completion. Nevertheless, there are vivid pictures of the commercial ventures of the time and the obstacles which they encountered, such as that of one vessel seized and condemned on five distinct grounds; or that disclosed by the hypothetical question put to the captains, in the famous case of the William Wilson, concerning the journey of that vessel to the north of Europe in 1810.

The American State Papers, Foreign, beside the voluminous diplomatic material, furnish excellent details of commercial ventures. The government received lists of captures and detentions by embargoes, generally from the insurance companies, and the losses were embodied in reports from abroad seeking restitution. The petitions of the merchants setting forth the interference with the traffic by the foreign restrictions is found in the State Papers, Commerce and Navigation. In the same series, the volumes, Finance, contain the reports of the secretary of the Treasury and furnish statistics of export and import.

Consular reports are also valuable, giving the month by month changes in the commercial outlook from such important centers as Hamburg, Amsterdam and Bordeaux.

There appear to be no complete customs records for any American port during the period. The officials of the port of Philadelphia, however, have recently handed over a wealth of early records, giving a part to the University of Pennsylvania, and the remainder to the Historical Society of Pennsylvania. The latter collection has now (1932) been catalogued in part, and is available to students. The customs records preserved in the manuscript division of the Library of Congress, are fragmentary in character.

There is a book which forms a sort of supplement and digest to the state papers on finance and commerce and navigation, which is indispensable to the student of the commerce of the period. This is Timothy Pitkin's *Statistical View*. It contains valuable tables of exports and imports by countries and by commodities over a long period of years. These have been made from unofficial reports, but the material has been arranged in a more convenient and usable form than that of the state papers.

The newspapers of the period, more durable fortunately than their modern successors, are still in existence, and are comparatively easy to read. They give lists of arrivals and departures, of vessels, the ports from which they came, and their destinations. They contain advertisements of foreign goods for sale, and mirror very exactly the rise of the carrying trade before 1807, and the misery of farmers and shippers under the embargo. Letters from private persons in many parts of the world, forwarded to the newspapers by their recipients often shed much light on commercial matters.

This study has grown out of the researches in connection with the seminar in the French Revolution and Napoleonic Period, conducted by Dr. W. E. Lingelbach at the University of Pennsylvania, 1909–1915. Dr. Lingelbach first suggested the study, and I wish to express my great indebtedness to him for encouragement and assistance during its prosecution. Thanks are due also to Dr. Frank Melvin, author of *Napoleon's Navigation System*, and to Dr. Verner Crane, for valuable suggestions; Mr. Victor Hugo Paltsits and Mr. Wilmer Leach of the manuscript division in the New York Public Library and Mr. Wm. Fitzpatrick and Miss Mitchell of the Library of Congress were of great assistance to me in collecting material.

CONTENTS

INTRODUCTION

The First Ten Years of American Commerce following the War of Independence, 1783–1793—Americans excluded from the British Navigation System—Persistence of trade relations between England and the newly freed states—Beginnings of American trade to the Far East—Laws of Congress in regard to commerce—Survey of American foreign trade in 1791.. 15

I

The War between England and France 1793–1801—Its Effect on American Trade—Opening of ports of French colonies to neutrals—British Orders, June and November, 1793—British seizures in West Indies 1794–Petition of American merchants to Congress–The Jay-Grenville Treaty—Work of the Commission—Treatment of American vessels in ports of France—Mission of Monroe—Decrees of Convention—Conditions in Santo Domingo—1795–97—British Seizures 1795—to Peace of Amiens... 27

II

Restrictions of Great Britain upon Neutral Trade 1803–1806—British Blockades, 1803–1806—The Santo Domingo Trade 1803–1806—The Indirect Trade of the United States 1793–1807—The Essex Decision. 51

III

The "Great Guns" of the Belligerents—The Berlin Decree, 1806. Its Application in Holland, Hamburg, and Bremen-American Protest—Order in Council, Jan. 1807 Enemy Coasting Trade forbidden to neutrals—Order of Nov. 1807—No neutral trade with Europe except through British Ports—The Orders in Operation—The Orders as an Economic Weapon—The Milan Decree.............. 92

IV

Jefferson's Policy of Non-violent Coercion—American Commerce on the Eve of the Embargo—Jefferson adopts the policy of non-violent coercion—The Embargo in Operation—The Embargo Abroad—The Embargo as a Diplomatic Weapon........................... 132

V

Repeal of the Embargo—Passage of Non-Intercourse Law,—Trade with England—June—August 1809 (suspension of non-intercourse) Trade under the non-intercourse law—Holland, North Germany and Denmark—Danish Seizures 1809–1810—Trade to Spain, 1809. Smuggled French goods exported through ports of Northern Spain—Trading to the "out ports" after Madison's Proclamation of August 10, 1809—Napoleon's Reprisal for the Non-Intercourse Law—Seizure of American vessels in Spain and Naples—Licenses proposed for American Trade.. 148

VI

The Macon Bill and its Enforcement Against England—Passage of the Macon Bill—Pretended Repeal of the Decrees of Berlin and Milan, by Cadore's letter of Aug. 5, 1810—The Trianon Decree, confiscating American vessels—Trianon Tariff—Baltic Trade 1810—Seizure of the New Orleans Packet—Madison's Proclamation reestablishing non-intercourse with Great Britain, Nov. 2, 1810..................... 182

VII

Repeal of the French Decrees and British Orders—The Mission of Barlow—Petitions for Repeal of Orders—Phillimore's Pamphlet—Repeal of the Orders in Council... 207

VIII

American Commerce—1811–12—Trade to Russia—Trade to Spain—Trade to the West Indies—Meeting of 12th Congress—The Merchants and the War—Conclusion.. 217

RESTRICTIONS OF BELLIGERENTS ON NEUTRAL TRADE
1793–1810

(NOTE: Restrictions of England, France and Spain, 1793 to 1808 inclusive will be found in American State Papers, Foreign III p. 262–292 passim. The following is a compilation based on this résumé and the latter restrictions of these powers and those of other powers from various sources.)

I. RESTRICTIONS OF GREAT BRITAIN.

     1793—March 25—Treaty with Russia
     May 25—Treaty with Spain
     July 14—Treaty with Prussia
     August 30—Treaty with Austria

These all contain clauses providing that no French ships are to enter the ports of these countries and no military or naval stores from them are to enter France. No neutral power, by reason of its neutrality is to give any protection to commerce or property of France.

1793—June 8—Instructions to the commanders of H. M's ships of war and privateers with respect to corn, meal, etc. Vessels with these destined to France shall be sent into England and the supplies purchased by His Majesty's government.

November 6—Detention of neutral vessels laden with French colonial productions. Etc.

1794—January 8—Revocation of last order and enactment of the following Detention shall apply to vessels from French West Indies to Europe or to French property in vessels from islands destined to any port. All vessels for French West Indies laden with military or naval stores to be seized.

1798—January 25—Orders of January 1794 to apply to colonies or settlements of France, Spain and United Provinces.

1799—March 22—Blockade of all ports of Holland. November 27—Suspension of the blockade of Holland.

1803—June 24—Direct trade between neutrals and colonies of enemies not to be interrupted, unless upon outward voyage, contraband supplies shall have been furnished by the neutrals.

1804—April 12—Blockade of Martinique and Guadeloupe, only applies to those ports which are actually invested, and after warning of blockade has been given to each vessel.

August 9—Blockade of Fécamp, Valery, etc., eleven channel ports of northern France and the river Seine.

1805—August 17—Direct trade with enemy's colonies to be subject to restrictions. Enemy colonies may trade to neutrals before November 1, 1805 if they have not violated provision of June, 1803.

1806—April 8—Blockade of Ems, Weser, Elbe and Trave to be strictly enforced.

May 16—Blockade from the Elbe to Brest. (The Fox Blockade.) Neutral ships coming from neutral ports may enter, *except* from Seine and Ostend.

September 25—Discontinuance of last blockade in part. Elbe to Ems is open.

1807—January 7—Interdiction of the trade from port to port of France and her satellite states. (Hamburg to Venice, except Portugal.)

June 26—Blockade of the Ems, Weser and Elbe.

October 16—Proclamation recalling seamen. Captains to demand British sailors from foreign vessels.

November 11—All ports and places of France, her allies and their colonies from which British vessels are excluded, shall be subjected to same restrictions as if actually blockaded by H. M's. vessels unless vessel has cleared out from British port under prescribed regulations. Vessels carrying goods with "certificates of origin" shall be good prize.

Goods enumerated in 43 George III may be imported into England, subject to such payment of duties as are now paid in ships navigated according to law. Sale of enemy ship to a neutral shall be declared illegal.

November 25—Dates at which above orders shall become operative at nearer and remoter ports.

Conditions prescribed for neutrals clearing through British ports.

1808—January 2—Blockade of Carthagena, Cadiz and St. Lucar.

March 28—Act of Parliament for carrying orders in council into effect.

April 11—Order in council permitting neutral vessels, without papers to carry supplies to the West Indies. (Intended to encourage violation of embargo.)

April 14—Act of Parliament prohibiting exportation of cotton wool, etc. Act of Parliament making valid certain orders in council.

May 4—Blockade of Copenhagen and island of Zealand.

June 23—Act of Parliament regulating trade between United States and Great Britain.

October 14—Admiral Cochrane's blockade of French Leeward Islands.

December—Repeal of duties laid March, 1808.

1809—April 26—Repeal of Orders of November, 1807, Blockade of Holland as far as Ems, of France and all their colonies and settlements and all ports of northern Italy, Orbitello to Pesara, inclusive.[1]

1810—Spring—Blockade of Elsineur—resulted in American vessels being unable to pay the Sound duties required by the Danish government.[2]

---

[1] *American State Papers*, Foreign, III, p. 241.
[2] *J. Q. Adams' Writings*, III, pp. 430–431.

II. Restrictions of France.

1793—May 9—Authorizes French vessels to arrest and bring into the ports of the republic vessels laden with provisions for an enemy port.

May 23—Exempts American vessels from the operation of the decree of the 9th.

May 28—Suspends the decree of May 23rd.

July 1—The decree of the 23rd again enforced.

July 27—The decree of May 23rd repealed and that of May 9th enforced.

1794—November 18—(25 Brumaire An III) General regulations—the most important is that merchandise belonging to the enemy is made liable to seizure in neutral vessels, until the enemy shall exempt from seizure French property similarly situated.

1795—January 3—(14 Nivose An III). Repeals the fifth article of the above and thus exempts enemy goods from capture in neutral vessels. (Secured by Monroe.)

1796—July 2—Neutral vessels shall be treated by France as they allow themselves to be treated by England.

1797—March 2—(17 Ventose An V). Enemy property in neutral vessels liable to confiscation; makes necessary rôles d'équipage. (Alteration of Treaty of 1778—retaliation for Jay Treaty.)

1798—January 18—(29 Nivose An VI). The character of vessels to be determined by that of their cargoes. (In force until December 13, 1800.) Foreshadows Berlin and Milan Decrees.

1799—March 18—(28 Ventose An VII). Explains the 4th article of Decree of March 2, 1797.

October 29—(8 Brumaire An VII).   Neutrals found on board enemy vessels liable to be treated as pirates.

November 14—(24 Brumaire An VII). Suspends the operation of the above decree of October 29th.

1800—December 13 and 19 (Frimaire 23 and 29 An VIII) a new convention with France—Repeals law of January 18, 1798. Enforces regulation of treaty of July 26, 1778.

1806—November 21. Berlin Decree. British Isles declared in state of blockade. All commerce with England interdicted for France and her allies. All English manufactures and goods coming from her colonies declared good prize.

1807—December 17. Milan Decree. Every vessel which shall have been searched by a British vessel, paid any duty to the British government, or be bound to or from any port of England or her colonies shall be good prize.

1808—April 17. Bayonne Decree. American vessels which come into ports of France, Holland, Hanseatic towns and Italy shall be placed under sequestration. They shall be presumed to be English, because the American embargo is in force.

1809—February 25. American vessels embargoed in ports of France, Holland and Bremen to be liberated.[3]

August 4. Rambouillet Decree (Secret). Every American vessel which shall enter ports of France, Spain or Italy shall be seized and confiscated, as long as the same measure shall be executed in regard to French vessels in the harbors in the United States. (Not published until March 23, 1810.)

November. Strict exclusion of American vessels from France, Spain, Naples, Holland, later from Prussia, Sweden and Russia (on ground that they were all English in disguise).

November. Decree of Napoleon confiscating vessels and cargoes entering Jahde, Weser and Elbe.

November 20. Decree of Napoleon prohibiting carrying of colonial produce to or from the city of Hamburg—ban lifted when Hamburg was annexed to the Empire, January, 1811.

December. Order to Berthier, commander in Northern Spain directing seizure of all American vessels in his control. Ships and cargoes to be considered good prize.

1810—February. New tariff, doubling duties on importation of colonial goods.

March 23—Rambouillet Decree. All American vessels in harbors of France and her allies to be seized and confiscated. In revenge for Non-Intercourse law. (See decree of Aug. 4, 1809 above.)

July 15—System of Permits announced for American vessels.[4]

August 5—Trianon Tariff—Enormous duties on colonial and American goods.[5]

Fictitious Repeal of Berlin and Milan Decrees.

Trianon Decree (secret)—American merchandise sequestered to be sold and proceeds placed in public treasury. Vessels seized but not yet disposed of to be sold and proceeds placed in public treasury.[6]

III. RESTRICTIONS OF SPAIN.

1800—February 15. Blockade of Gibraltar.

1807—February 19. 1st Aranjuez Decree (in imitation of Berlin Decree).

1808—January 3. 3rd Aranjuez Decree (in imitation of Milan Decree).

IV. COMMERCIAL REGULATIONS OF DUTCH GOVERNMENT, 1803–1808.

1803—July 5. Export of war materials, ship building materials and foodstuffs from Holland restricted. Import of British goods forbidden. For colonial goods, certificates of origin required.[7]

---

[3] *Consular Letters Bordeaux*, Vol. I cited by Melvin, p. 86.
[4] *A. S. P.*, Foreign, III, p. 400.
[5] *Ibid.*, p. 403.
[6] *Adams, Writings of Gallatin*, II, p. 197.
[7] Quoted by Hoekstra. *Thirty-seven Years of Holland-American Relations, 1803–1840*, from Rijks. Archief at the Hague: Staatsbewind.

November. Relaxation of above, neutral vessels forced into British ports to be permitted to land and unload if they bring no British goods. Certificate of origin dispensed with in certain cases.[8]

1805—May 31—British goods in neutral vessels stopping at Dutch ports to be seized. If brought in under false papers vessel to be seized as well.[9]

1806—November 21. Berlin Decree.

December 15. No vessel to leave port until permission of King granted; incoming vessels to be seized and investigated.[10]

1807—August 28. Incoming vessels to deposit double bond before unloading that they bring no British goods.[11]

September. Penalty for bringing in British goods, confiscation of vessel and entire cargo, neutral as well as British goods.[12]

1808—January 25. Embargo in Dutch ports.[13]

1810—February 3. Official notice to Bourne, that no American vessel would be admitted into ports of Holland (published in Poulson, June 18, 1810).[14]

V. Restrictions of Prussia.

1810—July 19. Prussian ports closed to Americans. "On account of abuse of American flag in facilitating British trade."[15]

1811—August 16. Colonial goods must be considered as coming from England, and must be confiscated even if paying tariff of October 2.[16]

VI. Restrictions—Mecklenburg.

1810—July 29. Ports of Wismar and Rostock closed to American vessels "because the North American flag has been abused by the English."[17]

VII. Restrictions of Denmark.

1809—November 3. No more colonial produce to be exported from Denmark.[18]

December. Sequestration of all West Indies products in Denmark for purpose of ascertaining its origin.[19]

---

[8] Hoekstra, p. 31.
[9] *Le Moniteur Universel*, June 19, 1805, p. 1113.
[10] Hoekstra, p. 44.
[11] *Ibid.*, p. 50.
[12] *Ibid.*, pp. 51-52.
[13] *Ibid.*, p. 63.
[14] Bourne to Secy. of State, Feb. 4, 1810, Consular Dispatches, Amsterdam.
[15] Forbes to Madison, July 26, 1810. See also *J. Q. Adams' Writings*, III, p. 467.
[16] *J. Q. Adams' Writings*, IV, p. 250.
[17] *Ibid.*, p. 477.
[18] Poulson, March 3, 1810.
[19] Forbes to R. Smith, Dec. 7, 1809, Consular Letters, Hamburg.

1810—January 3. Privateering ordinance. All neutral vessels which accept British convoy in Baltic and North Seas to be good prize.[20]

June 15. Ports of Tonningen, Husum and Sylt to be shut to Americans, ostensible reason to prevent smuggling of British goods from Heligoland.[21]

August 13. Remaining ports of Holstein closed to Americans.[22]

1810—September 8. Prohibiting entry of all vessels having on board colonial produce.[23]

VIII. RESTRICTIONS OF SWEDEN.

1810—September. Importation of colonial produce forbidden.[24]

---

[20] *J. Q. Adams' Writings*, III, p. 503.
[21] Forbes to Secy. R. Smith, July 12, 1810.
[22] *J. Q. Adams' Writings*, III, p. 478.
[23] Drumbahr vs. Marine Insurance Co., *Penna. Reports.* I.
[24] *Ibid.*

INTRODUCTION

The First Ten Years of American Commerce following the War of Independence, 1783-1793—Americans excluded from the British Navigation System—Persistence of trade relations between England and the newly freed states—Beginnings of American Trade to the Far East—Laws of Congress in regard to commerce—Survey of American foreign trade in 1791.

Americans Excluded from the British Navigation System

At the close of the war of Independence, the former colonies, while freed from the shackles of the navigation acts, had lost many solid advantages of Great Britain's commercial system. The thirteen states of the Confederation could obtain no commercial treaty from their former enemy. By act of Parliament of April, 1783,[1] the Privy Council was given power to regulate the trade between the two countries. This state of affairs prevailed until the signing of the Jay Treaty in 1795.

By the regulations of the Privy Council the goods exported from America to Great Britain were divided into three classes. First, were those goods which were upon the same basis as those from foreign countries, and paid the same duties. This class included the products of the whale fisheries—spermaceti, blubber, fins, also fish oil. The second class included goods which were to pay the same duties, as if they had come from the British possessions in America. This included all unmanufactured goods, also pig and bar iron, naval stores, pot and pearl ashes, indigo, masts, yards and bowsprits. All other products of wood from the former colonies were to come in free, although such articles from foreign countries paid a small duty. All these goods might enter in either British or American ships, and if in the latter, the "alien duty" required on foreign vessels was not to be exacted.[2] The West Indies market, so profitable to American trade in the colonial period, was still open to many American products, but only if imported in British vessels.[3]

---

[1] *Statutes at Large*, 20-25, George III, Vol. XIV, p. 330.
[2] J. Reeves, *History of Law of Shipping and Navigation*. Appendix; Order in Council of April 1, 1792.
[3] *Ibid.*, p. 353.

Meanwhile, the attempt of the new states to establish commercial relations with continental powers, Prussia,[4] Hamburg,[5] Saxony,[6] and especially France,[7] failed to produce satisfactory results.

Persistence of Trade Between England and the Newly Freed States

The bulk of American trade continued to be with England. Before the war of independence, American products had been compelled by law to seek the British markets, and forbidden to trade directly with European ports. Now when American shippers were free to trade with France and Holland, their continental supporters in the struggle against the mother country, and with all other European ports, it was found that such trade was not feasible. The best markets after all were those of Great Britain, where the Americans now found themselves regarded in some sense as foreigners. This superiority of the British markets arose from England's aptitude for maritime affairs, her many colonies, and wide trade connections, and her priority in the mechanical revolution in the production of goods. She had made herself the entrepôt of the world's trade, and almost any cargo of American produce could find a ready sale there, and an assorted shipload of China teas and nankeens, Dutch linens and English woolens, hardware or earthenware could be secured as a profitable return cargo for America. England was making the goods which America wanted, and making them cheaply, and no other country disputed the field. Add to this the fact that English capital was available on long term credits, to finance American undertakings and that there existed a common language and customs, and long established commercial connections, and it will be seen how strong was the pressure to continue in the old paths.

---

[4] J. Adams, *Works*, v. 8, p. 195; *Diplomatic Correspondence*, v. 1, 1783–1789, pp. 458–464.
[5] *Diplomatic Correspondence*, v. 1, pp. 46–49.
[6] W. E. Lingelbach, Saxon-American Relations, *American Hist. Review*, v. 17, pp. 517–539.
[7] Observations of Lafayette to Vergennes, *Diplomatic Correspondenec*, v. 1, pp. 282–290. T. J. Randolph, *Writings of Jefferson*, v. 2, pp. 392–393.

Beginnings of American Trade to the Far East

While the trade with England, in the years following the revolution, was hampered by the lack of a satisfactory treaty, and that with continental countries not firmly established, a new line of commerce had been opened. American captains made their way to the ports of the far east. In February of 1784, there started from New York the fine new ship, *Empress of China* of 360 tons, on a voyage to the antipodes. Robert Morris, Daniel Parker and other merchants of New York and Philadelphia were the backers of the venture. The cargo of the vessel was ginseng. With nine officers and a crew of thirty-four men, this vessel was the first American ship to undertake the voyage to China.[8]

Elias Haskett Derby of Salem, known as the father of American commerce to India, sent a vessel on a notable voyage to the East, in 1785. The ship was the *Grand Turk*, which had been employed as an American privateer during the Revolution. The first stop was at the Cape of Good Hope, where the captain sold a part of his cargo, consisting of rum, cheese, salt provisions and loaf sugar. He then proceeded to the Gulf of Guinea, where he sold rum and other articles for gold dust, but refused, by the owner's direction, to purchase any slaves. He returned to Salem, by way of the West Indies, where he purchased sugar and cotton enough to fill two ships.[9]

Derby was among the first Americans to challenge the great chartered companies of the European powers who had the monopoly of the oriental trade. His voyages extended to China, India, Mauritius, Madeira, Siam, and Arabia, as well as to

---

[8] Josiah Quincy, *Life of Samuel Shaw*. Shaw was the supercargo of the vessel. His full and interesting journal, covering the voyage and included in this volume, is fascinating reading. The Continental Congress commissioned Shaw as the first American Consul to China, on his second voyage in 1786. This Revolutionary officer, and eighteenth century merchant, may be said to have started the "entente cordial" between the United States and China. "His intelligence, business talents and fidelity to his duties and engagements, his amenity of manners and gentlemanly bearing," says Quincy, "greatly contributed to establish in that remote country confidence and respect for American people."

[9] Ralph D. Paine, *Ships and Sailors of Old Salem*, pp. 204-5.

Europe and the West Indies. He sent his son, Elias Haskett Derby, Jr., to India in 1787 for three years, where he established a very profitable trade. Young Derby visited Mocha in Arabia, in 1789, to secure a cargo of coffee. The natives had never heard of America, and his vessel was a nine days wonder in that distant port.[10]

The fine textiles of India, the pepper from Sumatra, gum from Senegal, and the products of the Spice Islands, of Bourbon and Mauritius were for the first time in these years brought to American ports in American vessels. Thus the overseas commerce of the young commonwealths weathered the critical years from 1783 to 1789.

It was largely the needs of commerce, as we know, which led to the replacement of the feeble Articles of Confederation by the Federal Constitution.

Laws of First Congress in Regard to Commerce

Spurred by the petitions of merchants in the ports the first congress promptly gave its attention to trade questions. Here the ideas long in the mind of Hamilton were the guide. The first tariff law of 1789 provided for a revenue and a moderate degree of protection by placing duties on almost all objects of import, but decreed a reduction of 10 per cent on such duties if the goods were imported in ships built or owned in the United States.[11] To encourage the far eastern trade, all teas brought in American vessels entered with lower duties. The carrying trade was encouraged by a provision that the duties on all goods which were imported and then exported within twelve months should be entitled to a drawback of all except 1 per cent of the amount. A tonnage act placed on American ships a small duty of 6 cents per ton, while all others were required to pay 50 cents per ton. The coast was divided into districts for the collection of the tariff and tonnage duties. A registration act provided for the certification of ships owned in America, requiring the dimensions of the vessel, the tonnage and the names of the owner and

---

[10] *Ibid.*, p. 210.
[11] *U. S. Statutes at Large*, Vol. I, pp. 23–28.

master to be set forth in the register. Vessels employed in the coasting and fishing trade were to be licensed.[12]

Survey of American Commerce—1791

Let us now note the routes which American trade was pursuing, and the articles carried, just after the establishment of the national government, and on the eve of the great twenty year period of war and upheaval in Europe growing out of the French Revolution and the rise of Napoleon.

The average ocean going vessel of the period was a small craft of probably less than 200 tons burden, with blunt prow and stern and with a width of one-third of the length.[13] Vessels of 300 tons were, however, not uncommon. When Stephen Girard's ship *Voltaire* was at the port of Antwerp in 1802 she aroused great interest on account of her size and beauty. The *Orizimbo*, a splendid vessel belonging to Mr. David Estabrook of Baltimore was of 533 tons, but was declared by her captain to be too large for ships' trade. Larger even than this vessel was the *Grand Turk*, belonging to Derby of Salem. She was of 564 tons. On the other hand a tiny craft like the Sloop *Experiment*, of only eighty-four tons and with a crew of only seven men and two boys successfully attempted a voyage to China in 1785.[14] The vessels which carried on trade with the ports of the West Indies were small vessels which could run away at any season of the year from any creek or bay with a large assortment of small articles, thus making a quick voyage and a small profit, and so had the advantage over larger and more expensive European vessels which came from a greater distance.[15] There were, of course, no lines of vessels making regular sailings from any ports; each voyage was a separate venture on the part of the merchant who owned or had chartered the vessel. In those days of slow and irregular communication, it was impossible for the merchant at home to predict the state of the distant market. Respon_

---

[12] Law of Sept. 1, 1789, amended Dec. 31, 1792—*U. S. Statutes at Large*, Vol. I, pp. 55–65, 287-299.
[13] *The Ocean Carrier*, J. Russel Smith, pp. 5–6.
[14] J. R. Spears, *Story of the American Merchant Marine*, p. 107.
[15] J. Adams to Sec'y. Livingstone, July 7, 1783, *J. Adams Life and Works*, Vol XIII.

sibility for the sale of the cargo and the purchase of goods in return was, especially in the case of voyages to the far east, in the hands of the captain, although sometimes there was a supercargo. In the case of long established trade, to Great Britain, France, or North Germany, there were generally one or more foreign correspondents of the American shipper in each large city, to one of whom the cargo was consigned.

An illustration of the fluctuation of the market and the fortunate result of a captain's "taking his own head" is seen in the account of the voyage of the *America* from Salem in 1804. The captain, Benjamin Crowninshield, had been ordered to go to the East Indies for a cargo of pepper, and under no circumstances to deviate from his instructions. Nevertheless when he learned, on stopping at the Island of Bourbon, that a cargo of coffee could be procured at Mocha, he proceeded to that place. At the Arabian port, he secured goat skins, gum Arabic, and sienna, but principally coffee. Meanwhile the bottom had dropped out of the pepper market, but coffee had greatly increased in value. The owners therefore were far from chiding the captain for his change of course on his return, for the coffee which he brought sold for a clear profit of one hundred thousand dollars in Holland.[16]

A good example of the responsibility placed upon the captain and the wide range of choices open to him, as well as of the variety of goods handled in the course of an eastern voyage, is seen in the instructions to the master of the brig *Enterprise*. This vessel, belonging to William Gray, one of the wealthiest of the Salem merchants, was dispatched on a trading voyage to South Africa and India in 1792. Gray's instructions to the captain of the Enterprise ran as follows:

"Proceed to the Cape of Good Hope, where sell part of your cargo, probably the Russian Duck and the coles; (from Liverpool) purchase 20 hhd. of brandy and 60–80 hhd. wine, such as is best calculated for the Isle of France market, also raisins and almonds; where (Isle of France) sell part of your cargo, or perhaps all. If you can find sugar, coffee, tea, indigo or cotton that

---

[16] Paine, pp. 485–486.

will pay 100 per cent profit, then I advise you to come back. If you cannot find goods to answer to come home from the Isle of France, then proceed for Calcutta in Bay of Bengal; there take sugar, salt peter and Bandanno silk handkerchiefs. If you have advice that nothing can be done to advantage at Calcutta, you may go to Canton; when you get to Canton, . . . take on Bohea tea, chinaware, nankeens and black satins; then proceed to this port. If you come home in winter, touch at St. Eustatius, and then lay till Spring, so that you may come on safer. Sell your whole cargo at Good Hope, if you can get 20 per cent profit, and purchase sugars or any other goods that will pay 50 per cent profit home. If you have opportunity to sell the Brig *Enterprise* at a good price, do it." In conclusion two different officers were suggested as successors, in case of the death of the captain, and five different European houses, to whom, or to whose correspondents, communications might be sent, at any time during the voyage.[17]

In the voyage of the vessel *Astraea*, to Batavia and Canton, already referred to, the directions of Derby, the owner, were very specific including the injunction not to violate any trade laws. At the end, however, he wrote as follows, "Captain Magee and Mr. Perkins, although I have been a little particular in these orders, I do not mean them as positive, and you have leave to break them in any part, except in regard to the acts of trade." In case of sickness Derby ordered the captain to add a clause to the orders, "putting the command of the ship into the person's hands that you think the most equal to it, not having any regard to the station he at present has on the ship."[18]

The principal exports of the United States remained the same as those of the colonial period, bread stuffs, tobacco, rice, lumber, salt fish and salt meats, pot and pearl ashes, indigo, and whale oil. For the year 1792 our total exports amounted to nearly twenty million of dollars. Of this amount by far the largest item was bread stuffs, which amounted to seven and one-half million. Next in value was the export of tobacco, which was

---

[17] Gray, *Wm. Gray of Salem, Merchant*, pp. 13–15.
[18] *Hunt's Merchants' Magazine*, Vol. 36.

valued at over four million, followed by rice which was worth a million and three-quarters. Wood products were valued at something over one million and salt fish at a little less than one million, while the exports of pot and pearl ashes were valued at about eight hundred thousand dollars. Naval stores were worth a little over two hundred thousand dollars.[19] Of these goods

VALUE OF EXPORTS FROM UNITED STATES
OCT. 1, 1790 - OCT. 1, 1791

BREAD STUFFS
TOBACCO
RICE
WOOD
SALT FISH
POT and PEARL ASH
SALT MEAT
INDIGO
FOREIGN GOODS
WHALE OIL
NAVEL STORES

PLATE 1

nearly one half, or over nine million dollars worth, were sent to Great Britain and her dependencies, over four and one-half million to France and her colonies, and over three million to Spain and Portugal and their colonies. The United Netherlands received nearly two millions, and Denmark something over two hundred thousand dollars worth. In return for all these commodities we brought back from England a flow of manufactured goods, consisting of cotton and woolen fabrics, earthenware, glass, iron mongery and leather goods. From France there came

---

[19] Pitkin T., *Statistical View*, p. 167.

brandies, wines, silks, and fine clocks and watches and other articles of luxury. From Holland, Hamburg, and Bremen linens and duck. From Spain and Portugal came wines and fruits, and from the West Indies, sugar, coffee and cocoa. From China we brought teas, nankeens and chinaware and from the East Indies, pepper, coffee and fine muslins.

DESTINATION OF EXPORTS FROM UNITED STATES
OCT 1, 1790 – OCT 1, 1791

GREAT BRITAIN and her DOMINIONS
FRANCE and her DOMINIONS
UNITED NETHERLANDS and her DOMINIONS
SPAIN and her DOMINIONS
PORTUGAL and her DOMINIONS
AUSTRIAN NETHERLANDS and GERMANY
EAST INDIES
DENMARK

PLATE II

As we look over the shipping news of the period, we are struck with the evident importance of the West Indies trade. Gaudeloupe, Hispaniola, St. Croix, St. Eustatius, Curaçao, even Montega Bay (Jamaica) and New Providence appear continually in the shipping lists. Although as we have seen, the British West Indies were ordinarily closed to American vessels, the governors of the islands were authorized to open their ports to Americans in times of emergency. Thereupon, as Professor Channing observes, famines and tornadoes seem to have occurred with alarming frequency. Nor do American shippers appear to have limited themselves strictly to the permitted ports in the French possessions. The Dutch Islands of Curaçao and St. Eustatius were open and were continually sought by Americans. They were important, not on account of their own products, but

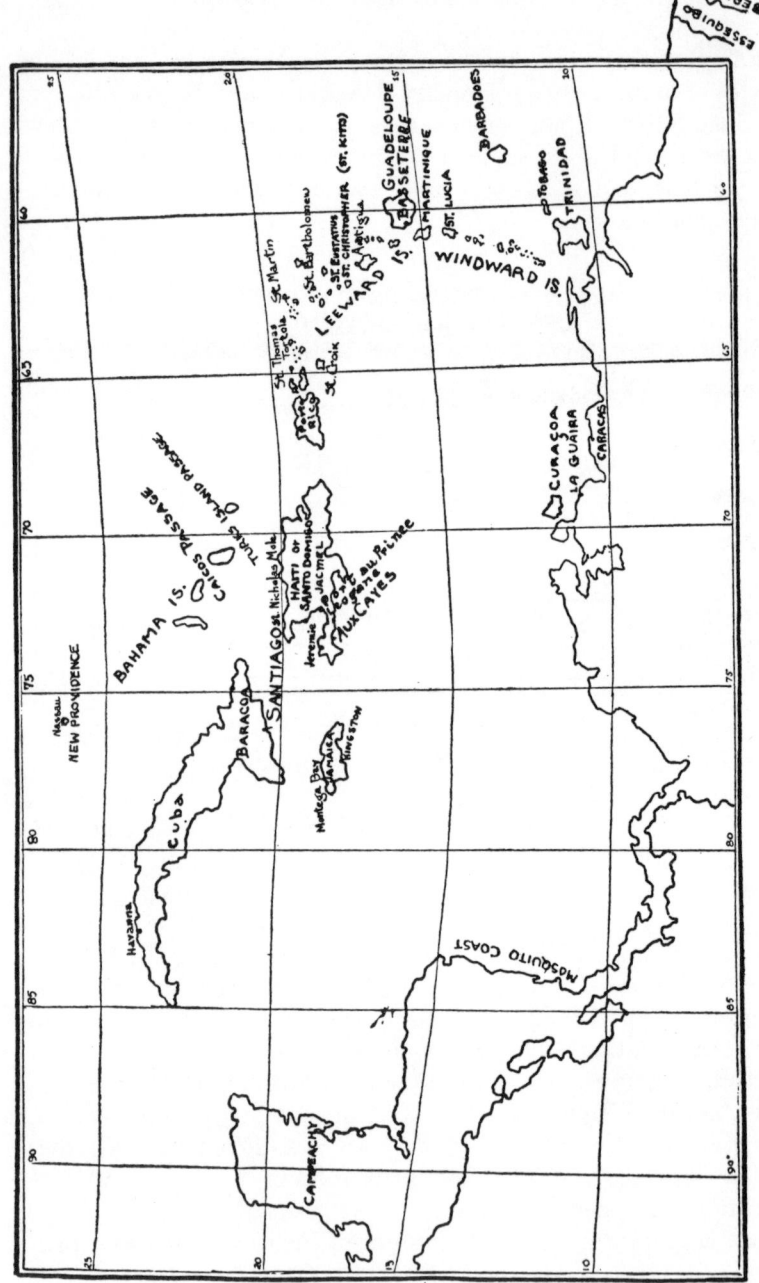

West Indies and Adjacent Territory

by reason of their favorable position and because they served as distributing centers for neighboring places. Curaçao was a small rocky island but seventy miles from the coast of Venezuela. It carried on a large trade with the Spanish colonies, the Dutch promoting its trade in every way, especially by low port charges. St. Eustatius on the way to and from the Windward and Leeward Islands, was made a free port by the Dutch, and became a great entrepôt for the West Indies trade, its advantages being shared by its smaller Dutch neighbor, St. Martin, and by the Swedish islands of St. Croix and St. Thomas. While Spain was notoriously illiberal in granting access to her colonial ports to foreigners, there seems to have been considerable trading to Havana.

The proportion of American commerce carried on under foreign flags in 1791 was two-thirds as large as that carried on in American vessels. The foreign tonnage declined steadily, until in 1806 and 1807, it was only one-tenth of that under the American flag.[20] It was principally British vessels which were supplanted by those of the United States. British observers

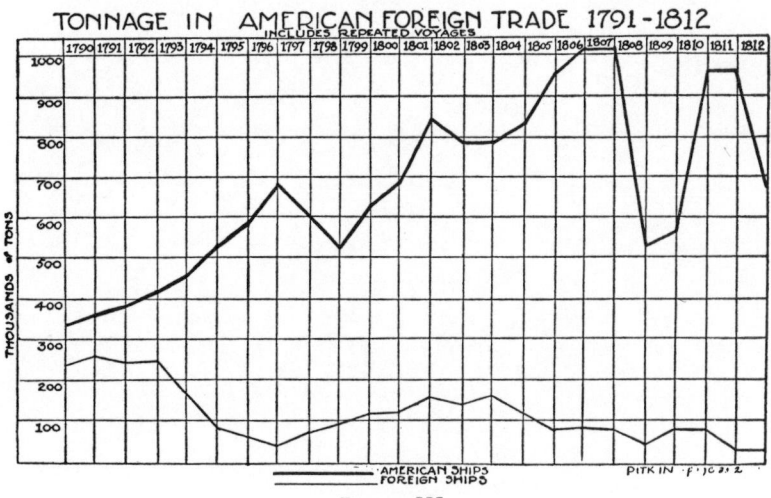

PLATE III

[20] Pitkin, Table, p. 352.

saw the change with concern. In his pamphlet, *Strictures on the Necessity of Inviolably Maintaining the Navigation and Colonial System of Great Britain*, Lord Sheffield gives figures showing the marked decline of British tonnage engaged in American trade. In 1789, the British tonnage was 72,000 and the American 21,000, but in 1800, British tonnage was 14,000, and American 110,000. Sheffield laid the blame for the decline, upon the law 36 George III C 17, and later laws which allowed the Privy Council to extend the privileges of trading to England to the vessels of foreign nations.

I

THE WAR BETWEEN ENGLAND AND FRANCE, 1793-1801

Effect on American Trade—Opening of ports of French colonies to neutrals —British Orders, June and November, 1793—British seizures on West Indies 1794—Petition of American merchants to Congress—The Jay-Grenville treaty Work of the Commission—Treatment of American Vessels in Ports of France—Mission of Monroe—Decrees of Convention—Conditions in Santo-Domingo, 1795-97—British Seizures 1795—to Peace of Amiens.

Effect on American Trade

Opening of Ports of French Colonies to Neutrals

The American government having done all that was possible by legislative action (1789-92) for the commerce of its citizens, the next step considered necessary was that in which the Continental Congress had failed, the securing of favorable commercial treaties with foreign powers. But before this could be accomplished, the entire situation was changed by the outbreak of war in Europe. The long struggle between France and England, beginning in 1793, opened the most flattering prospects to American commerce. It subjected the new government to years of humiliation and insult from both belligerents, inflamed party feeling in the United States an an unbelievable degree, seeming at times to threaten the union itself. Finally it resulted in a second short war with England which was to demonstrate the essential unity of the American people, and their determination to be a force to be reckoned with among the nations.

Very early the United States was concerned in the conflict. The French recognized in their maritime weakness a serious handicap. The firm of Samatan in Marseilles, had for several years been carrying on trade with Stephen Girard in Philadelphia. In March of 1793 the head of the firm wrote that Girard's ship was detained by a general embargo in the port, and even on its removal could probably not leave with safety because no convoy had been arranged. "It is evident," wrote Samatan, "that we shall not be superior, or even equal in strength to the other powers on any sea and our commerce will be totally unprotected."[1] It was for her colonies in this crisis, that France was chiefly concerned. It was necessary that they should be enabled to sell their raw materials as usual, and import their necessary food, and also the accustomed manufactured articles from the mother country. America, near at hand and eager for new commercial opportunities stood ready to perform this service.

The National Convention therefore in February, 1793, issued a significant decree in regard to colonial trade. The ports of the French colonies were declared open to American vessels and the goods which they carried in or out were to pay no higher duties than those in French vessels. This applied also to the French ports in the East Indies and the Isle of France and Bourbon.[2] In the following month, a similar decree of the convention threw open to the United States and other neutrals, under certain restrictions, the gum trade of Senegal.[3] In the flowery language of Genet, "The French republic, seeing in them (the Americans) but brothers has opened to them by decrees all her ports in the two worlds and has granted them all the favors which her own citizens enjoy in her vast possessions."[4]

Each of the belligerents, on the outbreak of hostilities had its eye on the food ships of the other. The harvest of 1792 had been poor in France, and so the government made arrangements to procure grain from America[5] and elsewhere. Some of these ves-

---

[1] Girard Mss.
[2] Duvergier, *Lois*, Vol. V, p. 200. Boyer Fondrede who spoke in the name of the Committee for the colonies in favor of this motion, voiced the views of the more enlightened and liberal element of the convention. "Our commercial system, said he, should change, like our political system. The colonies have been declared an integral part of our political system, but they have remained under oppressive commercial regulations. Prohibitions of neutral ships has always left the colonies a prey to famine." This was declared to be a homicidal policy. Since the French ship builders and manufacturers would be busy with military activity, this furnished an added reason why the colonial ports should be open to the United States; Moniteur, Feb. 19, 1793. Also *Archives Parlementaire*, Vol. 59, pp. 15–18.
[3] *Ibid.*, p. 284.
[4] Genet to Jefferson, May 5, 1793, *A. S. P.*, For. I, p. 147.
[5] Ternant, French minister to the United States applied to the American government for a credit of three million livres, to be furnished on account of our debt to France, the sum to be laid out in the United States in provisions

sels were seized by the British cruisers. The French wished to retaliate, but their treaty with the United States declared that in case either of the countries became involved in war, there should be full freedom of trade in the case of the neutral, without any exception, to come from any port to a hostile port.[6] To seize American ships laden with food and destined to England, would clearly violate this provision. But a decree of the National Convention of May, 1793 declared that the neutral flag was not respected by the enemies of France, and that for that reason she was absolved from her promises in the treaty with the United States. French ships were therefore authorized to bring into port neutral vessels laden with provisions belonging to neutrals, and bound for the enemy ports. The uncertainty and inexperience of the Convention were strikingly shown in their shilly-shallying over this decree, for on the strong protest of American Minister, it was declared two weeks after its issue, that American vessels were to be exempt. Five days later, the Convention changed its mind and took away the exemption. A month later, July 1, they again decided to make an exception in favor of American ships, but a few weeks afterward they finally settled that American food vessels should be seized as well as those of other neutrals.[7] The reasoning of the French government, in

---

to be sent to France. Jefferson, *Writings Ford ed.* 6, p. 190. The cabinet having assented Ternant ordered through the firm of Cunningham and Nesbit of Philadelphia a quantity of wheat, flour, and salt beef (Feb. 1793). On account of the rumors of war, Ternant declared it expedient to ship the whole to Havre or Nantes as American property. Corr. French Ministers to U. S. 1791-97. *Report Amer. Hist. Ass'n.*, *1903*, II, pp. 177-178.

[6] Treaty between United States and France 1778, Art. XXIII. W. M. Malloy, *Treaties, Conventions, etc. between U. S. and other Powers*, I, p. 476.

[7] Decrees of May 1, 23, 28, July 1, and 27, 1793. Duvergier, *Lois*, V. pp. 371-381, VI, p. 1, 71. There were not lacking men in the convention who wished to maintain the treaty with the United States at all hazards. The maker of the motion, July 1, to exempt American ships declared, "If we stipulate for the interest of privateers, without doubt we have no regard to a faithful ally. When we covenant for treaties, for public faith, one should not place in balance, the value of a few cargoes of food." *Archives Parlementaire*, Vol. 68, p. 33. This motion was carried, but the praiseworthy sentiments therein expressed were apparently forgotten a few weeks later, for the convention then heard the report of the commission of Marine on the petition of the owners of the privateer Le Sans Culotte of Honfleur, (who had taken a rich ship, the Laurens as a prize) that the decree of May 9 be maintained against all neutrals. They then decided finally to make no exceptions in favor of Americans. *Ibid.*, Vol. 69, p. 582.

basing its order for the seizure of the American vessels on prior action of the British government in taking such food-carrying vessels bound to France was the first instance of the tu quoque argument, which the two belligerents were to use throughout the twenty-year struggle, at the expense of the American republic.

The next year the National Convention formally declared its intention of seizing enemy goods in neutral vessels.[8] This likewise was a violation of one of the provisions of the treaty with the United States which provided that freedom of the ship should give freedom to the goods.[9] Here again the French claimed that the action of the British government made it impossible for them to observe their treaty, and that so long as English ships seized enemy property in neutral vessels, they should do the same.

British Orders of June and November, 1793

The war measures of Great Britain, in the meantime, had by no means left American commerce untouched. It had been a part of England's navigation system, to be so secured by favorable treaties, as to be able in case of war, to exert commercial pressure on her opponent. With Spain and Russia she had treaties of this kind, and these were now invoked. The plan of the British ministers was that the United States was to fall in line with these countries, and the neutrality of all was to be so construed as to bring about virtually an economic blockade of France. According to these treaties no French ship could enter the ports of the signatories, nor could military or naval stores from them enter French ports. The enforcement of the rule of 1756 was foreshadowed in the declaration that no neutral by reason of its neutrality should be able to give protection to the commerce or property of France.

The commanders of British cruisers, by an order of June 8, 1793, were to deflect all cargoes of grain or other provisions

---

[8] *A. S. P.*, For. III, pp. 285–286.
[9] Malloy, *Treaties, Conventions, etc.*, I, *Treaty with France, 1778*, Art. 23, p. 476.

from neutral ports, destined for France, to English ports instead, where the supplies were to be purchased by His Majesty's government.[10]

The plan of the Convention to allow American vessels to engage in commerce with French Colonies, was apparently to be frustrated by the Order in Council of November 6, 1793, which called for the detention of all neutral vessels laden with products from the French colonies, but this order was very soon changed (January 8, 1794) to apply only to vessels sailing directly from the French West Indies to Europe, and to French property in vessels from the islands, destined to any port.[11]

Thus within eighteen months of the first foreign decree designed to restrict American commerce the lines to be pursued by each belligerent had been laid down. Great Britain was to be on the watch for attempts of American vessels to carry French colonial goods directly to Europe, and for cargoes of food from America destined for France. As it was a part of her plan to seize the islands in the West Indies belonging to her rival, American vessels attempting to enter ports invested by a blockading squadron were likewise to be seized. France proposed to seize neutral vessels laden with food, on their way to English ports, and both belligerents were alert to seize enemy property in neutral vessels and disposed to look for such enemy property under neutral disguises.[12]

It was one thing to write down laws, orders and restrictions in London and Paris—quite a different thing to have them respected and obeyed in distant seas, when hundreds of alert and hardy American captains and crews were sailing their ships laden with produce for eager purchasers or seeking cargoes from ready sellers. To enforce these restrictions each nation employed its own armed vessels, as many as could be spared from the naval operations, and besides commissioned large numbers of privateers. Here the naval superiority of the English gave them a

---

[10] *A. S. P.*, For., III, p. 264.
[11] *Ibid.*
[12] Letter of LeBrun to Gouverneur Morris, March 29, 1793, *A. S. P.*, Vol. I, pp. 359–260.

great advantage, but French cruisers and privateers although weakened in morale by the Revolutionary propaganda were by no means impotent. Seizures of American merchant vessels began in the summer of 1793. By the following summer a representative of our government stood in London, with a long list of grievances demanding redress, and in Paris likewise, our minister demanded satisfaction for injuries.

The waters of the West Indies were soon alive with British cruisers and privateers ready to pounce upon American vessels from the French islands.

British Seizures in West Indies, 1794

One of the chief sufferers from these seizures was the Philadelphia merchant, Stephen Girard, who at this time, and for some years previously had been actively engaged in trade with Santo Domingo. Girard's fine brig *Sallie* was seized in March, 1794, by the British privateer *Hawk*, after leaving the Haitien port of Aux Cayes, for Philadelphia, with a cargo of sugar, coffee, and cotton. Although the papers carried by the ship were perfectly regular the vessel and cargo were condemned as French property, by the Vice Admiralty court in Jamaica. After some time, however, the *Sallie* was liberated because the orders of January, 1794 permitted a direct voyage between French colonies and a neutral, but the cargo was condemned, on the ground that the owner was a Frenchman.[13] On learning this, Girard immediately took steps to secure documents from the French consul in New York designed to prove that he had resided continuously in the United States since 1785 and was a bona fide American citizen. The next month another vessel of Girard's, the *Polly*, was seized after leaving the port of Basterre in Guadeloupe, laden with West India produce, on the ground that she had left a French port under blockade by the English. After the capture and condemnation in the Vice Admiralty court at Bermuda the captain tried to secure possession of the ship and cargo by purchase, as owners often did in such cases, but in this instance, the island authorities refused to permit it. Many of the Ameri-

---

[13] McMaster, *Life of Stephen Girard*, Vol. I, p. 272.

can vessels seized at this time were afterwards liberated when the cases came up in the British Vice Admiralty courts in the West Indies, but even then the loss sustained was serious, because some of them suffered a delay of four months, and the owners were obliged to pay all expenses and costs.[14]

The attitude of the British courts toward the trade with the French West Indies is well brought out in the case of the American Brig *Sally*. This vessel was seized by the British on the ground of her having on board the produce of a French colony. The British Admiralty court restored the ship and cargo to the American owners, but refused them the costs and damages which they claimed. An appeal on the case was heard in May, 1796.

On this occasion the counsel for the appellants denied the applicability of the Rule of 1756. This he declared had not been practiced by England during the American Revolution and he challenged the right of the captor to cite in his defence the Instructions of November, 1793, which he insisted were against the law of nations. The office of King's Advocate at this time was filled by the great lawyer, Sir William Scott, later Lord Stowell, whose interpretations of international law, were to touch American commerce so nearly in the period of the wars of the French Revolution and Napoleon. In his reply to the claimant's counsel, Scott, speaking for the captors, conceded that the neutral had the right to require that his commerce should not be disturbed by war, and that he should be at liberty to carry it on as at other times. This doctrine was based on Bynkershoek and other authorities. But that neutrals should derive advantages of new trade from a war, and snatch the enemy from the distress to which he had been reduced, that was an enlargement of neutral claims beyond the limits of justice. The reason why England had not invoked the Rule of 1756 during the American Revolution, Scott declared, was that France, in opening her colonial ports to neutrals, at that time, had announced that this action marked a change in her system, and was not due to the hostilities then existing. English authori-

---

[14] Claypoole, *Daily Advertiser*, July 4, 1794.

ties had doubted the sincerity of this statement at the time, and the event had proved them correct. But the English courts had given France the benefit of the doubt, and therefore the Rule of 1756 had not been put into practice. With the beginning of the French Revolution, when the power of the mother country over her colonies was weakened, proclamations had been issued in the French West Indies, "by persons in irregular possession of power" relaxing the commercial restrictions.[15]

In this case the High Court of Admiralty reaffirmed the decision of the lower court, refusing costs and damages to the claimant. Although the vessel was restored, because as we have seen in January, 1794, the order authorizing the seizure of the products of the French colonies carried in neutral vessels had been withdrawn, and the Sally had been captured after that date.[16]

In less than five months after the November, '93 orders, six hundred vessels were detained in British ports. One hundred and fifty of these were condemned in the spring of 1794, "leaving the crews stranded and without clothes to cover their backs." Wearing apparel was apparently considered good prize from the accounts of the American sailors.[17]

"The short time allowed for appeal," says Bemis, "from the island vice admiralty courts to the higher tribunals in England, and the temporary lack of funds of the ship captains, together with the impossibility because of time and distance, to communicate with the owners soon enough to start appeals, cut off all possibility of ultimate justice."[18] It was no exaggeration to say that this indefensible naval policy "created tremendous sensation" when the news reached the United States in the spring of 1794.

Petitions of American Merchants to Congress

The merchants of the Atlantic seaboard from Charleston to

---

[15] Scott here ignores the decree of the convention opening her ports in her colonies to Americans. *A. S. P.*, For. II, p. 147, Genet to Jefferson May, 1793.
[16] C. B. J. Gaskoine, Prize Cases in the Days of Stowell. Br. *Year Book of International Law, 1923*, pp. 85–88.
[17] Bemis, *Jay's Treaty*, p. 158.
[18] *Ibid.*, p. 159.

Portsmouth held meetings and adopted resolutions calling on Congress for redress. Complaints against Algerian pirates and the depradations of France appear also in these memorials, but their chief burden is the numerous and ruthless seizures by the British. The New York merchants emphasized the inconsistency of the ground for seizure, for they complained that British armed vessels took American ships trading not only with France and her colonies but in many cases those destined to neutral or British ports.[19] The Philadelphia merchants complained of the delay and expense in the case even of liberated ships, of the insult and violence perpetrated against the captains and crews, and the discouragement to commerce and agriculture, unless a remedy could be found. The principles of the Armed Neutrality of 1780 were extolled, by which neutral vessels were held inviolate, except when carrying contraband goods.

Meanwhile our government had not been idle. Three months after the order to the arrest of the food ships to France, England's first obnoxious order, Jefferson sent a vigorous letter of protest through Thomas Pinckney, our minister in London. Corn, flour and meal were not in the class of contraband, and we had a right to sell them to France. "It is not enough," wrote Jefferson, "for a nation to say, we and our friends will buy your produce; we have a right to answer that it suits us better to sell to their enemies as well as to their friends. To restrain us from sending grain to France is an act of partiality to Great Britain which may lead to a war with France. This is a dilemma which Great Britain has no right to force upon us."[20] The British minister to the United States, Hammond, replied that writers on inter-

---

[19] Dunlap and Claypoole, *American Daily Advertiser*, April 8, 1794.
[20] Jefferson to Pinkney, Sept. 7, 1793, *A. S. P.*, For., Vol. I, p. 239. The Declaration of London (1909) definitely placed food upon the list of conditional contraband. At the beginning of the World War (1914) the British government seized American food cargoes destined to German ports, ostensibly for the civil population of the country and also cargoes destined for neighboring neutral countries. Thus was begun the "hunger blockade" to which the German government retaliated by the submarine warfare. The American owners of the food cargoes were fully reimbursed for their losses by His Majesty's Government. For official American protests against the seizures, and the reply of Earl Grey, see *World Peace Foundation, Pamphlet Series* (1915), Vol. V, No. 4, Pt. II, pp. 89, 96, 110, 112, Pt. III, pp. 123–129.

national law expressly stated that provisions might in certain cases be considered contraband of war.[21]

In protesting against British interference in the trade between the United States and the French colonies, Jefferson could urge somewhat less clear support from the principles of international law than in the case of the food cargoes but here Pinckney's remonstrance was partially successful, for an Order in Council of January, 1794 as we have seen, mitigated the November decree, by restricting seizures of American vessels to those which were proceeding from French colonies to ports in Europe, or those which carried French property, or contraband. As this covered more than half of our trade with the French colonies, it operated to ease the tension against England.

Unfortunately there were other causes of complaint against that country which kept alive American resentment. The insistence upon the right to stop American merchant vessels wherever they might be, in order to apprehend deserting British seamen, and the retention of forts in the northwest, contrary to the Treaty of Versailles were two serious grievances. Public opinion, therefore, was importunate in demanding action. An embargo, March 26, 1794, on all foreign vessels in our harbor for two months was a mere gesture of protest.[22] As Pinckney's remonstrances had brought an unsatisfactory response, a special mission was determined upon.

The Jay-Grenville Treaty—Work of the Commission

We are not concerned here with the general provisions of the Jay Treaty, but merely with the protest against the vexations and spoliations under the orders of June and November of 1793. Here Jay secured some satisfaction. The treaty provided that in cases where the channels of the British Admiralty courts failed, appeal should be made to a special commission of five

---

[21] Hammond to Jefferson, Sept. 12, 1793, *A. S. P.*, For. I, p. 240.
[22] *Annals 3d, Cong.*, pp. 530–31.

members.²³ Enemy goods in neutral vessels were still to be liable to seizure, but an attempt was made to regulate the conduct of privateers by requiring their commanders to give bonds, and punishment was promised for injuries and violence to the officers and crews of captured vessels. The American contention that provisions should be excluded from the list of contraband was not granted; on the contrary, the list of contraband was made longer by adding naval stores and materials for ship building to the list.²⁴ Each country agreed to give the other the position of the most favored nation.

In the end the decisions of the joint commission resulted in a victory for the Americans on two important points, viz.: on that of food ships, and on the validity of the rule of 1756 under the law of nations. By an order in council of April, 1795, England receded from the position taken by Hammond in regard to the earlier food orders of 1793, which he had attempted to justify.²⁵ Cargoes seized under this order had indeed been paid for, but the contention of Hammond, backed by his government, was that they were contraband. The order of April, 1795, apparently gave up this claim, but directed the cruisers to arrest the food carrying vessels on their way to France, and send them in to British ports to be purchased by His Majesty's government.

Under this order the ship *Neptune* laden in part with rice, and bound from Charleston to Bordeaux was stopped by a British ship, and taken into the port of London. The Admiralty court ordered the sale of the cargo and the American owners received the ship, the value of the rice, as well as freight, demurrage and expenses. Not satisfied with the amount awarded, the owners presented a memorial to the commission and the whole question

---

²³ Wm. Pinkney, Christopher Gore, and John Trumbull were the American Commissioners, Dr. Nicholl and Dr. Swabey, represented the British government. In many cases which came before this commission payment was ordered to the American Claiments. The total amount of payments received under the Jay treaty, by American merchants for property illegally taken under British orders, exceeded ten million dollars. T. Pitkin, *Statistical View of the Commerce of the U. S. P.*, 374, see also H. Wheaton, *Life Writings and Speeches of Wm. Pinkney*, A. S. P., For. v. 2, pp. 119–123. *Public Treaties of U. S. in force in 1873*, in Revised Statutes of U. S. relating to District of Columbia, etc., 1875.

²⁴ *Treaty of Amity and Commerce with Great Britain*, Malloy I, pp. 590–606.

²⁵ Hammond to Jefferson, *A. S. P.*, For. I, p. 240.

of the legality of the order was thus brought before that body. The British members defended the seizures on the ground of the possibility of reducing their enemy by famine, and went to Vattel, Grotius and even Plutarch for justification. It appeared, however, that so far as the authorities on international law could settle the question, provisions could not be considered contraband, except in the cases of seige, blockade or investiture, nor had the usage of nations made them such.[26] A full indemnification was therefore decreed by the commission, for such losses.

When the seizures of American vessels trading with enemy colonies came before the commission, that body reversed the sentence pronounced even by the British Admiralty courts of the last resort, thus establishing the principle that the Rule of 1756 could not properly be considered a part of the law of nations.[27]

Treatment of American Vessels in French Ports

Meanwhile complaints were being received by the state department of injuries to American merchants in France. During the summer of 1793 there was a lengthy embargo laid upon foreign vessels in the port of Bordeaux.[28] The captains appealed to the American minister, Gouverneur Morris, protesting against the injustice of being prevented from sailing with their cargoes. They even petitioned the National Assembly, pointing out that Americans had braved all the dangers to bring into French ports supplies of flour, rice, sugar, coffee and tobacco, and had also gone to the relief of French colonies in want of necessities, but now the lading and exportation of every species of merchandise was prohibited, and the departure of those vessels already laden

---

[26] Wheaton, Henry, *Life, Writing, and Speeches of Wm. Pinkney, Case of the Neptune*, p. 310 passim. *Hist. of Law of Nations in Europe and American*, H. Wheaton, pp. 380–86.

[27] *An Examination of the British Doctrine*, etc., Madison's Writings, Ed. G. Hunt, Vol. VII, p. 267, footnote.

[28] This was apparently ordered by the Convention to prevent communication by the royalists with foreign powers. Yet the detention of American ships was a serious matter for it would discourage future shipments, and Bordeaux in 1793 was menaced by a serious famine. See Aulard, *Recueil des actes de Comité de Salut Public*, Vol. 2, p. 577; 3, p. 362. Also *A. S. P.*, For. Vol. I, pp. 373–374. For the protest of Fauchet against this embargo see Corrs. of French Ministers, *Op. cit.*, p. 321.

was forbidden. It was not until the following spring that this embargo was removed. Fenwick, the American consul at Bordeaux was able to secure a partial reimbursement for the captains, but the question of demurrage remained to be adjusted between the two countries.[29] The hostility of Morris toward the revolution made it impossible for him to be of further service to his country in Paris. James Monroe, a man in thorough sympathy with the new order, was therefore appointed in his place. On his arrival in France, in August, 1794, Monroe found many of his countrymen "laboring under embarrassments of the most serious kind."[30] The causes for this condition were various. One of the chief was the delay in payment for food cargoes.

Mission of Monroe—Decrees of Convention

The harvest of 1793 had been below the average in France, and there was danger of famine in various departments. Arrangements were therefore made through Fauchet, French minister to the United States, to supply the deficiency in part from America. One New York firm agreed to supply twenty thousand barrels of flour and by October, 1794, in pursuance of this order, thirteen vessels, eluding the British cruisers, had arrived in the French ports from Bordeaux to Brest. Here however, there was great confusion and bungling in receiving and paying for the cargoes. The convention had reason to fear that commercial channels were being used for anti-revolutionary propaganda, and for draining away the property of the emigrés and the wealth of the country. By a decree of October, 1793, therefore, all foreign trade was concentrated in the hands of the government which was weighed down by the burden of its complicated and unaccustomed duties.[31] The agents of the commission of commerce in the ports had no authority to deal directly for the cargoes, but had to await orders from Paris. The captains after waiting, sometimes for as long as two months, while fruitless correspondence went on, in some cases themselves went to Paris,

---

[29] Dunlap and Claypoole, *Amer. Daily Advertiser*, June 28, 1794. Consular Letters, Bordeaux, Fenwick to Randolph, April 23, 1794.
[30] *A. S. P.*, For. I, p. 675.
[31] *Writings of James Monroe*, Vol. II, pp. 70–71.

hoping to hasten a settlement, but their ignorance of the language and the forms only involved them in new difficulties. For the payment of the cargoes already accepted by the government, the commissaries of commerce and finance by their endless formalities and delays completely exhausted the patience of the captains. Even in cases where contracts for supplies had been made through the French minister in America, payment was delayed.[32]

In the French ports there were a large number of American vessels which had been seized, contrary to treaty stipulations, by French privateers. These vessels had not been condemned, but had been stripped of most of their crews, and now were wasting away, in the charge of the few or incompetent hands left on board. The papers of these vessels were in the hands of the Commission of Marine, from which they had to go to the commission of public safety, and repeated demands and entreaties from the captains could not procure them.[33]

Another cause of complaint was the two embargoes at Bordeaux, in 1793 and '94.[34] One hundred and three owners of vessels claimed damages on that score. Then there were unwarranted seizures of American vessels on the high seas. Eleven of these vessels were in French ports by October, 1794, their passengers kept on board prison ships and the cases still unsettled. The case of the ship *Mary* was typical. On her way from London to Boston, she was captured by a French vessel. The crew and cabin were ransacked, and the passengers, among whom

---

[32] *A. S. P.*, For. v. 1, pp. 749–51.

[33] In a letter to the Commissioner of Supplies, Dec. 6, 1794, Fauchet complained of the difficulty of securing further shipments of grain from America. "You know as well as we, citizens," he wrote, "that it was not only the fear of the English, which caused America . . . to hazard her property. There has been failure to promise him (the American shipper) that he will not be detained by any embargo; that he will be able to leave as soon as his cargo is delivered, that he will be able to bring back the value of that cargo, either in specie, or in goods not prohibited." In addition to all these uncertainties was added that of the payment for the cargoes. *Corr. of French Ministers, Op. cit.*, p. 507.

[34] The cause of the embargo of '94 was probably the Proclamation of the Department of Bordeaux, embodying three Arrêtes of the Comm. of Public Safety. "The object of them is to insure the certain supply of articles of the first necessity to this country, by confining the exportation of their own valuable commodities to those who enter into engagements under security to import equal numbers of necessary articles. Dunlap and Claypoole, *Daily Advertiser*, July 5, 1794.

were three American families, after being robbed of some of their effects, were hurried in small boats to a sloop of war, although it was late at night and the sea was running high.[35]

All these cases were reported to Monroe by Fulwer Skipwith, the American consul in Paris, in a report submitted in October 1794. He estimated that there were about three hundred American vessels detained in French harbors for the reasons just given. Of one hundred and seventy claims, he had secured partial payment for thirty-eight, but for the remainder nothing.[36]

The result of Monroe's labors at first bade fair to be successful, for on November 15, 1794, the Convention passed a decree ordering that vessels of all neutral nations should enter and leave port freely, that a method of payment for the cargoes purchased should be agreed upon, and that only contraband and enemy property should be seized on neutral ships. All pending claims were to be settled.[37] Two months later in January, 1795, the Convention decided to carry out its treaty obligations fully, by exempting enemy property from seizure, when carried on neutral ships.[38]

Rumors of the mission of Jay, and the possibility of a treaty between the United States and Great Britain prevented entire cordiality, but Monroe declared that as negotiations continued the attachment of France and the United States was daily progressing.

---

[35] Report of Fulwer Skipwith to Monroe, Oct. 1794, *A. S. P.*, For. Vol. I, pp. 749–751.
[36] *Ibid.*
[37] *A. S. P.*, For. I, p. 689. One of the cases which illustrates this regulation is that of the Brig *Samuel*, belonging to Welcome Arnold of Providence, with a cargo of sugar, coffee and other articles, the property of Gibbs and Channing of Newport, consigned to a firm in Amsterdam in December, 1793. The brig was overhauled by a French frigate and taken into St. Malo, but the French government, later decided that the vessel and cargo were neutral property, and ordered restitution, except of such articles as the republic was in need. Accordingly the coffee was paid for in money, and delivered to the agent of the Commission of Commerce at St. Malo, and the sugar, rice, and staves were put in requisition by the navy. The case was not finally settled until 1797. *Gibbs and Channing Letter Book.*
[38] *A. S. P.*, For. I, pp. 267–268, *Monroe Writings*, Vol. II, pp. 167–168. For a good account of Monroe's negotiations see B. W. Bond, Jr., *Monroe's Mission to France 1794–96*, John Hopkins Univ. Studies in Hist. and Pol. Sci., Vol. 25.

Conditions in Santo Domingo, 1795–1797

By this time, serious mischief was afoot in the waters of the West Indies, which was complicated by the political situation in the French islands. The revolutionary government in France had not been able to make itself master in all the islands. Where the adherents of the old royalist party were strong, they combined with the English naval forces to defy the authority of the Republic. In the island of Santo Domingo the English and their French allies for a time held all the ports except Leogane and Cape Francois. The party of emigrés also held the island of Martinique while the Republican leaders were in power at Guadeloupe.[39]

Even before they learned of the decree of July, '96,[40] the agents of the Directory in the West Indies had issued regulations which anticipated the sweeping provisions of that document, and surpassed it in severity. In Santo Domingo, the notorious Santhonax, and his partner Raimond began a course which opened the door for all kinds of violence and excesses against the hapless

---

[39] The ingenuity and deception to which American shippers resorted under these circumstances is well illustrated in the operation of Girard with Santo Domingo in 1795. Massac and Co., Girard's French correspondents at Port au Prince, reported that the regulations of the British authorities there as to articles permitted to be brought in by American vessels, varied constantly and at short notice. Dry goods were permitted one month, and forbidden the next. They suggested that a consignment of such goods, which they were anxious to receive might be landed by small boats sent out at night, after receiving the signal of a red flag at the mizzen mast of the American vessel. Captains who undertook voyages of this character had need of robust consciences, that honor and good faith among nations, which courts sometimes postulated, being not seldom laid aside. Captain Collady of the ship *Sally*, which Girard dispatched to Santo Domingo, in response to the suggestions of Massac, was provided with two different letters of instructions. The first directed him to go to the port of Leogane, and sell his cargo there. This was to be shown to French cruisers, in case any such should meet him. His real instructions directed him to go to Port-au-Prince, and when near enough to be seen from the shore, to hoist a red flag at the mast head, and to await instructions from Massac. In returning, if met by French cruisers, the captain was to have ready a plausible story that his original destination had been Leogane, but having been met by a British cruiser, he had been compelled to go to Port au Prince and sell his cargo there. The *Sally* arrived without mishap, and delivered her cargo at L'Archaye, a port in the possession of the English. She was laden with flour, wine, osnaburgs and other linens, and cheeses, described by Girard, as "the finest cargo that has ever left our continent for your port." The voyage was, an extremely profitable one for the consignor. McMaster, *Life of Girard*, I, pp. 313–318.

[40] "Neutral vessels shall be treated by France as they allow themselves to be treated by England."

Americans. In justifying their conduct to the Minister of Marine at Paris, (February, 1797) they naively explained that "having found no resource in finance, and knowing the unfriendly disposition of the Americans, and to avoid perishing in distress, they had armed vessels for cruising, and already eighty-seven cruisers were at sea, and that for three months the administration had subsisted, and individuals been enriched, with the product of those prizes."[41] At the same time Victor Hugues and Lebas, agents of the Directory in the Windward Islands, issued a decree, subjecting to capture and confiscation neutral vessels destined for all ports in the French islands delivered up to the English, and occupied and defended by the emigrés. They specified seven such ports—Martinique, St. Lucia, Tobago, Port au Prince, St. Marks, L'Archaye and Jeremie besides Demerara, Berbice, and Essequibo, ports in British Guiana, also any vessel that cleared out for the West Indies generally.[42] Under this decree occurred such a seizure as that of the schooner *Ariel*, on her way from Baltimore to Martinique, and condemned by the French Admiralty court in Guadeloupe for being "bound to an enemy's port, in rebellion against the French republic." Similarly the Brig *Sea Nymph*, laden with coffee at Jeremie (Santo Domingo) was seized and carried into Cape François on the same island and condemned on the ground of being laden with colonial produce of a revolted port in a state of seige, under the protection of the British government.[43]

The ship *Commerce* on her way from Hamburg to Newport was prevented from reaching her destination by the fierce storms of December, 1796. Her rudder and sails were disabled by repeated gales, and her commander was obliged to bear away to the West Indies for safety. Here the vessel was plundered of a part of her valuable cargo by a French cruiser. In their protest to Timothy Pickering, Secretary of State, Gibbs and Channing, the owners of the *Commerce*, stated that they had taken pains to

---

[41] *Annals 5th Cong.*, v. 3, pp. 3547–48; *A. S. P.*, For. II, pp. 57–63. See also *J. Q. Adams' Writings* (Ford ed.) II, p. 185. In the Council of Five Hundred, Pastoret expressed great indignation at this arming of cruisers against a friendly nation.
[42] *A. S. P.*, For. III, pp. 291–292.
[43] Yates, *Reports of Cases before Penna. Supreme Court*, v. IV, p. 160.

secure every official paper, issued by the custom house in the United States, for the verification of American property. In addition they had made declaration on oath before a notary public, of the ship and cargo being wholly their property, no foreign citizen or subject being interested therein, but even the official signature of the French consul to this document did not protect them from spoliation.[44]

A report of Secretary Pickering to President Adams, gives an account of French seizures from October of 1796 to June of 1797. This report revealed an appalling condition little short of piracy in the Carribean. Besides the pretext of going to or from British ports, American vessels were seized on the ground of defective papers. If on looking over those documents, the bill of lading or the sea letter or the list of passengers was lacking, or was in any way irregular, the vessel was seized and condemned. Neither the owners of the captured vessels nor their agents were admitted to trials before the Vice Admiralty courts, and captains and crews were beaten, insulted and even killed. No less than three hundred and sixteen American ships had been seized principally in the Carribean,[45] by the French between July, 1796, and June, 1797. The report included some seizures in French ports without any pretext, except that the captors wanted the prize. Some of these vessels were on their way from American ports to the islands with cargoes of provisions, lumber, or naval stores from the mainland, and drygoods and wine from Europe. Others were carrying cargoes of sugar, coffee, cotton, rum and molasses from the islands to American ports. A few came from European ports. They ranged in size and value from the small sloop *Honor* from New London valued at $3,000 to the large ship *James* from Baltimore, valued at $30,000. This latter vessel was, however, afterwards liberated. Twenty-three cases were given in full detail, with sworn statements from the captains,

---

[44] *Gibbs and Channing Letter Book.*

[45] *A. S. P.*, For. II, pp. 28–63. These lists in Pickering's Report were compiled from two Philadelphia newspapers, the *Philadelphia Gazette*, and the *Gazette of the United States.* It is perhaps unnecessary to say that the cases are not gathered from sensational scare head accounts such as we find in modern newspapers, but from obscure small type letters from correspondents in various quarters, and hence are probably entirely worthy of credence.

and the sentences of condemnation from Santo Domingo and Guadeloupe. The schooner *Betsey* from Curaçoa to New York was seized and condemned for want of a sea letter. The sloop *Rebecca*, from Jamaica to Philadelphia was condemned for coming from a British port. The ship *Eliza* from Barbadoes, and the brig *Lady Walterdorf* were seized for the same reason. The ship *Pattern* from New York to Jamaica with a cargo of codfish, rice and flour, was taken by a vessel which approached under English colors, but proved to be a French privateer from Santo Domingo.[46] Inured by their occupation to hardship and danger, the seamen who dared a voyage in these lawless waters, engaged in an extra-hazardous venture. More than thirty cases of violence are recorded in Secretary Pickering's report. These include pouring broadsides into a vessel, wounding four of the crew, exciting the crew to assassinate their captain, beating a supercargo with a sword, so that he died, and throwing a captain overboard. "American prisoners," it was said, "were dying in Guadeloupe in greater numbers than were ever known on board the *Jersey* prison ship at New York, during the American war."[47]

The period of growing friendship reported by Monroe in the fall of 1795 was interrupted by the news of the Jay treaty. This news resounded in Paris, to us Monroe's words, "like a clap of thunder". In February of 1796, the Minister of Foreign Affairs, De a Croix, informed Monroe that the French government considered that our ratification of the treaty with England annulled our treaty with France,—and that we had really taken our

---

[46] Among these greedy sea robbers, there were even some unprincipled Americans, who took their vessels to Guadeloupe or Santo Domingo, secured commissions from the agents of the Directory, and preyed upon their country men. *A. S. P.*, For. Vol. II, p. 40.
[47] *A. S. P.*, For. II, pp. 28–63, Lindsay, W. S., *Hist. of Merchant Shipping and Ancient Commerce*, I, pp. 359–362. Binney, H., *Report of Cases adjudged in Supreme Court of Penna.*, I, pp. 47–50. Watson and Paul vs. Insurance Co. of North America. For the capture of an American vessel by the French within sight of the Delaware lighthouses, and condemned by a French court in Santo Domingo on five grounds, See Murgatroyd vs. Crawford, J. Yeats, *Report of Penna. Cases*, II, pp. 420–428.

place with the "coalesced powers" against France.[48] He also charged the American government with alleged breaches of its treaty with France. Among these were the interference of American courts in certain French prize cases, the admission of English vessels into American ports, after having taken French vessels as prizes, and failure to allow the consuls of France their full power in American cities. No satisfaction was accorded Monroe for the wrongs of American shippers, against which he had protested, and in July, 1796, the Directory announced that the French Republic would treat neutral vessels, as to confiscation, search or capture, in the same manner as such neutral vessels should suffer the English to treat them.[49]

After the recall of Monroe, in November, 1796, occurred the unsuccessful mission of Charles Cotesworth Pinkney. While Pinkney, joined by John Marshall and Elbridge Gerry, were protesting against the seizure of enemy goods from American vessels, the Directory were ordering that in the future not only the goods, but the entire vessel should be seized. A decree of January, 1798 declared that the character of vessels should be determined by that of the cargoes. If loaded with the products of England or her possessions, they should be good prize, no matter who the owner might be. Moreover, no foreign vessel which had entered an English port should be admitted to a French port, except in case of necessity.[50] We have here the culmination of the attack of Republican France against the commerce of her rival, before the peace of Amiens. In the regulations of January, 1798 are foreshadowed those decrees issued from Berlin and Milan, by which Napoleon, a few years later, with nearly the entire continent at his back, attempted to batter down the solid walls of England's commercial prosperity.

Much of the earlier sympathy of the American people with the

---

[48] Cipher Dispatch, Monroe to Madison, Feb. 27, 1796. *Monroe Writings*, II, pp. 460–461. Fauchet in his official dispatches, declared that Sec'y Randolph had assured him that the object of Jay's mission was only to procure reparations for damages to American Commerce. Corresp. of French Ministers, *Op cit.*, pp. 375–77.

[49] A. S. P., For. I, p. 577.

[50] A. S. P., For. II, p. 182; Mahan, *Influence of Sea Power upon French Revolution and Empire*, II, pp. 249–250.

revolution was forfeited by these actions of the Directory. The suspension of commercial intercourse[51] and the state of quasi-warfare with that country followed.

The Convention of Morfontaine,[52] which relieved us from the burdens of our former treaties, concerning the defense of French possessions in America, and exclusive privileges to France, was ratified by the Senate, February, 1801. By this arrangement, the burden of the indemnities which Monroe had been sent to Paris to secure, nearly six years before, was transferred from the shoulders of the French government to those of the United States. This was a heavy price to pay for the accommodation of the difficulties with France, but the avoidance of war, and the securing of a new treaty, free from the entangling and burdensome provisions of the old arrangements were worth the cost.

The claims thus assumed by the American government were those for supplies, embargoes, and captures at sea, payment for which had already been claimed from the government of France before September 30, 1800.[53] Similar losses for which no claim had been made by that date, constituted a separate class of claims. These are the famous French Spoliation Claims, consideration of which proved a hard perennial among the lesser agenda of Congress from 1803 to 1891. Finally in the latter year, a law was passed authorizing payment.

British Seizures 1795 to Peace of Amiens

For some years after the Jay treaty there was comparative freedom from seizures by the British. But it was only comparative. There remained several grounds for taking American prizes, even before the new restriction of 1798, in regard to neutral trading with enemy colonies. One of these grounds was disputed ownership of a vessel. French ship owners in some cases tried to protect themselves from seizure, by a pretended

---

[51] *U. S. Statutes at Large*, I, p. 565. *Annals 5th Cong.*, pp. 1859–62, 2120–22.
[52] Malloy, *Treaties and Conventions*, I, p. 496.
[53] *Ibid.*, pp. 513–516; 517–520; *U. S. Statutes at Large*, 25, pp. 897–907. See also Webster, *Works, Curtis ed.*, II, pp. 152–178 passim. Report of Sec'y. of State, Papers on File in Dept. of State touching the unsettled claims of citizens of U. S. vs. France prior to July 31, 1801. Senate Documents 205. 48 Cong. 1st Session.

sale to Americans. Of this nature was the case of the ship *Bernon* which it was claimed had been sold in Bordeaux to an American, but which one witness declared, he believed to be the property of M. Chanon of Bordeaux. Although there was a certificate of American ownership taken, on oath before Mr. Fenwick, the American consul, the ship was condemned.⁵⁴ The ship, *Two Brothers*, had formerly been employed in French commerce, but in December, 1795, it was sold ostensibly to Walter Seaman, an American living in France. Taken by a British ship in 1799, it was condemned, because since its sale, it appeared never to have gone into a neutral harbor, the bill of sale was unauthenticated, and Seaman's actions toward the vessel did not seem to be that of owner.⁵⁵

Another class of seizures were those on the score of domicile and citizenship. Such was the case of the *Sallie*, belonging to Stephen Girard, returning from Hamburg and Batavia to the Delaware, and captured by the British brig *Cleopatra*, taken into Halifax and condemned. Although the owner furnished proof of having lived in America since 1774, the judge at Halifax declared that "Girard being born in France and owing his allegiance to France, and having been engaged during some years in a course of trade with the Isle of France, a French colony," the vessel and cargo were subject to condemnation. Girard, however, wrote to John Marshall, Secretary of State, protesting his American citizenship, and Rufus King, American minister to England, was directed to take the matter up in London.⁵⁶ But in the meantime the matter was settled by the captors paying to Girard the net proceeds of the cargo, each side paying its own costs and Girard receiving back his vessel.⁵⁷ The British

---

⁵⁴ Robinson, *Admiralty Reports*, Vol. I, pp. 101–106, London ed.
⁵⁵ *Ibid.*, pp. 131–134, London ed. In order to forestall any condemnation on the ground of enemy property, prudent American shippers took every precaution. Thus the Captain of the ship *John*, on a voyage from Newport to Surinam in the winter of 1796, was forbidden to take either freight or passengers on the homeward voyage, that there might be no cause for suspicion, and in addition to the usual custom house papers the vessel carried a declaration on oath before a notary that the vessel and cargo were solely property of the firm of Gibbs and Channing and this was further certified by the signatures of both the British and French consuls, *Gibbs and Channing Letter Book*.
⁵⁶ MacMaster, *Life of Girard*, I, pp. 383–385.
⁵⁷ *Ibid.*, pp. 391–92.

courts were inconsistent in this class of cases. They wished to count Girard a Frenchman because he had been born a Frenchman, even though he lived in America, but when they had before them the property of Fulwer Skipwith, the American consul at Paris, born in America, but living and trading in France, they counted him a Frenchman. Similarly, in the case of the *Betsey*, Furlong, which came before the Commission under the Jay Treaty, the British Admiralty courts had decided that George Patterson of Baltimore the part owner and supercargo of the vessel seized, who had remained for a short time in Guadeloupe on business was an inhabitant of that island, and therefore an enemy, and his vessel a lawful prize. Pinkney's arguments overthrew the decision in regard to the domicile of Patterson.[58] In the cases of Girard[59] and Skipwith American citizenship was finally admitted, but at the cost of considerable money, delay and annoyance.

On January 25, 1798, a new order in council was issued designed to give European neutrals the same rights which Americans enjoyed, by the January, 1794 order to secure colonial products for their own use. British vessels were authorized "to bring in for adjudication all vessels with their cargoes laden with goods the produce of any island or settlement belonging to France, Spain or the United Provinces and coming directly therefrom to any port of Europe, not being a port of this kingdom nor a port of that country to which such ships being neutral, shall belong." This was really a relaxation of the rule of 1756, as it affected European neutrals. It had no bearing on American trade.

---

[58] *Life and Writings of Wm. Pinkney*, H. Wheaton, pp. 242–46.
[59] Girard himself, however, was not consistent. In 1793 one of his vessels was seized by *Le Sans Culotte*, one of the Genet privateers, and in writing to Genet in protest, Girard describes himself as "Etienne Girard, a French merchant established for several years in this city (Philadelphia) where he has had constant business relations with the principal commercial cities of France, and particularly with citizen Samatan of Marseilles." "The wheat seized," he declared, "was for the account of a Frenchman, made by the order of an exporter who is French and an agent for Samatan, sole owner of the said cargo of wheat." *Life of Stephen Girard*, McMaster, Vol. I, p. 189.
[60] Binney, *Reports of Cases Adjudged before the Supreme Court of Penna.*, Vol. 6 Kohn vs. Ins. Co. of North America.

The ship *Gadsden*, sailing from Newport to Pasages in Spain, was seized by the British sloop of war, *Phaesant*, and taken in to Halifax, where part of the cargo, consisting of cocoa, tobacco, indigo and other articles was condemned, because they were proved to have come from Laguira in Venezuela, the original Spanish papers having been discovered on board.[60]

The order of 1798 requiring neutrals who came from enemy colonies to bring their cargoes to the ports of their own countries, or to those of Great Britain, was violated by the Danes and Swedes, who slipped into the ports of Holland on their way home. To prevent this an order was issued in March, 1799, declaring a blockade of the ports of Holland. This order was in force for about eight months and a number of American vessels were seized for attempting its evasion.[61]

In 1800 and 1801, the harbor of Cadiz was blockaded by the English, and several American vessels were seized for attempting to enter or leave this port.[62]

---

[61] The reports of the court trials of these blockade runners illustrate the persistance of American captains in seeking their desired havens, and the ruses of shippers in attempting to circumvent what they regarded as unfair restrictions. *Cf. Case of the Mercurius*, Robinson, I, p. 83; Columbia, *Ibid.*, pp. 154–157; Betsey, *Ibid.*, pp. 280–283; *Juno*, Robinson, II, pp. 116–120.

[62] The case of the *Peacock* presents several interesting features, Robinson, IV, pp. 154–160.

II

Restrictions of Great Britain upon Neutral Trade 1803-1806—British Blockades, 1803–1806—The Santo Domingo Trade 1803–1806—The Indirect Trade of the United States 1793–1807—The Essex Decision.

RESTRICTIONS OF GREAT BRITIAN UPON NEUTRAL TRADE 1803–1806

British Blockades, 1803–1806

After the brief breathing spell of twenty months ushered in by the Peace of Amiens, the first action of the belligerents to engage our attention is the remarkable series of blockades instituted by the British government, in various parts of the world. These, as we shall see, led to reprisals from the enemy, and started the warfare of orders and decrees which affected American commerce to a far greater degree than the restrictions of the earlier war.

In the campaign to seize enemy colonies, after the resumption of war in 1803, Great Britain declared a blockade of the islands of Guadeloupe and Martinique. In reply to Madison's inquiries as to the scope of this order, word was received from the Admiralty office, in April, 1804, that this blockade should only apply to those ports in the islands which were actually invested, and neutral vessels were not to be seized, in attempting to enter them, unless they had previously been warned not to do so.[1] What was most important, orders to this effect had been sent to Commodore Hood, the commander on that station, and to the Vice Admiralty courts in the West Indies and Nova Scotia.

This blockade, however, does not seem to have been very strictly maintained, for when the schooner *May and Eliza* went on a voyage from Boston to Surinam, in the spring of 1804, and stopped at Martinique, her master found no blockade existing there, although her owners, learning of the captain's intention,

---

[1] *A. S. P.*, For. III, p. 266.

had hastily purchased insurance to cover that contingency.[2]

There was also at the same time a blockade of certain ports of the island of St. Domingo, although there seems to have been no formal notification to that effect made to our State Department.

The vessel *Sukey and Polly* sailed from New Orleans, in August, 1803, for Cape François. On September 23, she passed through the Turk's Island Passage, and came in sight of the headlands of Hispaniola (Santo Domingo), between Cape François and Cape Nicholas Mole. Proceeding to this place, she was ordered away by a British ship of war, the commander of which declared that all the ports of the island in the possession of the French were blockaded by a British squadron, and endorsed her register to that effect.[3]

Another blockaded area in the West Indies was the small island of Curaçao belonging to the Dutch, and a busy mart of colonial trade. In March of 1804, Admiral Duckworth announced that he had decided to convert the seige of this island into a blockade.[4] This fact was communicated to Madison by Antony Merry, British minister to the United States, in April, 1804, but does not seem to have been clearly understood in American ports.

The schooner *Mariner* from New York, laden with meal, flour, fish and onions, started for Antigua, intending to go later to Curaçoa. The vessel on the way encountered a storm, and was obliged to put into the harbor of St. Croix, to refit. Here she sold part of her cargo. "As the vessel proved to be a dull sailor, the captain deemed it impracticable to beat up to Antigua against the winds and currents which there prevailed. He therefore proceeded to Curaçoa, to leeward of Antiqua. He was captured and taken into Jamaica and condemned, December, 1804, on the charge of the breach of the blockade. The master declared he did not know of any blockade, except from vague reports which he had not credited.[5] The blockade of Curaçoa in fact, was not made effective until December of 1806, when a

---

[2] Taylor vs. Sumner et al., *Mass. Supreme Court Reports, Tyng*, Vol. 4.
[3] Robinson vs. Marine Ins. Co., Johnson, *N. Y. Sup. Court Reports*, Vol. II.
[4] *A. S. P.*, For. III, p. 266.
[5] Kane vs. Columbia Ins. Co., Johnson, *N. Y. Reports* 2.

large fleet of English ships of war appeared.⁶ The island capitulated in 1807, and remained in the possession of the English until the end of the war.

On the other side of the world, a British squadron was blockading the Isle of France in 1805. The vessels which were ready for sea, however, eluded the men of war, as a correspondent wrote, by sailing in the night. There were five American vessels in the harbor at the time of his letter.⁷

In the summer of 1804, several American vessels made the journey to Curaçoa and traded without meeting any armed vessel near the island. In fact, it was possible to purchase insurance in New York for such a voyage for a premium of but 3½ per cent.⁸ The Brig *Lapwing*, the property of Snell and Stagg, of that city, had made one trip to the island safely, arriving August 23 and leaving September 5. The captain reported that at Curaçoa, the impression prevailed that the blockade had been lifted since July 21, when the British armed ship off the harbor of Amsterdam (Curaçoa) had disappeared. He reported this information on his return to New York, and made a second trip, during which he was captured by His Majesty's ships *Diana* and *Pelican*, off the eastern end of the island, November 12, 1804. At the trial of the case in the vice admiralty court in Jamaica, the captor cited the blockading order of Admiral Duckworth, which as we have seen, had been communicated to the American government in April of 1804. The master, however, denied that it was known in New York. The case was appealed by the owners to the High Court of Admiralty in London, and finally to the Lords of Appeal with the result that the appeal was granted and the vessel and cargo returned to its owners.⁹

In the following year, Sir Home Popham having withdrawn his fleet from the Cape of Good Hope, sailed westward to attack the settlements of South America. In June, 1806, without any

---

⁶ *N. Y. Evening Post*, Feb. 11, 1807.
⁷ *Appeals before Lords Comm. in Prize Causes*, Case of *Lapwing*. New York Ships.
⁸ *Ibid.*
⁹ *Poulson Daily Advertiser*, Oct. 19, 1805.

authorization from his government, he instituted a blockade of Montevideo. No notification of this was given to neutrals, until sometime afterward, nor was the blockade kept up with uniformity and rigor, several vessels managing to pass in and out, before September.[10]

In that month, the vessel *Rolla* from Philadelphia, under cover of a fog, passed the blockaders, who were lying seven or eight miles off shore. When the fog lifted, the English vessels pursued and fired upon the *Rolla*, but Spanish gunboats from the town came out for her protection, and she got safely in. On coming out, however, she was not so fortunate. On November 20, she was captured by the frigate *Medusa*, sent to England and condemned.[11]

The first blockade in Europe, after the rupture of the peace of Amiens, was that of Havre and the Seine, laid September, 1803.[12]

How American vessels tried to evade this blockade is illustrated by the voyage of the Brig *Shepherdess*. This vessel started with a clearance and all her other public papers for Embden, but the master had private instructions to go to Havre. In the channel, the *Shepherdess* was met by the British Cruiser *Pluto* and the master was warned of the blockade of Havre, but told that he might enter Fécamp. Paying no attention to this warning, however, the captain continued his course to Havre, and was seized while attempting to enter that port on September, 1804. The case came before the High Court of Admiralty, where the condemnation of both vessel and cargo was confirmed.

Sir Wm. Scott in pronouncing judgment, pointed out that although the blockade was known in America, the clearing out for Havre would not have been a ground for condemnation. On account of the great distance of America, it would be allowable for a vessel to clear out for a blockaded port, on the supposition that by the time of its arrival there, the blockade might be

---

[10] Ludlow vs. Union Ins. Co., Segeant and Rawle, *Penna. Supreme Court Reports*, Vol. II.
[11] *Ibid.*
[12] Robinson, *Admiralty Reports*, Vol. V, London ed., p. XI.

removed. This information must be sought at some English port, however, and not by approaching the port in question.[13]

A similar censure was incurred by the ship *Harriet*, which had attempted to enter the same port. This vessel started on March 16, 1804, from New York, where the blockade of Havre was not known officially, for the custom house granted the *Harriet* a clearance for that port. The vessel came to the mouth of the channel, where she met a British ship, which upon inquiry, informed the captain of the blockade of Havre. Nevertheless he attempted to enter the prohibited port. The *Harriet* was captured, and condemned in the Vice Admiralty court, on the ground that the blockade of Havre was known in New York at the time of sailing. The case being taken to the High Court of Admiralty, the Lords of Appeal decreed that the vessel should be restored, to the owner, subject to the captor's expenses. "We have to lament", so ran the record of the Lords of Appeal, "a want of prudence, in individuals, under such circumstances, that take the chance of information that they get at sea, and do not touch at a British port in the channel to inquire." It was no inconvenience, the court declared, to send in a boat to make inquiries.[14]

In April, 1805, a blockade was laid upon Cadiz, and the neighboring port of St. Lucar.[15] During the summer of 1805, seven ships of the line, under Admiral Collingwood maintained the blockade. There were several Spanish ships in this port, which the English wished to detain there to prevent their joining the French fleet. Six months later, this blockade was relaxed, admitting any goods except provisions and war materials. In November, 1806 (after Trafalgar), a correspondent wrote that the blockade had not been very strict of late. Nevertheless, he declared that business was at an entire standstill. When it was

---

[13] Case of the *Shepherdess, Ibid.*
[14] H. C. A. Miscellanea, 473.
[15] Robinson, *Admiralty Reports*, Vol. XI. A case arising under this blockade was that of the ship *Hare*, from New York, with a cargo of wine and salt, the *Hare* sailed from Cadiz, July 21, 1805, and was captured the same day, by His Majesty's Frigate *Hydra*. The case was appealed from the Vice-Admiralty Court, at Gibraltar by the owner of the vessel, Isaac Claason of New Prize Causes, March 1810, pronounced vessel and cargo lawful prize. *Appeals before Lords of Comm. in Prize Causes*. The *Hare*, N. Y. Ships.

impossible to land cargoes at Cadiz, the nearby port of Algeciras formed a convenient port of entry.[16]

Naples having been occupied by French troops, early in 1806, a blockade of that city by the British was in progress during the summer of that year. Nothing was able to enter the port except small craft, but the price of colonial goods was not thereby raised, partly because of the expectation of peace.[17]

In all the cases hitherto enumerated, American shippers suffered delay and expense, and in many instances seizure and condemnation of their property. Although a report of the senate described some of these blockades as spurious,[18] yet because all the orders applied to particular islands or ports, a show of legality might be urged for all of them. Since there were other more pressing grounds of complaint against England, our government made no very strong protest against them.

In addition to these, however, a new sort of blockading orders began to come from the Privy Council. These applied to great stretches of the coastline of northwestern Europe. Even the huge navy of Britain, with its thousand ships, distributed at points of danger in two hemispheres, could not spare cruisers and luggers sufficient for patroling such magnificent distances. These orders were therefore contrary to the principles of international law and to treaty stipulations. They led to reprisal from the French in the famous Berlin Decree, and began that war of commercial edicts between the two antagonists, which did not cease until the overthrow of Napoleon. During this time the commerce of the United States, as one shrewd Yankee captain put it, was like a whip top, struck at by both belligerents.

It will be remembered that shortly before the peace of Amiens, the English government had laid a blockade upon the entire coast of Holland.[19] This was the only extensive blockade laid in the first decade of the war, and it lasted only about eight months.

---

[16] *New York Evening Post*, Jan. 14, 1807, Acton, pp. 252–261.
[17] *Ibid.*, Jan 8, 1807. For the blockade of Genoa in autumn of 1804. See the case of the *Favourite*, in *Appeals before Lords Comm. in Prize Causes*, Phila. Ships.
[18] *A. S. P.*, For. III, p. 220.
[19] See ante chap. 2 p. 50

In August of 1804, however, a blockade was proclaimed by the British Privy Council of all the ports of the northern coast of France from Fécamp to Ostend, a distance of about two hundred miles. In this stretch of coast, eleven ports and the entrance to the River Somme, were declared closed to commerce. The blockade was to be a rigorous one, and Monroe was duly informed of it, by Lord Harrowby, Minister of Foreign Affairs.[20]

Since none of these ports except Havre, which was already blockaded, appear to have been much frequented by American shipping, this order made but little change in the routes of our merchantmen.

Eighteen months later, however, a more serious order was announced. Frederick William of Prussia, dazzled by Napoleon's promises of the imperial title, and the addition of George III's German kingdom to his dominions, had closed his ports to British vessels, and had occupied Hanover.[21] This province was bounded on its north sea frontage by the Elbe and the Weser. The English government therefore, in April, 1806, declared a blockade of these two great rivers of North Germany, as well as of the Ems and the Trave.[22]

American exports to Hamburg and Bremen, which at the beginning of our national period had been inconsiderable, had risen to nine million dollars worth in 1795, and to seventeen millions in 1799. Since the peace of Amiens, however, they had fallen to from three to six millions annually.[23]

In May of 1806, John Forbes, American consul at Hamburg, wrote to Madison, that contrary to expectations, the British were rigorously blockading all entrances to that city except Tonningen, a town in Schleswig, (Denmark) a few miles above Hamburg, which was destined later to serve for several years, as the port of entry for that great mart. Since vessels for Hamburg now landed at Tonningen, Forbes sought papers from the American consul at Copenhagen, allowing him to act as consul there.[24]

---
[20] *A. S. P.*, For. III, p. 266.
[21] *Annual Register*, 1806, p. 676.
[22] *Ibid.*, pp. 677–78. *A. S. P.*, For. III, p. 267.
[23] Pitkin, *Statistical View*, p. 237.
[24] Forbes to Madison, May 14, 1806, Consular Letters, Hamburg.

A month later, however, these arrangements were altered by a new order. This declared that the entire coast, including rivers and ports, from the Elbe on the east to Brest on the west, extending for over a thousand miles, was to be considered under blockade. Between the Seine and Ostend, no ships were to enter or leave, but beyond that strip, neutral vessels could come in and go out, to and from neutral ports, if laden on neutral account.[25]

This last order, commonly known as Fox's blockade, was in retaliation for Napoleon's instigation of Prussian hostility toward England. It was really a mitigation of the blockade of the northern ports of France, and of the German rivers. "While it professes, as Monroe, then American minister to England, wrote to Madison in May of 1806 to extend the blockade further than was heretofore done, nevertheless, it takes it from many ports already blockaded, indeed, from all east of Ostend, and west of the Seine, except in articles contraband of war and enemy property, which are seizable without a blockade."[26] From the wording of the order, Monroe believed that even colonial produce might be introduced into the ports outside the blockaded strip if it came indirectly, as he was convinced that the principles of the Essex decision, as we shall see later, had now been given up by the British government.

The exports of colonial goods from the United States, in the years 1806 and 1807, to the ports included in the Elbe to Brest Blockade, prove the correctness of Monroe's view. Forbes wrote that a number of American vessels came to Hamburg in the summer of 1806, on the relaxation of the British blockade.[27] In that year and the following, brown sugar to the amount of nearly 110 million pounds, and coffee to the amount of about 50

---

[25] *A. S. P.*, For. III, p. 267. The impossibility of blockading the west coast of France has been pointed out by Mahan. The heaviest gales on the Bay of Biscay blow dead on shore. "A vessel propelled by steam can keep a certain distance from shore for a long time, but for a sailing vessel, there is the necessity of gaining an offing, before a gale comes and the helpless drifting during its continuance . . . a blockade of the entire French coast does not seem to have been contemplated by the British ministry." A. T. Mahan, *Influence of Sea Power upon French Revolution and Empire*, I, pp. 99–100.
[26] *A. S. P.*, For. Vol. III, p. 124.
[27] Forbes to Madison, Oct. 8, 1806, Consular Letters, Hamburg.

million pounds was carried from the United States, to the ports of Holland,[28] and to Hamburg and Bremen.

The growing strictness in the exclusion of British goods from the latter ports, after the peace of Tilsit led the English government to relax still more the blockades of the German rivers. An order of September, 1806 withdrew the blockade entirely from the Elbe to the Ems inclusive.[29] This was done, because British goods, as we shall see later, were beginning to seek the cover of the American flag, in order to enter the continent, and it therefore became an object of the British government to facilitate instead of hinder the entrance of American vessels into the ports of North Germany.

There were a number of captures by British vessels during the period, on the ground of enemy property. A typical case is that of the Brig *Louisiana*, which left Philadelphia for La Guaira, laden with flour, dry goods and other articles. She was seized September 24, 1806, by the private ship of war *Patriot* and carried into Tortola, where a libel was filed against four boxes of merchandise and one box of vanilla as the property of Joseph Peries, the supercargo of the vessel, an enemy. During the trial at Tortola, Perez made deposition that he had been born in Milan, Italy, but he exhibited a certificate of naturalization as an American citizen, bearing date of August 28, 1804. The captors, however, were able to show a previous deposition of Jacques Peries, dated February 10, 1800, made in connection with the trial of another captured vessel, which showed that Peries had been born in France. The Judge at Tortola therefore pronounced the goods in question as lawful prize.[30]

The Brig *Favourite*, bound from New York to Pointe à Pitre, Guadeloupe, was captured July 2, 1806, and the case came before the Vice Admiralty court of Antigua. The charge of the captors was that certain goods on board the *Favourite* were the property of M. Seixas, an enemy. Thirty-two interrogations each were addressed to the master, mate, supercargo, and one

---

[28] Pitkin, *Statistical View*, pp. 157–161.
[29] A. S. P., For. III, p. 267.
[30] Case of the *Louisiana*—*Appeals before Lords Comm. of Appeal in Prize Causes*, Philadelphia Ships.

passenger, in regard to the vessel and its cargo. The affidavit of Seixes, showing his American citizenship was produced, but the court condemned the property. This decision was reversed, however, in June, 1810, when the case came before the Lords of Appeal.[31]

The Santo Domingo Trade, 1803–1805

After the period of friendly relations accompanying the sale of Louisiana, the first difference between France and the United States grew out of the Santo Domingo trade question.

In that unhappy island, the negroes, after the failure of La Clerc's expedition, had made themselves masters of a large part of the French domain. American trade was still carried on, and as usual, greatly enriched its promoters. As in the former war, the privateers commissioned by the French government attempted to prevent this trade with the ports in the possession of the blacks.

The schooner *Mars*, having brought a cargo from New York to Jeremie, (a port in the possession of the insurgents) was returning from that port loaded with sugar and coffee when she was captured in February, 1803, by two French privateers. The captan of the *Mars* returned to Philadelphia and there just after his arrival, he found in the market part of his cargo in the wrappings which he recognized. It had been bought up after seizure, transported to a Philadelphia warehouse, and offered for sale. The result was a lawsuit, which found its way to the Supreme Court of Pennsylvania, over the ownership of the cargo. The judgment of the court was that it was competent for France to vindicate her laws interdicting trade with her revolted colonists. The seizure was therefore justified, and the original owner was not able to recover his property.[32]

Even while the French authorities were obliged to flee, they attempted to prevent the blacks from receiving supplies. The

---

[31] Case of the *Favourite, Ibid.*, New York Ships. It appears that while British authorities refused to recognize certificates of American citizenship in the case of former British sailors, the admiralty courts, in the case of Seixes, and in many other cases held such certificates valid.

[32] *A. S. P.*, For. 2, p. 750, 747.

Brig *Neptune* of Baltimore, from Surinam, stopped at the port of Jacmel. She was captured after leaving that port by the French vessel *Le Serpant* and condemned by a tribunal sitting on a French vessel at sea, and claiming to be the court of prizes at the Mole,[33] but far beyond the jurisdictional limits of that place.

Piracy had for years been endemic in the waters of the Carribean, but the collapse of the French power in St. Domingo gave great opportunity for irregular seizures under the French flag, which American merchants called by that name. Barracoa and St. Jago, ports on the eastern coast of Cuba were the headquarters of these freebooters. During the spring of 1804, the schooner *Peggy* and the brigs *John* and *Joanna* of Newburyport were taken to these ports by vessels sailing as French privateers, and the American ships and cargoes were seized without any form of trial.[34]

In July of 1804 General Ferrand, representing what was left of the French authority in St. Domingo, issued a proclamation[35] designed to withdraw all commissions which had expired, been transferred, or irregularly issued, but this did not put a stop to the practice. In December, 1804, it was stated in Congress that the losses of the insurance companies of Baltimore alone, from these seizures amounted to nearly $500,000.[36]

Under these circumstances the American shippers attempted to protect themselves by arming their vessels. But under this guise it was not long before arms were being carried to the revolting blacks.

Conditions of this armed trade are well illustrated by the experience of the vessels *Hopewell* and *Rockwell*, which started from New York for Les Cayes, in June, 1804, the former armed with twelve six-pound cannon, and two twelve-pounders, as well as small arms, and a crew of twenty men. Before they reached their destination they were met by a French privateer, which

---

[33] Peters, *Admiralty Decisions*, District Court of U. S., Penna. District, Vol. 2, pp. 345-355.
[34] Cheriot vs. Foussat. *Reports, Penna. Supreme Court;* Binney, Vol. III.
[35] *Annals of Congress*, 8th Congress, 2nd Session, pp. 817–18.
[36] *Ibid.*, p. 818.

approached and began firing under English colors, in order to allay suspicion. After a short contest in which they suffered a loss of five men killed and several wounded, the American vessels were taken into Point à Pitre, Guadeloupe, where the officers, crew and passengers were lodged in prison. The master, in reporting the case to the owners, assured them that their ships and property had been defended with spirit until overcome by numbers.[37]

Clearly such a state of affairs did not comport with a state of friendship between the two countries for the armed American vessels, not being able to distinguish between the two, showed fight to Farrand's regularly commissioned privateers, as well as to those which carried no such credentials. Leaders in Congress, themselves, admitted that by the law of nations neutrals had no right to offer resistance to belligerent arrests, but must submit to capture, and seek relief through the admiralty courts of the nation making the seizure.[38]

A protest against the armed trade, and the carrying of arms to the blacks, was presented by the French chargé d'affaires, Pichon in May, 1804. He declared that, "American citizens under the very eye of the government, carry on a private and piratical war against a power with which the United States is at peace."[39]

Six months later, Jefferson brought the matter to the notice of Congress in his annual message. "While noticing the irregularities committed on the ocean by others, those on our own part should not be omitted, nor left unprovided for. Complaints have been received that persons residing within the United States have taken on themselves to arm merchant vessels, and to force

---

[37] *Annals of Cong.*, 8th Cong. 2nd Session, pp. 1291–1294.

[38] "That the right of visiting and searching merchant ships upon the high seas, whatever be the ships, whatever be the cargoes, whatever be the destination is an incontrovertible right of the lawfully commissioned cruisers of the belligerent nation. That the authority of the sovereign of a neutral country being interposed in any manner of mere force, cannot legally vary the rights of the belligerent cruiser. That the penalty for the violent contravention of this right is the confiscation of the property so held from visitation and search." Speech of Gold. *Annals 11th Cong.*, Pt 2, p. 1488. The quotation is from the judgment of Sir Wm. Scott, in the case of the *Mariah*. Robinson, I, p. 340. Scott is here giving the substance of the conclusions of Samuel Marshall in *A Treatise on Law of Insurance*, Vol. I, p. 312.

[39] *Annals of Cong.* 8th Cong., 2nd Session, p. 1290.

a commerce into certain ports and countries in defiance of the laws of those countries."[40]

Congress attempted to remedy the matter by regulating the conduct of the armed vessels. A bill was introduced which required all such vessels as cleared for the ports of the West Indies, to give heavy bonds to use their arms only "for resistance and defence in case of involuntary hostility" and to bring the arms back to the United States. The captains themselves were thus given the right to decide when to use force, although by so doing they might involve the country in war. Some members doubted the wisdom of conferring "the power of making war on any set of men, however virtuous and respectable, much less to the commanders of armed merchant ships, cruising in pursuit of wealth and plunder."[41] The bill, however, was passed and became a law March 3, 1805. But it gave no satisfaction to the shippers, nor did it prevent hostile encounters in the Carribean.

An American captain writing from Havana in the summer of 1805, described the experience of the Brig *Jane* of Baltimore, which mounted sixteen guns, and had a crew of forty-five men. She was captured by a French privateer of four guns, after a fight in which the American vessel lost twenty-eight men, including her captain, who it was reported, had shot his mate, and two of his crew, for attempting to haul down the colors.[42]

Unarmed vessels which passed through these waters were likely to suffer the fate of the Brig *Betsey* and the Schooner *Betsey*, which started from New York for the Mosquito Coast, with a cargo of dry goods, iron-mongery and lumber. On August 30, 1805, in Caicos Passage, they were boarded by a French privateer under English colors. The captors plundered the vessels of everything of value in the cargo, as well as stores and provisions, opened every cask of water on board except one, and finally put on board five captive American seamen, taken from some other unfortunate vessel, and obliged the two vessels to make for Jamaica.[43]

---

[40] Richardson; *Messages and Papers of the Presidents*, I, p. 370.
[41] Speech of Eppes, *Annals of Congress*, 8th Cong., 2nd Session, p. 820.
[42] Poulson, *Daily Advertiser*, Aug. 7, 1805.
[43] *Ibid.*, Oct. 23, 1805.

Shortly before this (February 5, 1805) General Farrand, who represented the authority of Napoleon's government in the island, had issued a savage proclamation decreeing the punishment of death to those who attempted to enter ports occupied by the rebels, or were encountered at sea, within two leagues of such port.[44]

Even this drastic order did not deter American shippers. They secured clearances for Tobago, St. Thomas, Curaçoa, Jaimaca or Havana, but made for the ports of Santo Domingo instead. In June, 1805, Ferrand issued another decree in regard to the trade. Several of the most respectable houses of New York, Philadelphia and Baltimore, as appeared from correspondence which had fallen into his hands, were keeping up a trade of long standing with the revolted blacks. The ship *America* of thirty-four guns, the *Connecticut* of twenty-two, and the *Indostan* of fourteen, were cited as American ships not only engaged in this trade, but transporting arms and ammunition from port to port, for Dessalines, the leader of the negroes.[45]

Ferrand authorized the commanders of French privateers to conduct such American vessels into any neutral or allied ports in the West Indies. The governors of the islands were urged to open their ports to receive them, because in measures for the suppression of the revolt in Santo Domingo, "all nations ought to concur." The papers from these vessels were then to be transmitted to Santo Domingo for examination. He also decreed a "black list" of all merchants, captains and supercargoes found to be engaged in the forbidden trade, whose property, no matter under what flag, or proceeding to what destination, should be good prize.[46]

Napoleon now made an insistent demand that the American trade to Santo Domingo should be entirely forbidden by the government of the United States. Turreau, the French minister at Washington, called upon Madison to do so, in the fall of 1805.[47] Two notes had already been received by General Arm-

---
[44] *A. S. P.*, For. III, p. 292.
[45] *A. S. P.*, For. II, pp. 728–730.
[46] *Ibid.*
[47] Turreau to Secy. of State, Oct. 14, 1805, *A. S. P.*, For. II, p. 725.

strong, our minister at Paris, protesting strongly against the trade. "This system of immunity and tolerance", wrote Tallyrand, "can no longer continue, and his Majesty is convinced that your government will think it due from its frankness, promptly to put an end to it."

Clearly, unless the United States wished openly to recognize the negro republic under Dessalines, it could no longer permit those armed expeditions whose successful returns were celebrated by feasts in American ports at which, as Talleyrand charged, the success of the new government of Haiti was openly toasted.[48]

It was not until February of the following year, that Congress acted in the matter. A bill was introduced, prohibiting trade with those ports of the island not in the possession of the French. To some members this appeared as a weak surrender to the peremptory demand of a foreign power.

The people of Santo Domingo had declared their independence of the French government. The United States, being an outsider should preserve an attitude of impartiality between these two parties to a civil war—so argued those who wished no interference with this lucrative traffic. By one of those investigations into not very remote history by which it is often possible plausibly to defend a given course, when the ministers of a government seek to erect into a universal rule a course of action which at the moment suits their convenience, it was shown that France, before 1778, had carried on commerce with the revolting English colonies, and had denied that England had any right to interfere.[49] Nevertheless, the bill passed both houses, and became a law, February 28, 1806.[50]

The law, however, did not succeed in stopping the trade. Admiral Willaumez, putting out with the French fleet from Martinique, in September, 1806, fell in with a convoy of eight American vessels, escorted by two small frigates, and conveying a quantity of coffee from the forbidden ports to New York.

---

[48] Talleyrand to Armstrong, July and Aug. 16, 1805, *A. S. P.*, For. II, pp. 726–727. Same to Same, *Annals of Cong.*, 9th Cong., p. 1219.
[49] *Annals of Cong.*, 9th Cong., I, p. 118.
[50] *U. S. Statutes at Large*, II, p. 351.

Baffled by a storm, Willaumez was not able to carry out his intention of hanging the captain and supercargo to the yard arm, as a warning to their country-men in New York.[51]

During this time, was there any interference by the French government with American vessels and cargoes in European waters?

Napoleon, having conferred with his ministers, as to the means of doing the greatest damage to British commerce, decreed, in June, 1803, that thenceforth no goods from Britain or her colonies should be admitted to the ports of France, nor could any ship coming from any English port be allowed to enter.[52] This was virtually an anticipation of the Berlin decree. To insure that colonial goods admitted were the product of France and her allies, and of these only, the neutral ships bringing such commodities must carry certificates of origin. These were documents designed by the French consuls at the point of starting testifying that the goods were not the product of England or her colonies. Any captain who failed to have a certificate of origin, by reason of having forgotten the regulation, or having changed his course, was not to be admitted to the ports of the republic, except on condition of taking as return cargo a quantity of French manufactures equal to the incoming cargo. The securing and carrying of these certificates of origin was not particularly objected to by the Americans. When the English later made the presence of the certificate of origin a ground for the seizure of American vessels, it was conceded,[53] by our government, to be a fair municipal regulation.

The prohibition of English goods, and the requirement of certificates of origin, were included in a law promulgated in Holland, only a month after its publication in France.[54] As Napoleon's power extended, the same principle was applied to the countries newly brought under his control.[55]

"We cannot sufficiently caution shippers and owners of ves-

---

[51] *New York Evening Post*, Jan. 24, 1807.
[52] Duvergier, *Lois*, 14, p. 335, *cf.* Also Napoleon, *Correspondence*, 8 p. 365.
[53] Madison to Erskine, March 25, 1808, *A. S. P.*, For. III, p. 213.
[54] Hockstra, *Thirty-seven Years of Holland-American Relations*, 1803–1840, p. 21–29.
[55] *Corr. de Napoleon*, Vol. 8, p. 322.

sels," wrote a merchant of Antwerp in December, 1806, to an American correspondent, "to be particular that the French consul's certificate corresponds with the manifest. In sending vessels here or elsewhere, they expose the property and vessel to seizure for the smallest omission. The French laws are herein very strict, and require the utmost exactness."[56]

How strictly the law of June, 1803 could be enforced we may see from the case of the *Young Eagle*, which sailed from New York for Bordeaux, in August, 1803. She was stopped by an English cruiser, on suspicion of carrying enemy property, and sent into Bristol, but was afterward liberated. Continuing her voyage to Bordeaux, the vessel was detained at the mouth of the Garonne, and after weeks of delay, was ordered to leave, without unloading any part of her cargo.[57]

The Indirect Trade of the United States, 1793–1807

Thus far we have been concerned with the seizures and depredations upon our commerce, practiced by the two belligerents. Yet American foreign trade, in the same period, instead of being crippled and diminished actually expanded. This was because of the opportunities offered to our shippers in the carrying trade. It began as we have seen with the opening of the ports of French colonies to the Americans at the commencement of hostilities in 1793.

Beginning in 1794, one may notice in American newspapers, a change in the merchants' advertisements. Enormous consignments of pepper, sugar and coffee have arrived, and these are noted as "entitled to drawback". Wines and brandies in unprecedented quantities, and linens and muslins in bewildering varieties are advertised, as "suitable for export", or "adapted to the West Indies market".

The ends of the earth were ransacked to furnish goods for this new and lucrative trade. Sugar was brought from Benares, as well as from Santo Domingo, Havana and St. Croix. Cargoes of coffee arrived from Mocha and Java, from "that storehouse

---

[56] *N. Y. Evening Post*, Feb. 19, 1807.
[57] Speyer vs. New York Insurance Co., Johnson, *New York Reports 2*, see also Lee to Madison, March 1, 1804, *Consular Letters*, Bordeaux.

of the eastern world" the Isle of France, and from the West Indies. Pepper came from Sumatra and Calcutta, mahogany and logwood from Campeachy, and hides from the river Platte. A typical cargo of Bengal goods, landed at Philadelphia in 1795, included printing cloths, checks, baftas, cassias, callicoes, gurrahs and mulmuls.[58] The ship *Sampson* from Canton in 1794 brought taffetas, sewing silk, nankeens, chinaware and tea sets.[59]

A wide variety of wines and liquors are listed among the goods imported for sale. There are advertisements of red and white wine from Bordeaux, besides other kinds from Madeira, Lisbon and Teneriffe, rich old port from Oporto, and sherry of unspecified origin. There was also old Jamaica spirits, Antigua and West India rum, cognac, French and Peach brandies, London porter and Holland gin.[60]

Dry goods, including satins and lutestrings, also silk stockings, umbrellas and kid gloves, were sent from Bordeaux. The fast sailing vessels so frequently announced as seeking freights for Hamburg brought back hemp, bar iron and German linens, platellas royal, and blue cottons. From Amsterdam came cheeses, sail cloth and many sorts of fabric. From Dublin and Cork came linens, sheetings and damask. Hemp and duck came from Russia, and from Italy, olive oil, silks and laces. All these goods were imported in addition to the customary spring and fall consignments of cottons and woolens, hardware, earthenware and miscellaneous articles from British ports.

Poulson's *Daily Advertiser*, for July 1, 1805, contained the following advertisement of goods for sale in Philadelphia, under the heading, Goods Entitled to Drawback: "Fine Cambricks, Laces, White Holland, Wahrendorps and Giffenberg Linen, Swiss Sheeting Linen, White Silesia Linen, Fine Dutch blue and white checks, Seltzer water, Nuremburg wares and window glass." The firm of Cope and Thomas, of North 2nd Street in the same city advertised 120 packages of German goods from Frederickstadt, "the whole entitled to drawback". The lot included Brown Platellas, Britagnas, Dowlas, Ticklenburgs,

---

[58] *American Daily Advertiser*, June 23, 1795.
[59] *American Daily Advertiser*, July 9, 1794.
[60] *Ibid.*

Coutils and Tickings," also "a general assortment of European and East India goods among which are several adapted to the West India Markets."[61] B. A. Pettit of South Front Street advertised articles lately arrived from Bordeaux, "Sweet oil, Anisseed Cordial, Brandied fruit, etc." and an invoice of Dry Goods, "put up for the West India Market."[62]

Many of these goods, of course, were intended for domestic consumption, but as the advertisements and other evidence shows, a considerable part of them entered into a strong current of trade, from the colonies of France, and later from those of Spain and Holland through the United States to the mother countries of Europe, and a return flow of their goods, to the colonies. The maritime superiority of England prevented her opponents from attempting to continue communications with their colonies in their own ships, and compelled them to open the trade to neutrals. While the opening of the colonial ports of France beginning in 1793, which we have already noted, was perhaps to a certain extent a part of the liberalizing policy of the national convention, in breaking down old barriers,[63] necessity would in any case, soon have compelled it.

By so much as this trade benefitted France and her allies, by so much did England desire to thwart it. To do so, would be for her a short cut to victory. Therefore England, by the Order in Council of November, 1793, as we have seen, reverted to her practice in the Seven Years War, which had become known as the Rule of 1756. This was the principle that a trade not open to a neutral in time of peace, could not be opened to him in time of war. The relaxation of the November order, in less than two months, in favor of the Americans, so that they could transport French colonial produce to the United States, was granted, as

---

[61] Poulson, *Daily Advertiser*, Jan. 2, 1805.
[62] *Ibid.*
[63] In a flowery speech of the type which the revolutionist evidently greatly admired, Boyer Fonfrède, in the convention declared (Feb. 19, 1793,) that the colonies formerly subjects had now been declared an integral part of the French nation. Their ports should be open to the merchants of the American states, "so blessed by liberty and so rich in grain . . . The flags of the two free peoples should fly together" *Archives Parlementaire.* First Series, Vol. 59, pp. 15-18.

Lord Grenville informed Thomas Pinckney, to preserve understanding and harmony between the two countries, and to take away the pretext of evil disposed persons who wished to cause irritation between them.[64] This policy James Stephen, the English defender of the rule, pronounced a "costly courtesy", on the part of Great Britain. Once stored in American warehouses or landed on American wharves, it was not difficult to transport the colonial produce to good markets in Europe. Since the trade was highly profitable, it is difficult to see how it would do otherwise, than deflect itself to conform to the new regulations. A system arose by which this colonial trade was carried on through American ports. This simply made the trade slightly more inconvenient and added to the cost of the goods, but rendered the trade, for a time at least, perfectly safe.

Stephen Girard was one of the merchants who was engaged extensively in the carrying of coffee, sugar and log wood to Antwerp and Hamburg during this period. A vessel of his, coming from the Isle of France, was on its way to Hamburg when the captain, hearing the rumor of war, put into the harbor of Cowes for information. There the vessel was seized by a British man-of-war, on suspicion of having on board Dutch or French property. Mr. Auljo, the American consul wrote to Girard, that the vessel was sure to be restored to him, but he continued, "In the future I would recommend your bringing your goods to America, before you send them to Europe, as much the safest and least troublesome way of carrying on the business."[65]

A firm actively engaged in this system of the carrying trade was that of Gibbs and Channing of Newport. In 1797 we find them ordering a consignment of Platellas, Ticklenburgs, Brabant linens and green baize from London, after assuring themselves that these goods were entitled to drawback on exportation from America. They requested a certificate with the shipment of the goods from England, in order to facilitate the securing of the drawbacks.[66] It was necessary, however, for the American

---

[64] *A. S. P.*, For. I, p. 430.
[65] McMaster, *Life of Girard*, I, p. 380.
[66] Gibbs and Channing to Hugh Pollack and Co., Sept. 13, 1797, *Gibbs and Channing Letter Book*.

shipper to deposit a bond with the custom house at home which was released when the exportation of the foreign goods had been consummated. Thus Gibbs and Channing on reshipping similar goods to Cuba, sent to their correspondents in Havana a certificate of the shipment, requesting them to sign it, and have it certified by the American consul there, and return it to Newport in order to cancel their bond.[67] In 1803 the same firm shipped sugar and Bourbon coffee to Amsterdam.[68] During the year 1805 prices for colonial goods were especially good. On sending an assorted cargo of mahogany, logwood, fustic, coffee, sugar, cotton and nankeens to a firm in Copenhagen, the consignors wrote: "From the brisk demand and advanced prices of coffee and sugar in France, Holland and other parts of Europe, we calculate on your being able to effect prompt sales of them at beneficial prices."[69] In the same year this Newport firm shipped a large consignment of pepper to France, specifying that the return cargo should consist of Britannias, linens, silks and other goods suitable for the West India market.[70]

Another Newport firm active in the carrying trade was that of Champlin and Robinson. For example, we find them sending a cargo to Antwerp, in 1803, containing among other articles, "India piece goods", and logwood.[71] The next year they sent to the same port, a fine cargo consisting of sugar and cotton of the first quality, and a quantity of "Campeachy chipt logwood", specifying as usual the return "of consular certificates for the cancelling of our bonds given for the payment of the duty on the sugar imported by us."[72]

A study of the comparative amounts of the foreign and domestic products exported, commencing in 1796, the first year when the records of the two classes of goods were kept separately shows that beginning at twenty million in 1796, the

---

[67] Same to Messrs. St. Maria and Cuester, Oct. 14, 1797, *Ibid.*
[68] Champlin Correspondence, Memo of July 27, 1803, Wetmore Collection.
[69] Gibbs and Channing to Messrs. Hyberg and Co., April 17, 1805, *Gibbs and Channing Letter Book.*
[70] Same to Minturn and Champlin, March 23, 1805, *Ibid.*
[71] Cargo of Brig Rowena, March 25, 1803, Wetmore Collection.
[72] C. Champlin to Robinson Potter, April 10, 1804, *Champlin Letter Book*, Newport.

value of the foreign goods exported from our shores rose to forty-five millions in 1799. Checked by the non-intercourse law with France, July, 1798 to 1800, it again rose to fifty-six millions in 1801. The brief peace period of 1802 caused it to fall to thirteen millions, showing that France and her allies again took the trade with their colonies into their own hands. On the resumption of the war, the value of the foreign goods exported again mounted, reaching its maximum in 1806. In that year the trade totalled sixty million and in 1807, fifty-nine million. Comparing this with the amount reported in 1792, of little more than one-half million, we see what golden opportunities, the war offered to the American shipper. The foreign goods began to exceed the domestic goods in value, beginning in 1797 until by 1799, they were worth thirteen million more, after the rupture of the peace of Amiens, the value again rose, until by 1806, it exceeded that of domestic exports by twenty million.[73]

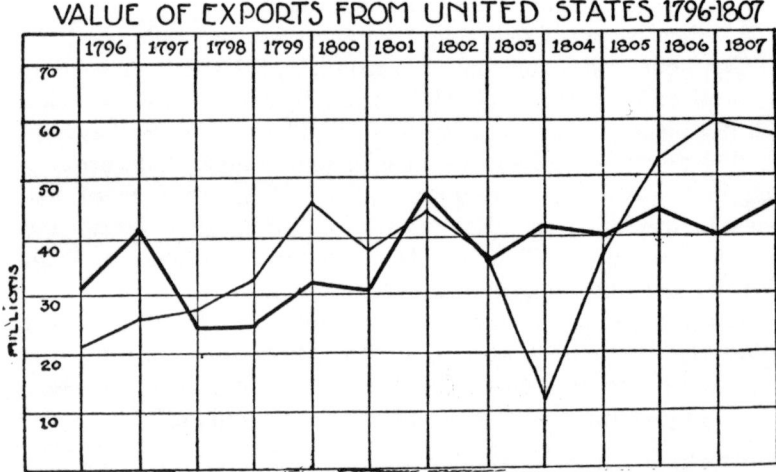

If we consult the accompanying charts, illustrating the export of colonial produce from American shores, we shall see that, beginning with insignificant amounts of coffee, sugar, cocoa and

---

[73] *Pitkin*, p. 370.

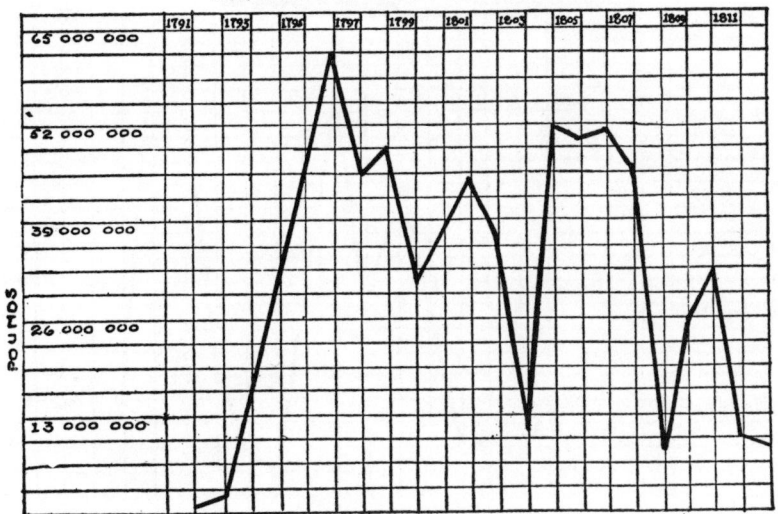

EXPORT OF COFFEE—1791-1812

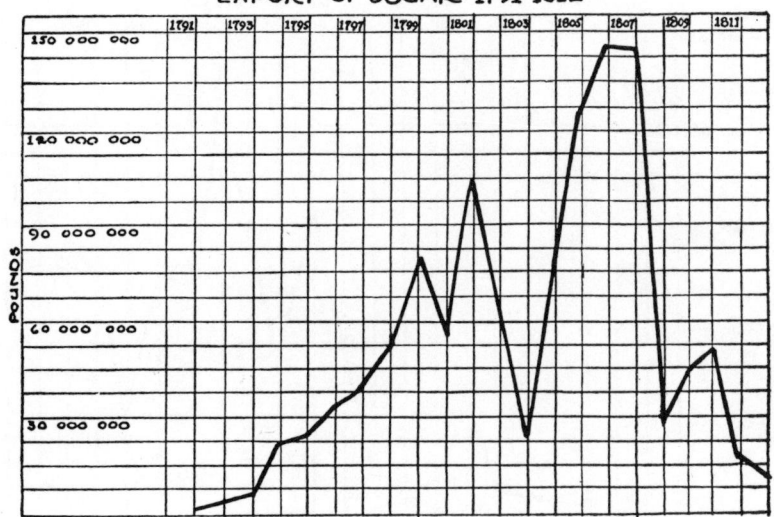

EXPORT OF SUGAR—1791-1812

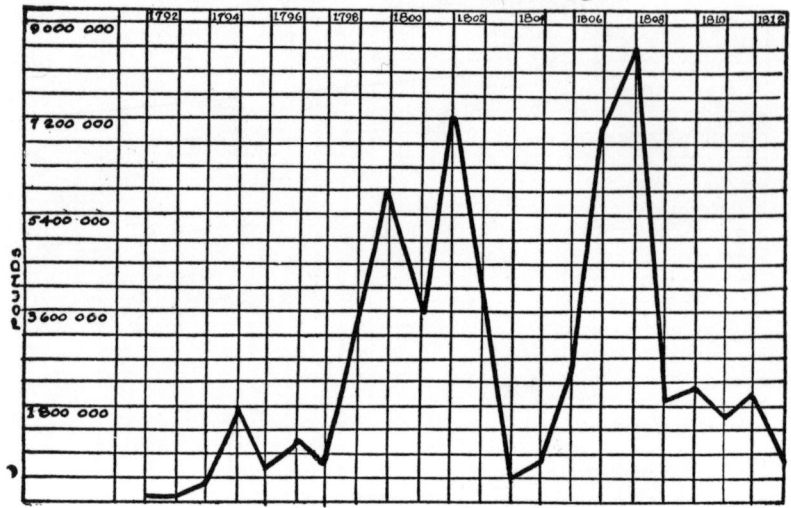

EXPORT OF COCOA - 1791-1812

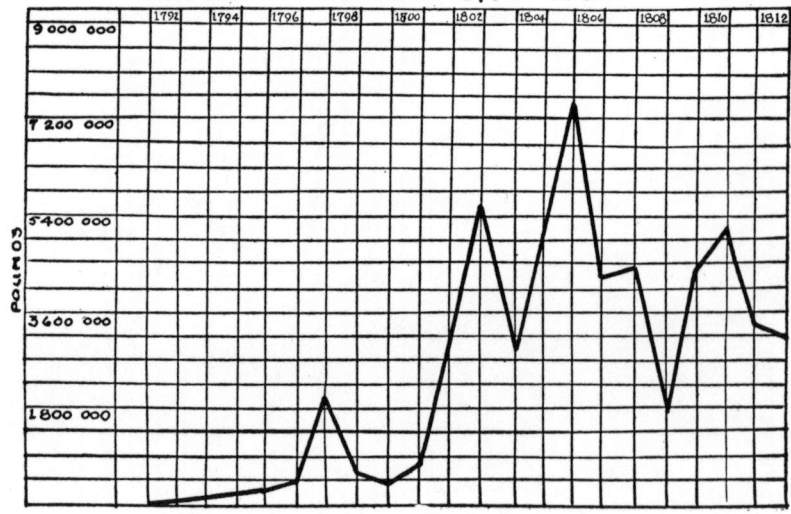

EXPORT OF PEPPER - 1791 - 1812

pepper, in 1791, a steady climb begins, reaching to amazing heights by the time of the peace of Amiens, and rising still higher in the five year period from 1803 to 1808.

The amount of sugar exported from this country in 1791 was about 75,000 pounds but by 1802, it had arisen to thirteen hundred times that amount, and by 1806 to nearly two thousand times the amount exported in 1791. Fifty times as much coffee was exported in 1798, as in 1791. Of pepper, less than 500 pounds was exported in 1791, but over five million pounds in 1802, and over seven million in 1805. The value of the cocoa exported shows similar rapid expansion. The figures representing the annual tonnage employed tells the same story.

The seizures in the brief period between November, 1793 and January, 1794, came before the commission under the Jay treaty, to which allusion has already been made. Restoration was decreed even for seizures of colonial goods in American ships going directly to European ports.[74] Thus the Americans believed a precedent was established for setting aside the Rule of 1756. How much more, then, reasoned American shippers, should the indirect trade through American ports be lawful. As the board of commissioners under the 7th article of the treaty of 1794, in revising the decisions of the British courts founded on the instructions of November 6, 1793, condemned this doctrine, there was just cause to expect that it would never be revived.[75]

For two or three years after the ratification of the Jay treaty, as we have seen, there was comparatively little interference with

---

[74] "One of the results of that treaty (of 1794) comprehends a most important sanction from Great Britain against the doctrine asserted by her. Art. 7 of the treaty stipulated compensation to citizens of the United States for damages sustained from irregular and illegal captures and established a joint board . . . to decide on all claims, according to equity, justice and the law of nations. These claims were founded in a very great degree, on captures authorized by the British instructions of Nov. 6, 1793, and depending therefore on the question whether a neutral trade with belligerent colonies shut in time of peace was a lawful trade in time of war. The board on a full consideration, reversed the sentences pronounced even by the admiralty tribunal of last resort, in pursuance of those instructions and consequently as the commission were guided by the laws of nations, the reversal decided that the instructions and the principles on which they were founded, were contrary to the law of nations." Madison, An Examination of the British Doctrine. *Madison Writings*, G. Hunt, ed., Vol. VII, p. 267, footnote.
[75] Monroe to Lord Mulgrave, Aug. 12, 1805, *A. S. P.*, For. 3, p. 104.

our commerce from the British. American shippers, therefore, entertained no misgivings as to the safety of the indirect trade. They were the more confirmed in this view, by the decision of the High Court of Admiralty in London, in the case of the ship *Polly*. This decision seemed to warrant American merchants in assuming that provided certain formalities were complied with, such voyages might be prosecuted unmolested by British cruisers. The *Polly*, an American vessel, was seized on her way from Marblehead to Bilboa in Spain, and condemned in the vice admiralty court at Halifax, because she was carrying Havana sugar and Caracas cocoa to the home country. The High Court of Admiralty in London, however, to which appeal was made, decided that since the goods were evidently American property, had been landed in America, and by documentary evidence, were proved to have paid duty, they could not be seized. Restoration was therefore secured. The theory of the English courts was that landing the goods and paying duty, absorbed the goods into the domestic stock of the country.[76]

The language of Sir Wm. Scott, in this decision, however, was very guarded. The opinion of the court appeared to be tentative. In furnished no clear cut and unequivocal guide for the American shipper, nor did it give them unmistakable assurance that similar voyages in the future might be sure of a similar decision. "It is not my business," declared Sir Wm. Scott, "to say what is universally the test of a bona fide importation. It is argued that it would not be sufficient that the duties should be paid, and that the cargo should be landed. If these criteria are not to be resorted to, I should be at a loss to know what should be the test, and I am strongly disposed to hold, that it would be sufficient, that the goods should be landed, and the duties paid." Thus, as Madison shrewdly remarked, "the judge tied a knot to bind himself, but avoided drawing it closely, in order to loosen it again, if occasion should require.

On the other hand two decisions of an adverse nature were rendered at this period. These were the cases of the *Immanuel*

---

[76] Robinson, *Admiralty Reports*, II, p. 361–371.
[77] Madison, *An Examination of the British Doctrine Works*, ed. by G. Hunt, Vol. VII, p. 314.

and the *Mercury*. The former was a Hamburg ship, which, in a voyage from her home port stopped at Bordeaux, took on French goods as a part of her cargo, and proceeded to Santo Domingo. In war, declared Sir Wm. Scott, a neutral had a right to carry on his accustomed trade, but no other. The economic isolation of a colony from any but the parent state, he picturesquely described by declaring that Guadeloupe and Jamaica could have no more trade connection with Germany, either in peace or in war, than if they were located on the mountains of the moon. The Bordeaux goods in the *Immanuel's* cargo were declared forfeited. The rule of 1756 was thus upheld, although the court admitted that a relaxation had been permitted in the case of the Americans.[78]

Similarly, the rule was upheld in the case of the *Mercury*, which was decided two years later. This was an American vessel laden with Havana sugar, seized in going from Charleston to Hamburg. The shipper had not given himself the trouble of landing and reloading his goods, and had paid no duty in America. His cargo, by no stretch of imagination, could be considered as having become absorbed into the general stock of the country. His touching at Charleston, therefore, was declared by the court to have been for the mere purpose of giving the voyage the color and appearance of having begun there, and the cargo was condemned.[79]

These two decisions, of 1800, and 1802, as well as that of the *Freeport* in 1803 and the *William* in 1804, might have aroused fears in the minds of American shippers, lest the practice of 1756 might be revived in full force, but there had issued from the Advocate General in England in the year 1801, a communication which appeared to justify their confidence. This statement was called forth by the decisions of the Vice Admiralty courts of the West Indies in regard to the seizure of the *Leopard* by a British cruiser in 1800.

The American brigantine *Leopard*, laden with Malaga wines, which had been imported into the United States, had been

---

[78] Robinson, 2, pp. 186–206.
[79] *Ibid.*, 5 p. 400; see also Ship *Gadsden*, Kolme vs. Ins. Co. of North America, Binney 6, pp. 219–220.

seized by a British cruiser on her way to the Spanish colonies, taken into the Vice Admiralty court at Nassau, and the cargo condemned in October, 1800, on the ground that the wines were "the production of the Spanish territory in Europe, and bound to the trans-Atlantic parts of that empire." Emboldened by this decision, numerous captures of similar cargoes had followed resulting in similar sentences from the Vice Admiralty courts at Nassau and Jamaica.

These decisions were made the subject of protest by Rufus King, then American minister in London, to Lord Hawkesbury, Minister of Foreign Affairs, with the request that precise instructions be issued to the proper officers in the West Indies and Nova Scotia to correct the abuses arising from such seizures.[80]

In reply, a carefully qualified statement was forwarded from Dr. John Nicholl, the King's Advocate General. In the main it upheld the American contention. "What is a direct trade," wrote Dr. Nicholl, "or what amounts to an intermediate trade importation into the neutral country, may sometimes be a question of some difficulty; a general definition of either, applicable to all cases cannot well be laid down. The question must depend upon the particular circumstances of each case. Perhaps the mere touching in the neutral country to take a fresh clearance may properly be considered a fraudulent evasion, and in effect the direct trade; but the High Court of Admiralty has expressly decided (and I see no reason to expect that the court of appeal will vary the rule) that landing the goods and paying the duties in the neutral country, breaks the continuity of the voyage, and is such an importation as legalizes the trade although the goods be reshipped in the same vessel, and on account of the same proprietor, and be forwarded for sale to the mother country or the colony."[81] Another report of similar tenor, came from Dr. Nicholl two months later. In this he declared that the English tribunals had held that neutrals could not be admitted by the enemy, on account of the pressure of

---

[80] *Life and Corr. of Rufus King*, Chas. R. King, III, pp. 403-404.
[81] *A. S. P.*, For. 2, p. 491.

war, to carry on his colonial trade, from which in time of peace, they were wholly excluded. But this principle had on account of special circumstances, been relaxed during the war then going on.[82]

Thus fortified, just before the peace of Amiens by an opinion of great weight, apparently authorizing their activities, the American shippers promptly resumed the indirect trade, in the war which began in 1803.

In fact American trade suffered little interference from England during the first eighteen months of the war. James Monroe, writing to Madison from London in July 1804, declared that our commerce never enjoyed in any war as much freedom, and indeed favor, from the British government as it then did.[83]

The Essex Decision

These halcyon days, however, were not destined to last. There were men in England who saw with growing concern, the increasing commercial activity of the United States, in the colonial trade with France and her allies. Their sentiments found expression in the celebrated pamphlet, *War in Disguise or The Fraud of the Neutral Flags*, by James Stephen, published in London in 1805. In this work, the British government is represented as the victim of its own generosity. In spite of the stress and burden of twelve years of war, France and her colonies appeared to be highly prosperous. This, Stevens believed, was because their capital was really at work earning high dividends under the cover of the flags of neutrals, especially that of the United States. The leniency of the British government in tolerating the indirect trade, had been most ungratefully requited. The orders of 1798 led Americans to pretend a British destination. Vessels cleared out from American ports for Falmouth and Cowes and a market, but they put into the British merely to learn from their business agent there, to which enemy port they had best proceed to procure the highest prices. In case a British cruiser hove in sight the

---

[82] *A. S. P.*, For. III, p. 265.
[83] Monroe to Madison, *Monroe Writings*, Hamilton, ed., Vol. IV, p. 218.

captains destroyed or concealed such papers as disclosed their destination. The excuse of the captains from American ports, seized with colonial goods, and proceeding to enemy ports, had become proverbial. They invariably professed that they had intended importation to America, but news of the better markets abroad had caused them to alter their course. Since condemnations resulted from papers on the vessel and the replies of the captains and their agents, the questions had now come to be well known, and the officers were drilled before hand to answer all questions readily. Since England of all nations upheld the cause of civil liberty, while the aim of Napoleon was to establish a despotism, Stephens, therefore, arrived at the conclusion that England should no longer tolerate the neutral carrying trade.

Similar ideas were apparently beginning to possess the minds of the government leaders. In September of 1805 the ships returning from England brought the news that British cruisers and courts were evidently acting in conformity with new orders. The *Daily Advertiser* of Philadelphia reported on September 21, that Captain Follansbee of the ship *Perseverance* had just arrived in Baltimore with information that American vessels laden with cargoes from enemy ports were being seized and condemned, even though the goods had been entered and discharged in American ports.[84] Two days later a London letter published in the same paper declared that a late decision showed that the landing of the cargo and the payment of the duties would be no safeguard against confiscation.

---

[84] One of these vessels was the *Brig Rowena*, belonging to Christopher Champlin of Newport. This vessel started from the latter port, April 25, 1805, laden with Martinico sugar and coffee, for the port of Antwerp, her cargo being certified by the Collector of the port at Newport, as not being the product of any British colony. The *Rowena* was seized by the British armed cutter *Griffin*, on June 10, and carried into the Downs, and condemned on July 23, 1805, by the High Court of Admiralty. In Dec. 1808, the appeal of the defendants was still pending, but the London agents of Champlin, feared that the capture would be sustained "on the ground of continuity of the voyage." Chris. G. Champlin to Robinson Potter, April 25, 1805. Same to President and Directors of Newport Insurance Co., Sept. 16, 1805. Champlin Papers, R. I. Hist. Soc., Providence. In the same place will be found the copy of a certificate of importation, which accompanied a cargo of coffee sent to Antwerp in a similar transaction, in March of the same year. This document, signed by the Collector of the port of Newport, gave the Island of Bourbon as the origin and the date of the importation. A small part of the consignment remained in the United States.

James Monroe, on his return from Madrid to London, in August, 1805, found twenty or thirty American vessels brought into that port, under such circumstances. He wrote to Armstrong at Paris, that a recent decision had declared the formalities of landing and paying duty in America as fraudulent and evasive.[85] This was the famous case of the ship *Essex*, which had been seized in the former war. A decision was rendered in 1803, but the case having been carried to the Lords of Appeal, the final decision was pronounced in July of 1805. The judgment of the court was written by Sir Wm. Grant, the Master of the Rolls.

The *Essex*, a Salem ship had come from Barcelona, and having stopped at Salem, she was proceeding with her Spanish cargo to Havana, when she was seized. The Lords of Appeal declared that it had evidently been the intention of the owner to go to Havana, in the beginning; he had never planned to sell in America. The voyage was therefore a continuous one, and the condemnation pronounced in the lower court in 1803 was confirmed.[86]

Monroe presented a vigorous protest against the recent seizures and the decision, and asked Lord Mulgrave, the Minister of Foreign Affairs, whether new orders had been issued. Answered that there had been no new orders, Monroe replied that the decision had the force of an order. Lord Mulgrave failed to offer any explanation. Although a number of the captured vessels in the port of London were afterwards released,[87] the decision in the case of the *Maria*, handed down in the High Court of Admiralty in September, 1805, further elucidated and confirmed the doctrine of the continuous voyage.

It was declared to be an inherent and settled principle that "the mere touching at any port without importing the cargo into the common stock of the country" would not alter the nature of the voyage. No new principle had been laid down in

---

[85] Monroe, *Writings*, ed. Hamilton, Vol. IV, p. 310.
[86] This decision in the case of the *Essex* was never apparently published. We learn its main features from references in the case of the *Maria* (Robinson, *Admiralty Reports*, pp. 365–372), and the case of the *William*, tried before the Lords of Appeal, but quoted by Robinson, Vol. 5, pp. 385–406.
[87] *Monroe Writings*, ed. Hamilton, Vol. 4, p. 311.

the *Essex* case, which was merely the first case of the kind which had come before the Court of Appeals. But the court would have rendered an exactly similar decision, had a similar case occurred earlier. As a proof that the continuous voyage had been held illegal, even when the vessel had touched in America, the court cited the case of the *Enoch*. Here a charter party had been found on board disclosing the intention of the owner to make the voyage to an enemy colony, thence to America, and from there to the mother country in Europe. This vessel was condemned, as was the *Rowena*, whose previous voyages between the enemy port in Europe, and the enemy colony, with America as the "half way house" created a strong presumption, that when captured it was engaged in a similar undertaking.[88]

Eight months after the condemnation of the *Essex*, occurred the decision of the Lord of Appeal in Prize Cases, in regard to the *William*, March 1806. This was an American ship which had come from La Guaira to Marblehead, in May 1800, with a cargo of cocoa. Having briskly unladen, cleaned and slightly repaired the vessel, the owners obtained a certificate that the duties had been secured, promptly reloaded the vessel, and within four days of their arrival cleared out for Bilboa, in Spain. At the trial they claimed that they had expected to sell the cocoa in the United States, but hearing of better prices in Spain, they had determined to seek that market. The Lords of Appeal decided however, that they had neither tried nor intended to sell in America, but had proceeded with all speed to go through the forms of landing, not because importation was intended, but "because it was thought expedient that something should be done which in the British Prize court might pass for importation." The voyage was therefore declared illegal, and the sentence of condemnation pronounced in the lower court (1804) was affirmed.[89] In connection with this case, the judges adverted to the case of the *Freeport*, which had come up in 1803. This vessel had carried a cargo of goods from Cadiz to Boston, and at the time of capture was proceeding to the Spanish West

---

[88] Robinson, *Admiralty Reports*, V., pp. 325–33.
[89] *Ibid.*

Indies. The captain, who was also part owner, did not even assert any purpose of importation into the United States, and the vessel was therefore condemned.

The protests against the *Essex* decision had by this time reached England. The American merchants, according to Sir William Grant, who rendered the decision, claimed that they "had by our former decisions, been led to believe that proof of landing and payment of duties in America would in every case, be held absolutely decisive of the legality of the voyage." This was denied by Grant. "After looking attentively over all the cases," he wrote, ". . . in which this sort of question has occurred, I conceive not only that it will be impossible to point out a judgment, in which any such unqualified doctrine has been laid down, but that the judgments antecedent to that in the *Essex* case had clearly and unequivocally negatived the existence of the alleged rule of decision," i.e., Case of the Polly, 1800.

The Lord Commissioner then reviewed two other cases. One of these was that of the *Mercury*, which we have already examined.[90] The other was that of the *Eagle*, a vessel which had carried a cargo from Bilboa to Philadelphia, and thence to Havana; there being no clear evidence of Havana as the ultimate destination, the vessel and cargo had been released. The object of the review of these cases, wrote Sir William Grant, was "to examine whether there be any inconsistency in their principles." He maintained that there was none. "The alleged novelty (in the *Essex* decision), he concluded, "in departing from the supposed principle of holding that landing and payment of duties in America did absolutely and under all circumstances legalize the subsequent voyage" was negatived by the fact "that there was not one decision in which any such principle had been asserted or implied, and that there were at least two decisions which stood in direct contradiction to it, the Freeport in 1803 and the William in 1804.[91]

An examination of a number of cases which were appealed

---

[90] See ante, p. 77
[91] Robinson, V. pp. 385–406.

to the High Court of Admiralty during the years 1804 to 1806 inclusive, gives some idea of the grounds upon which that court based its decisions. The Lords of Appeal laid it down as a general rule that: "If the goods were brought in to America with any intention of being immediately conveyed to Europe, especially to the country from the colony of which the produce is to be considered as coming,"[92] the voyage was to be considered an indirect or continuous one. In reading over the minutes of the trials one is impressed with the patient study evidently given to each case, the attempt to find the facts, and to render just decisions, within the rule laid down by the court.

One of the first questions to be raised by the Lords of Appeal in the cases of alleged continuous voyages, was as to the payment of duties in America. This was shown in the case of the *Eliza*, which came before the court January 21, 1804. This vessel had brought a cargo of sugar from Martinique to an American port, but then having obtained a new clearance, went on to Nantes. The Lords of Appeal held that if there was real importation into America, with payment of duties, tonnage, etc., without drawback, they should consider that the case involved two distinct voyages. Nevertheless they declared that indulgence to America in such cases would give Great Britain's own subjects nothing. If the United States declared a small duty or no duty, this would make the indirect trade entirely too easy. A call was therefore made on the appellants for proof as to duties paid, the amount, and whether subject to refund.[93] Final decision in this case was not recorded. The fact was, as we have seen, that foreign goods reexported from America were subject to a drawback of all but $3\frac{3}{4}$ per cent of the duty paid,[94] and the Court, having ascertained this fact, never afterward considered the payment of the duties alone a ground for holding the importation a bona fide one.

Several of the cases show that the plea of low prices for colonial produce in America and better markets abroad was often sufficient to secure the freeing of the captured vessel.

---

[92] Case of the George Washington, H. C. A., Misc., 473.
[93] H. C. A. Misc., 473 Case of the *Eliza*.
[94] Ante Chap. i, p. 18 By the law of May 13, 1800, the drawback of $1\frac{1}{4}$ was raised to $3\frac{3}{4}$, *Laws of U. S.*, 2 pp. 82–83.

A good example of a vessel freed under these circumstances is the *John Bulkley*. This vessel was captured April 16, 1805, when on a voyage from Philadelphia to Amsterdam, with a cargo of sugar, coffee and pepper. A large part of this cargo had been imported in the same vessel from Batavia, having reached Philadelphia at the end of the preceding May. The goods were landed at the custom house, the duty having been paid and offered for sale by their owner Wm. Waln, in notices inserted in *Poulson's Daily Advertiser* of July 4th, and 18th. Waln not being able to procure his price, according to his appeal against the capture, determined to export the goods to Europe. The decision of the High Court of Admiralty was that the importation had been genuine, and the vessel was ordered by an interlocutory decree to be given up to the owner, while nine months was allowed for further proof by the claimant of intention to sell in America. The captor's lawyers were able to show that Waln had been interested in an earlier voyage from Amsterdam direct to Batavia, although the pretended destination of the vessel was Canton. They produced letters which raised a strong presumption that the goods had been intended for Amsterdam from the start. Nevertheless, the Lords of Appeal finally (February 8, 1810) sustained the decision of the lower court, and the claimant received vessel and cargo, being obliged, however, to pay the captor's legal expenses.[95]

In the case of the *Palinurus*, appealed May 2, 1806, it was held that the appellant had established the fact of a fair attempt to sell the goods brought from Guadeloupe to America. The goods had been entered at an American port, the duties having been paid, and then removed from the quay. Prices having failed however, shipment to Europe was determined on. The voyage was thus declared not continuous. A similar decision was reached in the case of the *Ambition*, appealed July 8, 1806, although this vessel arrived at New York with sugars from Havana, on August 17th, and sailed on September 16th, for Amsterdam with the same cargo.[96]

---

[95] *High Court Admiralty, Appeals in Prize Causes*, 1803–1811, Philadelphia Ships I.
[96] H. C. A. Admiralty Court, Misc. 473, Case of the *Palinurus*.

Another example of the court's leniency was that of the *Respect*. This vessel brought a cargo of sugar from Martinique to an American port. The owner, Clark, made an affidavit that he had wished the master of his ship to purchase coffee at Martinique, which he had expected to sell in America. When sugar was substituted, and the American market was unfavorable for this commodity, while that of Amsterdam held out better prospects the owner determined on sending his sugar to that port. The court decided, January 16, 1807, that this was not a continuous voyage.[97]

On the other hand, the *Little Cornelia* and her cargo were condemned. This vessel, carrying a cargo of sugars from Martinique, landed in New York on July 25, 1805. The cargo was landed, hauled away from the wharf and the duties were paid. But on the 29th of the same month the owners began to reload the same cargo, and on August 13th, the vessel cleared for Amsterdam. At the trial the owners gave proof of their offering and advertising the sugars for sale in New York. But the time allowed for this was certainly brief. After four days they decided to ship to Holland. On October 2, 1805, the *Little Cornelia* was captured. The case having been carried to the Lords of Appeal, they rendered a decision in March 1809, upholding the capture of the vessel and sugars, except that ten tons of logwood, which had formed part of the cargo, was restored to its owners.[98]

In the case of the *Fame*, which came before the High Court of Admiralty October 30, 1805, the facts in the charter party furnished the ground for condemnation. According to that contract a cargo was to be taken on at Havana, then carried to Newport in America, and thence delivered to Tonninger or Hamburg, if not blockaded. Going to Newport, the Court believed, was for a new clearance only. The rule to which the country adhered, was that trade with the colony of the enemy not allowed in peace was illegal in war, notwithstanding the temporary relaxation of the enemy. "The principles on which

---

[97] *Ibid.*, Case of the *Respect*.
[98] Appeals in Prize Causes, New York Ships, the *Little Cornelia*.

this country acted in the last war," according to the minutes of this case, "was allowing some modification by instructions."
. . . If such principles press on neutrals, "they can have recourse to the government which has power to relax the extremity of our belligerent rights, attending to what the consideration of other countries may appear to require, but the court can give no relaxation."

The question was raised, in connection with this case, as to whether the law applied to the colonies of Spain also, France only being named. In the last war, the construction had applied to the colonies of all nations, since the ground policy of colonial trade was the same for all. There was then, only a short question for the court. Large and liberal consideration of policy might have force elsewhere, but not with the court. The voyage of the *Fame* was therefore held to be illegal.[99]

In the case of the *Eagle*, appealed September 17, 1805, there was a cargo of 133 hhd. of sugar imported from Guadeloupe, which was brought to America and then shipped to Cherbourg. Here the Lords of Appeal declared that if the goods had been imported long before, or by different parties, the importation might be considered a genuine one, but in this case, the period before reexportation had been hardly longer than necessary for quarantine. The court believed the reexportation to have been by the same parties. They found no proof of intention to sell in America. Unity of vehicle was not essential, provided the court found unity of intention. They pronounced the voyage of the *Eagle* continuous.[100]

The news of the *Essex* decision reached America in September. The merchants of the coast cities had by this time a list of accumulated grievances but the blow at the carrying trade was the chief burden of their complaint. They now called upon Congress for relief. Petitions were drawn up in New York, Philadelphia, Baltimore and other places.

The New York petition called attention to the lack of warning on the part of England, and to the injustice of the new ruling.

---

[99] H. C. A. Misc. 473, Case of the *Fame*.
[100] *Ibid.*, Case of the *Eagle*.

The petitioners pointed out that the profits arising from the trade were spent largely in England.[101] The Philadelphia merchants professed themselves willing to make any sacrifices which the government might require, to secure redress. A list of 69 captures by the British, as reported by the Philadelphia Insurance Company, was enumerated. This petition, however, also complained of the pillaging of the "pirates and plunderers" in the West Indies, the proclamations of Ferrand in San Domingo, and the hovering of the vessels of the belligerents at the entrance to our harbors.[102]

The Baltimore petition was the work of William Pinkney, who had been one of the American commissioners under the Jay treaty, and was soon to be sent to England, to assist Monroe. Pinkney attacked the British position that a new trade, unaccustomed in peace, should not be permitted in time of war. "If we accept the truth of this position," so ran the petition, "the converse should also be true." If there can be no enlargement, there should be no restriction." The plea that our interference in the trade of the colonies of Britain's enemies was unlawful, because they were benefitted by it could not stand, Pinkney argued, because the trade was permitted to British subjects.[103]

All Americans, were not such enthusiastic defenders of the carrying trade, however, as the merchants. In New York there appeared a pamphlet by Clement C. More, entitled *An Inquiry into the Effects of the Foreign Carrying Trade upon the Agriculture Population and Morals of the Country*. The author argued that agriculture and manufacture should be the chief occupations of the American people. The carrying trade deflected them from farming, brought in large profits and luxuries and embroiled the country with foreign nations. While More did not go so far as to urge that the trade be given up entirely, he did hold that no risks should be run in its defense, since it

---

[101] *A. S. P.*, For. II, pp. 737–739.
[102] *Ibid.*, p. 740–741.
[103] *A. S. P.*, For. II, pp. 750–756, passim. This was also the view expressed by Madison in his Examination of the British Doctrine, *Op. cit.* Madison declared that neither authorities on international law, nor the public treaties of Europe since 1648, supported the British position.

was of only temporary nature, and with the coming of peace, the Americans would be shut out of Europe with their colonial cargoes.[104]

In protest against the decisions of the British courts, the Senate (February 13, 1806) adopted resolutions, declaring the new position a direct encroachment upon the independence of the United States.[105] By way of retaliation, the closing of American ports to British goods was suggested. But when the members of Congress faced the plan for the total exclusion of British goods it was perceived that the incidence of such a blow would be so heavy upon the United States that it had to be given up.

The report of the Secretary of the Treasury on American exports and imports, showed how inextricably our commercial concerns were bound up with those of Great Britain. We imported each year from that country and her domains about twelve million dollars worth more than we exported to those countries.[106] This difference we paid by exchange on London, resulting from our excess of exports over imports to European countries and from goods sold by us in the West Indies. The direct trade was therefore bound up with the indirect. Great Britain was finding us a good customer, precisely because the indirect trade made us more wealthy.

Our total imports from Great Britain and her dominions for the last preceding year, had reached the sum of thirty-five millions, the revenue from which had amounted to five millions, while on goods from all other countries it amounted to six millions.[107] If we should cut off nearly one half of our revenue, the loss would have to be made good by internal taxes.

Those who opposed the principle of non-importation declared that the trade which we were seeking to protect, in this drastic manner was not the ordinary peace trade of the country, but "a mushroom growth, the mere fungus of war," as John Ran-

---

[104] For verification of More's prediction, see figures for exportation of colonial goods from America, 1816–1833, *Pitkin Statistical View*, pp. 146–147.
[105] *Writings of J. Q. Adams*, Ford ed., III, p. 133–134.
[106] *A. S. P.*, Commerce and Navigation, 1, p. 640.
[107] *Ibid.*

dolph termed it, which profited only a few individuals.[108]

Congress finally passed a bill for partial exclusion of British goods. The law permitted the introduction of coarse woolens, of Jamaica rum, of Birmingham and Sheffield cutlery, and of salt, articles which could not be procured elsewhere, but all other goods which could either be made at home, or imported from other countries, were excluded.[109]

The measure was adopted April 18, 1806, but it was not to go into effect until the following November, because Pinkney in London, held out hopes of accommodation with Great Britain before that date.

To Monroe's repeated remonstrances against the seizures of the summer of 1805, Lord Mulgrave returned only evasive answers. Great Britain, thought Monroe, did not wish to give a definite promise, because she wished to be free to act, in case the alliance with Russia and Austria proved successful against France. "In the meantime," as he wrote to Madison in September, 1805, "she seeks to tranquillize us by dismissing our vessels in every case that she possibly can. It is evident to those who attend the trials, that the tone of the judge has become more moderate, that he acquits whenever he can acquit our vessels, and keeping within the precedent of the *Essex*, seizes every fact that the papers or other papers furnish in the cases which occur, to bring them within that limit."[110]

Upon the death of Pitt, Charles James Fox became Minister of Foreign Affairs. Fox, the old friend of America, was able to effect a compromise. For the Order in Council of May 16, 1806 (Fox Blockade) which was now issued, virtually set aside the Rule of 1756. This order which we have already discussed,[111] allowed neutral vessels to enter ports, from the Elbe to Brest (except in the strip from the Seine to Ostend) "if they had not

---

[108] *Annals, 9th Cong.*, p. 559. For the view of British merchants as to the mutual advantages of Anglo-American trade, see *Petition of Merchants against Orders in Council*, Hansard, pp. 1050–1060.

[109] *U. S. Statutes at Large*, II, p. 379.

[110] Monroe to Madison, Sept. 25, 1805, *A. S. P.*, For. III, p. 106. The cases of the *John Bulkley*, the *Ambition* and the *Respect* already discussed and others found in H. C. A. *Miscellanea and Appeals to the Lords Com. of Appeal in Prize Causes*, bear out Monroe's statement.

[111] See ante, p. 58.

been laden at an enemy port, or if departing, they were not destined to an enemy port." In other words no question as to the origin of cargoes was to be raised. Statistics of the export of coffee, sugar, and other colonial products, from American to continental ports, during 1806 and 1807, prove, as we have already shown, that up to the laying of the "long embargo" in America, the carrying trade continued to flourish.

Meanwhile, the attempts of Pinkney and Monroe to secure reparations, and to negotiate a new treaty ended in failure, and the Chesapeake Affair widened the breach between the two countries.

The absorption of most of the colonies of France, Spain and Holland by England, as the war progressed, tended to throw more of the colonial trade into British hands. After the issue of the Orders in Council of November 1807, interest in America was shifted to other phases of the question of neutral rights. In public discussion in the United States, we hear no more after this of the Rule of 1756, and of the *Essex* decision.

III

The "Great Guns" of the Belligerents—The Berlin Decree 1806—Its Application in Holland, Hamburg, and Bremen—American Protest—Order in Council, Jan. 1807 Enemy Coasting—Trade forbidden to neutrals—Order of Nov. 1807—No neutral trade with Europe except through British ports—The Orders in Operation—The Orders as an Economic Weapon—The Milan Decree.

THE GREAT GUNS OF THE BELLIGERENTS

The Berlin Decree, 1806

The hegemony of the continent after the brilliant victories of 1805–1806, offered Napoleon new opportunities. At last it seemed possible to carry out the long cherished dream of Frenchmen, to close England's markets over a wide area, and so undermine her commercial stability. The Grand Empire had been built up of France and her surrounding marches, whose heads appointed by Napoleon from his family and his most trusted followers, might apparently be counted upon for absolute cooperation.

From the Imperial Camp in the capital of conquered Prussia, Napoleon launched the bolt of the new warfare. His decree of November 21, 1806, begins with a recital of England's misdeeds. Some of these were simply trumped up, but two of them were genuine—the paper blockades and the seizure of enemy property on neutral vessels.

Against English blockading orders, Napoleon objected that they took in entire coasts and even a whole empire, including unfortified places, and ports before which she had not a single ship. This he declared was contrary to the principles of international law. On this point the American Department of State fully agreed with him. Madison, writing to Erskine in March 1808, referred to these same blockades as "never legally established according to recognized definitions."[1] In spite of the

---

[1] *A. S. P.*, For. III, p. 212.

assurance given Fox by the heads of the British navy, the Elbe to Brest blockade could not be maintained by his Majesty's cruisers.

Napoleon also affected to hold it as a great reproach against the English, that they did not respect enemy property in neutral ships. But such property, by being thus carried, did not, by the law of nations, become neutral, not can we think for a moment, that Napoleon candidly believed that it did.[2] As a champion of the "modern law of nations," Napoleon was not convincing. That collector of cash levies from conquered cities, and wholesale snatcher of national art treasures from fallen enemies surely could pretend to no tender conscience where the principles of international law were concerned.

Having proved that England had in one particular violated the principles of the recognized law of nations, Napoleon issued a fiat which went much further in that direction, to be in force until she should change her practice, respect private property on the sea as well as on land, and alter her blockading policy.

The British isles then were declared to be in a state of blockade. All commerce with England was forbidden, and there was to be no handling of British merchandise. No vessel from England was to be admitted to any port of France or her allies. Any vessel attempting a false declaration was to suffer confiscation.[3] "No continental markets for British goods," might be said to sum up the purport of the decree.

Notice of the decree was to be sent to the kings of Spain, Naples, Holland, Etruria, and the other allies, whose citizens, declared Napoleon, were fellow victims of England's maritime code. There was no formal notice to the government of the United States.

From the first, Armstrong suspected that the new decree boded no good to his country. "Much is said here," he wrote to Madison, "of qualifications which are to be given to the arrête of November 21, and which would indeed make it very

---

[2] Article 14 of the Convention of 1800, between France and the United States, especially provided that "free ships shall give a freedom to the goods."
[3] Duvergier, *Lois*, etc., 16, p. 67.

harmless, but these are rather to be hoped for than believed in."⁴

Decrès, Minister of Marine to whom Armstrong applied, for an explanation of the new regulation with respect to America, ventured the opinion that the decree would make no modification in the regulation then observed by France with regard to neutral navigation, and that the arrangements of the conventions of 1800 would still obtain.⁵ But he hastened to disclaim any official information on the subject, and he referred Armstrong to the Count of Benevento, Minister of Foreign Affairs. For months no definite statement on the subject could be secured.

Meanwhile, a few American vessels were seized, in various European ports, and in the waters of the West Indies, although the Berlin decree did not specifically authorize captures at sea.

Insurance from British to American ports rose from 3 per cent to 10 per cent. In anticipation of the closing of European markets the prices of American and colonial goods dropped in London.⁶

In all the ports on the West coast of France, there was a great stir of privateers fitting out for the capture of neutral vessels. A few days after the promulgation of the decree, eighteen had been equipped in St. Malo alone.⁷ From Guadeloupe armed vessels prepared to capture American merchant men bound to or from British ports in the West Indies.⁸

The first seizure of American vessels under the Berlin Decree occurred in the Mediterranean, where vessels were captured early in 1807, and taken into the port of Leghorn. The first of these to come before the Council of Prizes, was the *Hibernia*. Part of the cargo, consisting of rum and ginger were of British origin, but since the vessel had left America on November 6th before the decree could have been known in America, and since she was bound to a neutral port, the Council decided that she could not be seized. She was therefore liberated and her captors

---

⁴ Quoted by H. Adams, *Hist. of U. S.*, III, p. 390.
⁵ *A. S. P.*, For. II, pp. 805–806.
⁶ Ellis and Allan Papers, London letters, Dec. 8 & 13, 1806.
⁷ *New York Evening Post*, Feb. 13, 1807.
⁸ *Ibid.*, March 6, 1807.

were obliged to pay costs and damages.⁹ Another of the vessels captured at this time was also liberated, and the two remaining ones were allowed to depart, after they had given moderate bonds, to abide by the later decision of the Council of Prizes.¹⁰

At Naples the brig *Fitz William* of Boston, bringing freight for Leghorn, was captured and condemned, on the ground that she had cleared for Messina, a port in the possession of the English.¹¹

From Bordeaux, the American consul, Wm. Lee reported that in April, two American vessels had been captured by the French privateer, *Eve*, from Bayonne. One of these was the *Walker*, belonging to Hicks, Jenkins and Co. of New York, which had started from London for America with a cargo of sundries. The other was the *Zulema* of Philadelphia, on her way to Liverpool with a cargo of flour.¹²

The ship *Bordeaux Packet* on her way to Amsterdam with teas, was stopped by an English cruiser, and had her papers endorsed, warning her not to enter any port of the enemy or his allies, nor Hamburg or Lübeck. Later she was boarded by another British cruiser, and carried into Plymouth, but soon liberated. The *Bordeaux Packet* then continued her journey to Antwerp, where she was seized, under the Berlin Decree, February 1807, on the suspicion that the cargo was British property. Mr. Ridgway, the American consul at Antwerp, to whose house the teas were consigned, made strenuous efforts for her liberation, but without success. In July 1808, the Emperor directed the property to be sold and the money placed provisionally in the sinking fund until he should be assured that the owners were not English. Proofs of American property were furnished, but Ridgway could obtain no redress.¹³

In July of 1807, came the ringing of bells in French cities, as Lee wrote from Bordeaux, announcing the peace with Russia, by which it was said that Alexander and Napoleon had divided

---

⁹ *A. S. P.*, For. III, p. 247.
¹⁰ Consular Letters, Leghorn, April 13, April 27, 1807.
¹¹ List of Arrivals at Naples, July 1–Dec. 28, 1807, Consular Letters Leghorn.
¹² Consular Letters, Bordeaux, April, 1807.
¹³ Brown vs. Phoenix Ins. Co., Binney, *Penna. Supreme Court Reports*, Vol. 4.

between themselves, the east and the west of Europe. This strengthened the hands of Napoleon. It seemed to make the combination against England invincible. With Russia and Turkey added to the French side, and Denmark and Portugal compelled to enter the system, Napoleon foresaw the English vessels loaded with merchandise, ranging the shores of Europe, from the Sound to the Hellespont, seeking for an entrance and finding none.[14]

Signs of the more energetic prosecution of this "war for the independence of commerce" now appeared. The Spanish government at Napoleon's bidding, had passed the Decree of Aranjurez, in February, 1807. By this the Berlin Decree was proclaimed as the law of Spain.[15] As a result of this several American vessels were captured upon the high seas, and taken into Spanish ports. Upon the protest of Erving, the American chargé d'affaires at Madrid, he was told that the final decision in regard to these captures would coincide with that of the French government, in similar cases in France. Erving therefore referred the matter to Armstrong.[16]

One of the vessels already seized under the Berlin Decree, the *Hibernia* at Leghorn, had, as we have seen, been freed by the Council of Prizes at Paris on March 24,[17] others (perhaps the *Walker* and *Zulema*) had also been liberated, for Armstrong, in writing to Champagny, August 9, 1803, in regard to the Spanish seizures, expressed the hope that the decisions in these cases would not be less favorable than those already rendered, and that the stipulations of the Convention of 1800, were not affected by the Berlin Decree.[18]

Instead Armstrong received a few days later, an unfavorable reply. To the question whether, under the Decree of November 21, armed vessels could seize English property or goods of English origin in neutral vessels the Grand Judge Regnier had given an official answer. This, needless to say, embodied, not

---

[14] *Correspondence Napoleon*, I Vol. 15, pp. 659–660.
[15] *A. S. P.*, For. III, p. 6.
[16] Melvin, Napoleons Navigation System, p. 38.
[17] Appleton to Madison, Consular Letters, Leghorn.
[18] *A. S. P.*, For. III, p. 243.

his own opinion, as a jurist, but the decision of Napoleon.
Since the Emperor had not thought proper to express any
exception in his decree there was to be no ground of exception
in the execution of it, in any respect.[19] On the question of
whether French armed vessels might seize neutral vessels going
to or from England, even though they had no English merchandise on board, the Emperor had not as yet made up his mind.

Eleven months had now passed since the announcement of
the blockade of Britain, and, as Champagny wrote, the European
powers, instead of protesting, had adopted the principle. It
was beside the point to mention treaties, "since England's
infraction of the rights of all maritime powers rendered their
interests common."[20] Indeed, from the rumors in diplomatic
circles in Paris, at the time, Armstrong half expected that the
United States would be asked to join the continental union
against England.[21]

No such proposal was ever broached to him, but on November
11, 1807, just about a year after the first enunciation of the
Berlin Decree, the first unfavorable decision was rendered by
the Council of Prizes, in the case of an American vessel. This
was the famous *Horizon* decision.

That vessel had collected a cargo in the Spanish colonies of
Buenos Aires and Montevideo, and was making for an English
port, when she was captured by an English cruiser, and her
cargo condemned, as the product of an enemy's colony. The
ship, however, was restored to the captain. Loading his vessel
with a cargo partly of British goods he started for Lisbon, but
his voyage was ended by a shipwreck off the coast of France,
near Morlaix, in May of 1807. The remains of the vessel and
the cargo were sold by the French authorities and the proceeds
of the British goods were confiscated, but the rest of the proceeds
was returned to the captain.

The decision seemed to the Americans a particularly harsh
one. As Armstrong pointed out in his letter to Champagny,
had the *Horizon* voluntarily entered a French harbor, the

---
[19] *Ibid.*, p. 245.
[20] *A. S. P.*, For. III, p. 245.
[21] *Ibid.*, p. 243.

worst fate she could legally have suffered under the Berlin Decree was refusal of permission to enter, but having had the misfortune to experience shipwreck, this vessel of a friendly power must forfeit a part of her cargo. The opinion of the Grand Judge Regnier as to the scope of the decree rendered in September should not be retroactive to cover an event which had occurred many months before.[22]

To Armstrong's representations against the decision, Champagny replied, that since the United States submitted to search from English vessels, and observed England's absurd rules of blockade, they could have no complaint against France, who was only acting in retaliation for prior injuries inflicted by England.[23]

Another condemnation in the fall of 1807 was that of the ship *Victory*. This vessel started from New York, in the summer of that year, for Cherbourg, with a cargo of potashes and fustic, bona fide American property. Stopped by an English brig, she was compelled to put into Plymouth, but after a stay of only six hours, her papers were returned and she was allowed to proceed. On the arrival of the *Victory* at Cherbourg in September of 1807, the custom officer reported the case to Paris, and in reply was informed that the Emperor had decided that the 7th and 8th articles of the Berlin decree "should have full sway." No vessel that had touched in England should be admitted, and in case of false declaration, the vessel should be seized. The captain of the *Victory* had declared that he had not been in an English port since November, 1806, but he had been seen to tear up a paper on the approach of the French officials, which being pieced together proved to be a certificate of the American consul at Plymouth, that the vessel had been there. The vessel and cargo were therefore condemned.[24]

More fortunate was the brig *George Washington*. She too had been carried into England, released and then had reached her original destination, Bordeaux. The owner of the cargo, evidently a Frenchman, had petitioned the Emperor that the

---

[22] *Ibid.*, pp. 245-6.
[23] *Ibid.*, pp. 247-248.
[24] Mumford vs. Phoenix Ins. Co., Johnson, *N. Y. Supreme Court Reports*, Vol. 7.

vessel might be admitted. Instead Napoleon ordered the author of the petition to be arrested, and declared for the strict and rigid execution of the November decree. The *George Washington* however, managed to slip out of the harbor, just one hour before the officer appeared to seize her.[25]

We shall now give some account of the effort to enforce the Berlin decree at various places outside of France.

The Berlin Decree—Its Application in Holland

When the Berlin Decree was issued, strict and detailed regulations[26] for the keeping out of British goods were already theoretically, although not actually, in force in Holland and Louis Bonaparte, king of the country since June 1805, planned to make no change in his practices. The new regulation would be executed, he declared only "insofar as the measures already adopted shall not be sufficient to effect the general blockade of the enemy's country."[27]

His imperial brother had other ideas. He insisted on active cooperation in Holland. Louis therefore determined to investigate all arrivals and clearances. By a decree of December 15, 1806, he ordered that no vessel should leave the ports of Holland, but by his permission, and after the captain's giving a bond, that he would not deliver his cargo in an enemy port. Incoming vessels were to be seized at once, until their cargoes and papers should be investigated.[28]

The Dutch merchants hardly knew how this order would affect their activities. "We remain much in the same disagreeable state of uncertainty," wrote one of the correspondents, of Taylor, a Baltimore shipper, "in regard to the ships going and coming . . . all communication with England is at a stand, except by private opportunity now and then . . . If you send any of your ships this way, I would not advise you to let them call first in England."[29]

---

[25] Consular Letters, Bordeaux, Oct. 20, 1807.
[26] *Corr. de Napoleon*, X, pp. 36–40.
[27] Hoeckstra, *Thirty-seven Years of Holland-American Relations*, 1803–1840, p. 31.
[28] *Ibid.*, p. 29.
[29] Letter to Taylor, Jan. 7, 1807, Taylor-Bourne Papers.

A letter from the same correspondent a month later shows that anxiety had been removed. "Everything in regard to entering and clearing of ships," he wrote, "is now properly regulated here . . . the papers must be sent to the Hague for the king's signature, and we get them back in four or five days." Arrivals of American vessels were awaited with coffee, Havana sugar, Maryland and Virginia tobacco, Georgia cotton and Carolina rice.[30] Departing vessels suffered only a temporary delay. Backer, another Amsterdam correspondent of Taylor's wrote in March: "All the ships which have detained for some time under a sort of silent embargo, by the king's not granting his signature, for departure, have now leave to sail."[31]

In June of 1807, Focke and Company, Amsterdam correspondents of the firm of Ellis and Allan in Richmond, reported that the prices of both sugar and coffee were low on account of considerable arrivals from America.[32] The next month, however, suspicion began to be directed toward some of these cargoes. Four vessels laden with sugar ostensibly from New York, were found upon investigation to have come from England. When the reputable houses to which they were assigned understood their character, they protested that they had no interest in the cargoes.[33]

An examination in this case seems to have convinced Louis, and his Minister of Finance, Gogol, that the carrying of false papers was more wide spread than they had supposed. All precautions seemed vain against that which Louis describes as a "horrible evil which ought not to be tolerated by neutrals in spite of all the enmity among nations."[34]

Notwithstanding, Louis was not able to prevent the connivance of his own officials at the practice. George Rex Curtis, American consul at Rotterdam, reported a mysterious American vessel detained for some time by the authorities in that port during the summer of 1807, and finally proved to be a British smuggler.

---

[30] J. B. Forbes to Taylor, *Feb.* 1807, *Ibid.*
[31] Backer to Taylor, March 2, 1807, *Ibid.*
[32] Ellis and Allan Papers.
[33] Hoeckstra, p. 47.
[34] Louis to Napoleon, Aug. 19, 1807, Dubosq, A. *Louis Bonaparte en Holland, d après ses Lettres,* 1806–1810.

French Revolution and Napoleon, 1793-1812 101

The custom house officials finally allowed her to slip away in safety.[35]

In Holland, as elsewhere, the peace of Tilsit marked a turning point in the enforcement of the Berlin Decree. Little more than a month after the signature of his highly advantageous pact with Alexander, Napoleon threatened to end the laxity in Holland by sending 30,000 French troops to that country, for the enforcement of his decree. Gogol in desperation replied that there was one unfailing way to prevent the entrance of English goods, and that was by putting a stop to all commerce. In that case, however, he reminded the Emperor, stores for the French and Dutch navies, and other necessities, would also be cut off.[36]

Nevertheless decrees were issued in August and September, which were designed to make the admission of British cargoes under neutral flags well nigh impossible. The August decree set forth that twenty-two vessels at that time under sequestration, were to be judged before the proper tribunals "with the greatest severity." Incoming vessels were obliged to deposit a "double bond" as security that they carried no English goods, and had not touched at a British port. If a vessel was guilty of these offenses the bond was forfeited and she must leave port. One month later this penalty was altered. The offending vessel was to be confiscated together with its entire cargo, neutral as well as British goods.[37]

American vessels which were directed away from the Elbe and the Weser at this period and urged to seek Dutch ports instead,[38] found conditions but little more favorable in Holland.

The American consul at Amsterdam, Sylvanus Bourne, had protested nine months earlier, at the Decree of December, 1806, which required outgoing vessels to give bond not to visit an enemy port. He had reminded the Dutch government that this was contrary to the terms of its treaty with the United States,[39] assuming for diplomatic purposes, that the government was

---

[35] Curtis to Bourne, July 8, July 18, Aug. 1, 1807, Taylor-Bourne Papers.
[36] Hoeckstra, pp. 49-50.
[37] *Ibid.*, p. 50-52.
[38] Curtis to Bourne, Nov. 12, 1807, Taylor-Bourne Papers.
[39] Bourne to Madison, Dec. 18, 1806, Consular Letters, Amsterdam.

acting as a free agent in the matter. Naturally Bourne's protest was of no avail.

The stringent decrees of August and September 1807 induced Bourne to attempt a warning to shippers in America.[40] On September 22, he wrote to Madison: "The rigorous execution of the decrees of this government which forbid entry in this country of either ships, cargoes or persons which have been in England, has given rise to many difficulties and embarrassments of a perplexing nature, and will render it expedient that the commerce of the United States should be duly advised thereof, in order to avoid trouble. It would be well that vessels destined for Holland should not contract in England for orders, and that no travellers should attempt to come here via England. I submit to you the propriety of making a public communication of this advice."[41]

Less than two months later however, Armstrong was sending out circulars to all consuls in France, Holland and Italy, advising the return of all American vessels to their home ports.[42] Since indications pointed to an increasing stringency in the enforcement of the Berlin Decree, the representative of the American government in the country of the offending belligerent agreed with the president upon the wisest step—the withdrawal of our vessels from the theatre of depredation and seizure.

Those captains who delayed in following this advice were caught by the embargo laid in the ports of Holland at the beginning of the new year. The seamen of these vessels were for the most part discharged with the payment of two months wages required by law in such cases, and then set adrift. They promptly made their way to the American consul of the port and clamored for passage home.

Curtis at Rotterdam was especially hard pressed. "There are ten ships in this port," he wrote to Bourne, "the masters of which seem all disposed to make me a legacy of their crews, in the event of the embargo continuing, and these added to the

---

[40] Moniteur Nov. 7, 1807, 1202, Phila. Aurora, Dec. 10 and 18, 1807. Aurora, Nov. 21.
[41] Bourne to Madison, Dept. 22, 1807, Consular Letters, Amsterdam.
[42] Curtis to Bourne, Nov. 7, 1807 Taylor-Bourne Papers.

ten men belonging to the *Sultana*, lately wrecked, would form a much larger family than I could well look after."⁴³ In addition, Ridgway, consul at Antwerp, was sending on American sailors recently liberated in France. In the end the Dutch government was petitioned to allow a vessel to return to America, carrying these men.

The Berlin Decree—Its Application in Hamburg

The experiences of American traders at Hamburg from November 1806 to the close of 1807, furnish a good illustration of the uncertainty as to the meaning of the decree, the confusion of authority among the various officials, and their shocking venality.

Forbes, the American consul, in a letter to Madison of November 22, described the coming of the victorious Army of the North into the city, under Marshall Mortier, one month after the battle of Jena. "The garrison of Hamburg was disarmed, the whole police taken over by the French, and all British goods ordered to be declared within twenty-four hours.⁴⁴ . . . It is universally admitted," wrote Forbes, "that this measure, will give a most tremendous shock to the commerce of all Europe. This has always been the central knot of those great exchange operations which not only give life to trade, but are interwoven with the finances of every government in Europe. If the object is a blow at English commerce, it will involve every country in Europe in no less injurious consequences."⁴⁵

The Army of the North soon left, but a force of 1500 Italian troops remained to garrison the city, and an embargo was laid upon all the shipping in the port. Five American vessels were among those detained, without warning of any kind. Forbes immediately began to solicit for their release, but could get no satisfaction.⁴⁶

Meanwhile, it was probable that more American vessels would be arriving, some having left America before the new regime in

---

⁴³ Curtis to Bourne, March 10, 1808, *Ibid.*
⁴⁴ Consular Dispatches, Hamburg.
⁴⁵ Consular Dispatches, Hamburg, Forbes to Madison, Nov. 22, 1806.
⁴⁶ Same to same, Dec. 12, 1806, *Ibid.*

Hamburg was known, others having touched at England, or carrying questionable goods. It became apparent that the sweeping decree of the Emperor was to be made the occasion of all kinds of irregularities on the part of the French authorities.

Since there seemed no security for American trade, Forbes issued a circular of warning to American vessels approaching the city. It was dated January 7, 1807, and advised putting in at Glückstadt, a port in Holstein, farther down the Elbe, 80 miles nearer the sea than Hamburg, and to which the British blockading cruisers would permit neutral vessels to go. The circular read as follows: "All American vessels arriving at the mouth of the Elbe, proceed to the port of Glückstadt, on the Danish side of the Elbe, there to wait such further instructions as they may receive from me, or their consignees. Keep as near as possible to the Danish shore, and make no entry previous to their arrival at Glückstadt."[47]

The reason for this advice was that the French consul had made it known, that a vessel coming from England would be seized, but if it came from Glückstadt, "means night be found to facilitate its entry." The implication was that the austerity of the agent must be softened by pecuniary means.[48] Forbes declared that he would leave the expediency of such means to the consignees.

Again pressed, in February 1807, to grant permission for the embargoed American vessels to depart, Bourrienne, the French minister at Hamburg, half promised it, but refused to put the matter into writing. A few days later, an American vessel from Philadelphia arrived. Here Bourienne raised the difficulty that he had no authority to admit it, but if he visited it to verify the declaration of the captain, it might come in. Forbes then inquired if there was a settled tax or duty in such cases. Bourrienne replied evasively, "That will be ascertained afterward."[49] More greasing of palms!

Forbes had requested that all measures in regard to commerce should be given greater publicity. The public agents of

---

[47] Consular Letters, Hamburg, enclosure to Madison.
[48] *Ibid.*
[49] Forbes to Armstrong, Feb. 24, 1807, Consular Letters, Hamburg.

Napoleon declared that the Emperor had issued an order for the blockade of the Elbe and the Weser, but there had been no mention of the stoppage of arrivals and departures of neutrals in the ordinances issued by the French authorities since their arrival.

"It is very remarkable," wrote Forbes, "and certainly according to my apprehension totally repugnant to the rights and usages of nations, that from the first occupation of the city by the French troops, not one of the extraordinary measures so immediately affecting commerce have been officially communicated to me, nor can I learn that such a form has been observed toward any other foreign agent here."[50]

Protesting against these unfair practices, not only in the name of the United States, but of all those suffering from similar treatment, Forbes reserved the right of his government to demand satisfaction for all damages.

Bourrienne's reply to this spirited protest was a shameless invitation to Forbes to come down from his high horse, and join in the "pickings." "He proposed," wrote Forbes, "that I should not consider the subject as a diplomatic business, but understand myself with the French consul to participate in the advantages resulting from the present circumstances." Happily the American consul was a man of integrity and the invitation was rejected. Forbes by this time perceived the reason why no commercial regulations were officially issued, and naturally it was not a pretty reason. "The whole mystery of this conduct," he wrote, "is explained by the following fact, well known, to almost everyone here, although not susceptible of legal proof. There is a very considerable trade going on here with England, in face of the existing decrees. This trade pays of course, an immense tribute to the French agents, which has so completely contaminated every fiber of their moral circulation that they can see or feel nothing but through the medium of corruption."[51]

Forbes expressed himself as very unwilling to surrender the splendid neutral commerce of his country to the persecution or

---
[50] *Ibid.*
[51] Forbes to Armstrong, Feb. 24, 1807, Consular Letters, Hamburg. cf. Bourrienne, *Memoires.*

dearly bought protection of these harpies, while they carried on their trade with their enemies, "which they so boastingly pretend to annihilate." He therefore addressed an appeal to Marshall Brune, the Governor General of the Hanse towns. From him redress was equally hopeless. He offered only the strict letter of the November decree, reserving the right to admit such vessels as Bourienne approved.[52]

Having laid the matter before Armstrong at Paris, Forbes received from him only the old opinion of Decrès which had followed the announcement of the decree, that it would not affect the commercial relations between the two countries.[53] When this reply was shown to the French minister at Hamburg, he declared that he was not bound by the explanations made at Paris.[54]

In the continued refusal to publish any rulings, Forbes could only conclude that the object of the French authorities was "to extort heavy tribute from each individual case." He was disinclined to pursue further his humiliating and ineffectual applications to Bourienne, or to appeal to Governor General Marshall Kellerman, as Armstrong advised, for he perceived that the French system was "to protract as much as possible a reign of suspense and arbitrary application of measures to neutral trade, professedly intended only against the commerce of their enemies."[55]

Turning from the French authorities, Forbes presented a protest to Herr Syndic von Sieden of the Hamburg Senate, setting forth that five ships belonging to citizens of the United States were detained by a pretended blockade of the river Elbe, which had never been officially announced to the American consul.[56] The Syndic replied briefly that he could do nothing, as the city was in charge of a "force majeur." The embargoed vessels, however, having suffered a delay of five months, were finally allowed to depart in April, 1807.

No American vessels seem to have arrived during the spring

---
[52] *Ibid.*
[53] Armstrong to Forbes, March 10, 1807, Consular Letters, Hamburg.
[54] Forbes to Armstrong, April 15, 1807, *Ibid.*
[55] Forbes to Madison, April 20, 1807, *Ibid.*
[56] Forbes to Von Sienen, March 18, 1807, *Ibid.*

French Revolution and Napoleon, 1793-1812

and early summer of 1807. The British blockade of the Elbe, the Weser and the Ems, which had been completely removed in September, 1806, had been reestablished in June, 1807, on account of the position of the French upon the continent, which enabled them to control the navigation of these rivers. The English consul at Altona informed Forbes, however, that American vessels might be admitted at Glückstadt, or even at Altona, directly below the city, on the Danish border, if the vessels came from neutral places with neutral cargoes. Between Glückstadt, and Altona, however, at Stade in Hanover, the French commanded the river and put on each passing vessel one or more marines, who might if they chose, compel the vessel to proceed to Hamburg, or to pay the tribute which they chose to demand. Vessels clearing out from Hamburg, however, were liable to capture, by the English cruisers. Glückstadt therefore remained the safest port in the vicinity, for the time being.

Eudel, the director of customs, reputed a zealous servant of Napoleon's, now induced the Emperor to take more strenuous measures against British goods. Accordingly, in August of 1807 the Emperor issued a new decree, retroactive in its operation, requiring a certificate of origin for goods presumed to be of British origin and destined for Hamburg.[57] From the state of affairs already described in the city, we should not expect to find the new regulation honestly enforced. Nor was it.

A strikingly unjust seizure under the certificate of origin order was that of the *Julius* of Baltimore. This vessel started from the Chesapeake August 23rd, only 16 days after the order was issued by Napoleon, the shippers naturally knowing nothing of the decree. She was laden with a cargo warranted to be American property—Havana sugar, besides coffee and tobacco, which however, did not come from a British colony. Arriving at the mouth of the Elbe, she was stopped by French custom officers, and sent into Hamburg, where she was seized in spite of the protests of both Forbes and Armstrong. The ground of her seizure was her want of a certificate of origin, and the seizure

---

[57] A copy of this decree, dated St. Cloud, Aug. 6, 1807, was enclosed in Forbes' letter to Madison, Aug. 20, 1807, Consular Letters Hamburg. The decree is not found in the Napoleon Correspondence.

was confirmed, not by the tribunal at Paris, but by the decision of the Emperor, who at the same time condemned many other cargoes (January, 1808).[58] Later all seizures made by the close of 1807 in both Hamburg and Bremen on account of the lack of certificates of origin, were confirmed by the same authority.[59]

The harsh measures of England having driven Denmark to the side of Napoleon, restrictions in Danish ports were now added to those already fettering commerce in the Elbe. "The French and Danish governments," wrote Forbes in November, "rival each other in blindly and indiscriminately persecuting all commerce, under the pretext of distressing the British trade."[60] On account of the usefulness and value of the commodities introduced, the commerce in question continued to be the most favored. How far theory was opposed to practice might be seen in the admission of two vessels which Forbes declared he was morally certain had been loaded and cleared from England, and the rigid sequester of an American vessel from Baltimore.[61]

The extreme indulgence which the British trade received in Hamburg lasted until the close of 1807. British goods then began to seek the American flag, as a cover for entrance into Hamburg and Baltic ports.

Napoleon, having returned to St. Cloud after his triumph at Tilsit, turned his attention to conditions at Hamburg. October 23, 1807, he issued a drastic order, interdicting in the severest manner the navigation of the Elbe and the Weser to all vessels. Although this regulation does not seem to have been enforced so far as American vessels were concerned, Forbes considered it of sufficient seriousness to issue, November 4, a circular warning American captains away from both of the great German rivers. This circular appeared in American newspapers by the close of January, 1808.[62] By that time the American embargo would have prevented legitimate sailings in any case, but those shippers who obeyed the law could take comfort from the fact that their

---

[58] Smith vs. Del. Ins. Co., *Penna. Reports*, Sergeant and Rawle, Vol. II, pp. 73–85.
[59] Wichelhausen to Madison, Sept. 3, 1808, Consular Letters, Bremen.
[60] Forbes to Madison, Nov. 13, 1807, Consular Letters, Hamburg.
[61] *Ibid*.
[62] e. g. Poulson, *Amer. Daily Advertiser*, Jan. 30, 1808.

ventures in the direction of Hamburg and Bremen would probably have ended in failure. The warning stresses the trade restrictions of both the belligerents and the immediate enforcement of unexpected regulations.

The circular was dated at Hamburg, November 4, 1807, and read as follows: "To the masters of American ships bound to Hamburg: In the present unprecedented crisis such great and almost daily changes take place, and the measures affecting commerce are put into such immediate operation that it is impossible for the most prudent with the best intentions, to avoid the injuries which on every side lay in wait for neutral trade. . . .

"The French custom house officers or douainiers, without any official intimation to the foreign agents here, have some time since, in virtue of an imperial decree applied the commercial regulations and laws of France to the trade of this city, and without any exception, required certificates of origin, signed by the French consul at the place of shipment, for all articles attempted to be introduced here. In addition to the inconveniences which the prompt and unexpected execution of this measure presented within a few days, a new order of the French Emperor, has interdicted in the strongest manner, the navigation of the Elbe and the Weser, to all ships whether going or coming; and in consequence, the American ship *Julius*, from Baltimore, was seized and the cargo sequestered. The ship was liberated, but without freight, and must remain here under an embargo, the terms of which cannot be foreseen . . . Under this state of things it must occur to every one that it cannot promote the interests confided to you to enter either of these rivers," J. M. Forbes.[63]

The seizure of the cargo of the *Julius* by Eudel the Collector of Customs, was confirmed by the decision of the Emperor, several months later. British goods still attempted entrance under the American flag. In November, the ship *Lucy*, of Plymouth, Mass., appeared at Hamburg, purporting to have come from Norfolk, Va. The French customs officials suspected her of being English. Forbes, after examining her sea letter,

---

[63] Consular Letters, Hamburg.

came to the conclusion that the signatures of the President and the Secretary of State were forged, as indeed the captain later confessed them to be. Forbes then secured the arrest of the captain, wishing to convince the French authorities that the American government frowned upon the fraudulent use of its flag and ships papers, and hoping thereby to secure consideration for the legitimate trade.[64]

The American consul expressed the belief, however, that similar cases of American vessels covering British goods had occurred in the Baltic at Rostock, Wismar, Stettin, Königsburg and Danzig.[65]

This seizure of the *Lucy* at Hamburg marks the beginning of a new kind of "fraud of the neutral flags" undertaken this time for the benefit of English shippers, and destined to expand greatly, as we shall see, in the period from 1809 until the end of the struggle.

In issuing his warning to American captains, Forbes had not acted too soon. On November 11 was issued the British Order in Council requiring all neutral vessels destined for the ports of France and her allies to stop in English ports[66] and on December 17, came Napoleon's Milan Decree marking for seizure any neutral vessel which had so much as been visited by a British vessel.[67] Eudel seems to have interpreted the latter as authorizing the arrest of every American vessel arriving at the port.

One enterprising Yankee merchant had a pilot boat at the mouth of the Elbe to turn away his captain to the nearest Dutch port.[68] In spite of warnings, however, some American vessels continued to reach Hamburg and the October order, interdicting navigation in the river, seems to have counted for little. In December, Forbes issued a third circular giving the latest regulations in regard to certificates of origin. These were, as usual, designed, in theory, to sift out British goods. Cargoes were to be admitted under the American flag, if they came from a neutral port, and had not touched in England. "You will be

---
[64] Forbes to Madison, Nov. 13, 1807, Consular Letters, Hamburg.
[65] Same to same, Feb. 14, 1808, *Ibid*.
[66] *A. S. P.*, For. III, p. 269.
[67] *Ibid*., pp. 290–291.
[68] Consular Letters, Rotterdam, letter of G. R. Curtis, Consul.

French Revolution and Napoleon, 1793-1812   111

called upon," ran the circular, "to declare from whence you come and at what ports you have touched during the voyage. In case of making false declaration, you will be exposed to the forfeiture of your ship and cargo, and will be imprisoned, both master and crew until the master shall have paid 6000 francs, and each seaman 500 francs, fine, imposed by a late decree."[69]

Nevertheless, at the close of 1807, Forbes expected the total suspension of American commerce at Hamburg and talked of resigning his consulship, as there was no salary attached thereto. He remained at his post however.

The Berlin Decree—Its Application in Bremen

The experiences of American shipping at Bremen during the year 1807 corresponded to those at Hamburg. General Dumonceau, the commander of the district assured Wichelhausen, the American consul, in December, 1806, that American cargoes could pass freely if only accompanied by proper documents.[70]

Although the blockade of the Elbe and the Weser by the British had been supposedly removed in September, 1806, and not reestablished until June of 1807, yet British cruisers stopped American vessels even before the latter date, warned them away from Bremen, and advised them to seek Tonningen, as the nearest open port. Such a warning was given to the ship *LeRoy*, which sailed from New York in April of 1807, laden with a cargo of sugar, coffee and Nicaragua wood valued at $175,000. The captain having been taken into Plymouth, but soon released, made for the Danish port of Tonningen. Here his goods were delivered to the agents of the consignees at Bremen, and the goods were forwarded to the latter city in lighters. It appeared that the British government on a remonstrance from the city, had relaxed the blockade so far as to permit importation in that manner.[71]

By July, however, the importation of rice, flour and rum by water was forbidden by the British from Tonningen to Hamburg

---

[69] Consular Letters, Hamburg, Dec. 4, 1807.
[70] Wichelhausen to Madison, Dec. 31, 1806, Consular Letters, Bremen.
[71] Low vs. Day. (U. S. Insurance Co.) Binney, *Penna. Supreme Court Reports*, Vol. V.

or Bremen, on the ground that these might be used to supply the French armies. Land transportation was not feasible, on account of the heavy charges, and the many middlemen required.

In spite of the British blockade a few American vessels reached the city, and these were subjected to heavy charges, by both the French and the German authorities, to which Wichelhausen raised objection. But the trail of the serpent was over the Bremen trade also. Major General Abemma was an honest and liberal-minded man . . . wrote Wichelhausen, "who would yield if he were not under the influence of the French and Dutch (German) consuls, whose personal advantage it is that these measures be not repealed, it having increased their income very handsomely."[72]

Later in the year, several American vessels which reached the city, were detained upon their arrival, on account of having touched in England.[73] "More French Ship!" was the ironical comment of an American newspaper at this news. Very reluctantly, American shippers were learning that they came within the scope of Napoleon's decrees.

American Protest Against the Berlin Decree

To the pretensions of the Berlin Decree the American government urged two principal objections: that they were contrary to the principles of public law and to the convention of 1800. Article 12 of the latter treaty ran as follows: "It shall be lawful for the citizens of either country to sail with their ships and merchandise (contraband goods always accepted) from any port whatever, to any port of the enemy of the other and to sail and trade with their ships and merchandise, with perfect security and liberty, from the countries ports and places of those who are enemies of both, or either party, without any opposition or disturbance whatsoever and to pass not only directly from the places and ports of the enemy aforesaid to neutral ports and places, but also from one place belonging to an enemy to another place belonging to an enemy, whether they be or be not

---

[72] Wichelhausen to Madison, July 4, 1807, *Ibid.*
[73] *Ibid.*

under the jurisdiction of the same power, unless such ports or places, shall be actually besieged or invested."[74]

While this language is very sweeping, it does not seem specifically to authorize that if one of the parties b came involved in a war, the other party, being neutral, might sail from the port of the enemy to the ports of the other party to the treaty. Therefore it is a question whether the Berlin decree violated Article 12 of the treaty. On the other hand, when the treaty was signed in 1800, there was no anticipation of such a situation as obtained in 1806, when the bounds of France were extended to include Holland, North Germany and Italy.

But even if the decree did not run counter to Article 12, it certainly violated Article 14, which provided that "free ships shall give a freedom to goods, and that every thing shall be deemed to be free and exempt, which shall be found on board the ships belonging to the citizens of either of the contracting parties, although the whole lading, or any part thereof, should appertain to the enemies of either, contraband goods being always excepted."[75]

Such were the arguments used by Madison in his first letter to Armstrong, after the news of the Berlin decree reached Washington.

In July the letters of Armstrong were still favorable but seizures of American vessels in the Spanish ports and in Antwerp aroused his misgivings. On August 9th, the American minister wrote to Champagny, Minister of Exterior Relations, for an explanation.[76]

In the end however it was the Grand Judge Regnier who answered the request, and in a brief note announced the determination of Napoleon to include American vessels within the scope of the decree.[77]

Any last lingering hope of special favor for Americans was blasted by the *Horizon*[78] Decision, rendered one month later

---

[74] Malloy, *Treaties* I, p. 500.
[74] Malloy, Treaties I, p. 500.
[75] *A. S. P.*, For. III, p. 242.
[76] Armstrong to Monroe, July 7, 1807, *A. S. P.*, For. III, p. 242.
[77] *A. S. P.*, For. III, p. 244.
[78] See ante, pp. 97–98.

(October, 1807), but not known to Armstrong until November. In giving their reasons for the decision, the Council of Prizes referred to opinion of the Decrès letter[79] as a private interpretation, "of which the council had at no period partaken."[80]

What is the true explanation of the change in French policy toward American trade in the summer of 1807? Partial reasons may be found in the growing power of Napoleon on the continent after the agreement with Alexander, and the English bombardment of Copenhagen which emphasized more clearly than ever that this was a struggle of the whole continent against one small island. A still stronger reason is doubtless found in the open disobedience to the decree in Holland and in the North German ports, and the extensive bringing in of British goods by neutrals under false papers. If neutrals undertook to flout his attempts to keep British goods out of the continent, the author of the Berlin Decree was the last man to neglect such a circumstance as an excuse for tightening the screws. In December, 1807, came a new decree from Milan:

Order in Council, January, 1807—Enemy Coasting Trade Forbidden to Neutrals

We shall now see what measures of reprisal had been undertaken by England. The first act of retaliation to the Berlin Decree on the part of the British government was the coasting order of January, 1807. This order emphasized the futility of the enemy's declaration of the blockade of the British coasts, "when the fleets of France and her allies were confined within their ports by the superior valor of the British navy." His Majesty's government, would be justified in declaring a blockade of the coast of France and her allies, but was unwilling, so ran the order, to proceed to an extremity so distressing to neutrals. The King in Council therefore forbade trade from one enemy port to another.[81]

Most of the seizures under this order appear to have taken

---

[79] See ante, p. 94.
[80] *A. S. P.*, For. III, pp. 247–249.
[81] *Ibid.*, pp. 267–68.

place in the Mediterranean. The report of Thomas Appleton, consul at Leghorn, for July, August and September of 1807, gives details of the cases decided in the Vice Admiralty court at Malta for that period. There were among these seven or eight condemnations of vessels under the January orders. These included the *Fair American*, on her way from Naples to Leghorn, and the *Nymph*, from Gallipoli to the same port.

In the case of the latter vessel, the claimant pleaded that the January Order was not known when he left Gallipoli; but the judge ruled that it must have been known in Leghorn before he left that port for the east. The *Joshua Potts*, from Gallipoli ostensibly for Lisbon, was evidently bound for Marseilles, for a letter was found on board from Degas, American consul at Naples to the owner residing in that city in France, referring to the need of "assimilated papers" for Lisbon. The British judge therefore condemned the vessel, and ordered that no faith should thenceforth be attached to the signature of Degas. Other voyages hindered by these condemnations were from Leghorn to Manfredonia, from Naples to Barcelona, and from Valencia to Naples.[82] "Under this new law of the ocean," declared Jefferson, in his message at the special session of Congress in October, 1807, "our trade in the Mediterranean has been swept away by seizures and condemnations, and that in other seas is threatened with the same fate."[83]

Monroe and Pinkney were occupied in London during the summer and fall of 1807, with negotiations looking toward a new treaty, and with the Chesapeake Affair. Neither of these matters progressed successfully, and in October, Monroe terminated his mission, and returned home. Immediately after his departure, Pinkney was confronted with the new problems created by the Orders in Council of November, 1807.

Orders in Council—November, 1807

These celebrated regulations were issued, so it was declared, in retaliation for the Decree of Napoleon issued one year before.

---

[82] Consular Letters, Leghorn, 1807.
[83] Richardson, Messages and Papers of the Presidents, I, p. 427.

They announced that all the ports of Europe belonging to France or under her control, or from which the British flag was excluded, and also all ports of enemy colonies, were to be considered as strictly blockaded, even though no vessels patrolled their entrance. His Majesty, however, being by his own confession, very regardful of neutrals, announced two great modifications of this sweeping blockade. One was that neutrals might trade between their own countries and enemy colonies. The second modification was the remarkable proposition that neutral vessels, although strictly forbidden to sail directly from their home ports to enemy ports, might freely and legally do so if they came first to British ports and there submitted to certain regulations later to be prescribed. So far as their language went, the British ministers apparently saw no reason why the United States, the principal neutral carrier, should not obediently and gratefully acquiesce in this arrangement.

Not only were neutral vessels to exercise the privilege of entering enemy ports as a favor at the hands of England, but if any such neutral vessel conformed to French regulations by carrying a certificate of origin, that was to be ground for the seizure of the vessel.[84]

As an added inducement to neutral ships to seek English ports, a second order of the same date provided that any goods legally importable into England might be brought in by any eutral ship.[85] Formerly these goods could be brought only by British vessels, or by those of the country of origin of the commodity. By the new regulation England would become, to a greater extent than ever, the entrepôt and storehouse for the products of the whole earth. The right of neutrals to enter any port of Europe under the control of Napoleon which was taken away with one hand by the November orders, was virtually given back with the other by the institution of the license system. According to an order of November 25, 1807, neutral vessels might lade in British ports with goods the growth and manufacture of his Majesty's dominions or with

---

[84] *A. S. P.*, For. III, pp. 29–31.
[85] *Ibid.*

foreign goods legally imported, provided a license[86] for this purpose had been secured, and proceed to any port not actually blockaded although coming under the restrictions of the said order. Foreign sugar, coffee, brandy, snuff and cotton required a special license.[87]

Four months later, the British system was still further shaped and strengthened by a law laying considerable duties on a long list of articles exported from the United Kingdom.[88] The object of the law was increased revenues for the government. It affected practically all the articles American ships might carry as they stopped at English ports on their way to the continent. These articles must now virtually come to England to be taxed, before they proceeded to continental markets, lest they be seized by British cruisers.

As soon as the blockading order was made public, Canning requested an interview with the American minister, not, as he made plain, to discuss the propriety of the orders, but merely to forestall possible misconstructions. Pinkney however was not anxious to learn the munutiae of proposed enforcement.[89] Instead, he protested against the whole system as menacing with absolute ruin the trade of the United States. The French decree, Pinkney argued, did not apply to American vessels on the high seas, as the letter of Decrès plainly showed. The touching at British ports, the handling of British merchandise, and the carrying of certificates of origin, were only municipal regulations of France.[90] He denied Canning's charge that the decree had recently been enforced with increasing rigor.[91]

When the Orders in Council came up for discussion in Parlia-

---

[86] *A. S. P.*, For. III, pp. 270–271.

[87] A license in this connection is a special permission to an individual to carry on a traffic forbidden by law.

[88] 48 George, III, ch. 26, March 28, 1808, *Statutes at Large, U. K.*, 47–49, George, III, pp. 336–348.

[89] *A. S. P.*, For. III, p. 203.

[90] *Ibid.*

[91] *Ibid.* Pinkney was here evidently relying on the reassuring letter of Armstrong of July 7. Although the *Horizon* decision was not known to him, it seems remarkable that he had no official knowledge of the opinion of Regnier, which was issued in Sept. He must certainly have heard the ominous news in regard to the fate of American vessels in the ports of Holland and North Germany.

ment, during February and March, 1808, the whole policy was vigorously denounced from the benches of the opposition. In the House of Commons, Lord Henry Petty criticized the orders on the score of their legality. The arrest of vessels for carrying certificates of origin, was illegal, for the protection of foreign merchants was guaranteed in Magna Charta. Laws as far back as the reign of Edward III provided that no ship should be arrested on the high seas, or compelled to come to England without the consent of the master of the ship. Petty quoted Coke and Chief Justice Hale to prove that short of Parliament, no power could forbid foreign ships from entering or leaving the kingdom.[92]

In the Lords, Erskine attacked the orders as hostile to British industries, then in a state of unprecedented prosperity, in spite of the prolonged hostilities. American shippers, he declared, were bringing their products to every port of England, and carrying British commodities and manufactures into every corner of Europe.[93]

The same point was emphasized in the petition of British merchants trading to America,

"Our intercourse with the United States," said they, "at all times valuable, is infinitely more so since we are excluded from the continent of Europe." . . . The neutrality of America, was declared to have promoted the prosperity of Great Britain. "The produce of our colonies in the West Indies, of our empire in the East, and of our fisheries on the banks of Newfoundland, has frequently found a foreign market by this means."[94]

The Orders in Council in Operation

The pressure of the Orders in Council was felt by American vessels at once. Some even which left port before their issue were confronted with them on entering European waters.

The perplexing situation in which captains found themselves between the British and French regulations is well il-

---

[92] Hansard, 10, pp. 314–320.
[93] *Ibid.*, Speech of Erskine, March 8, 1808.
[94] *Ibid.*, pp. 1056–1060 passim.

French Revolution and Napoleon, 1793-1812 119

lustrated in the case of the ship *Hero*. This vessel left New York November 1, 1807, bound for Leghorn, carrying as a large part of her cargo, nearly nine thousand pieces of Chinese nankeen. These were insured at a premium of 5 per cent, and were declared in the policy, as was usual in such cases, to be warranted American property, proof of which was to be made in New York only. If turned away from the port of destination by blockade, the captain was to be allowed to proceed to a neighboring port not blockaded. When sixty or seventy leagues from Leghorn, to which she was making her way in the face of a Levanter, the *Hero* was boarded by a British cruiser. Her papers having been examined, her register was endorsed as follows: "His B.M.'s Sloop Grasshopper January 9, 1808. Pursuant to his B.M.'s Order in Council you are hereby warned to discontinue your voyage to the port of Leghorn, upon pain of confiscation of ship and cargo. And you are pursuant to further orders of H.M. hereby informed that if you are found proceeding to any port or place of France, Spain, Portugal, Holland, Denmark, Tuscany, Naples, Ragusa or the Seven Isles, or from which the British flag is excluded, your ship and cargo will be confiscated as lawful prize to the captor, the above mentioned ports being declared in a state of blockade."

The captain of the *Hero* then made for Gibraltar, where he found twenty or thirty sail of American vessels bound up the Mediterranean, many of which had also been stopped by British cruisers. While at Gibraltar, he learned of the Milan and Aranjuez decrees. On account of the number of French and Spanish privateers in the Mediterranean, he believed that he would certainly be captured and condemned if he prosecuted his voyage. He therefore attempted to return to the United States, but was refused a clearance for an American port, and told by the British authorities that should he proceed to the United States without one, he ran the risk of capture by British cruisers. He therefore proceeded to England under convoy and abandoned his voyage.[95]

---

[95] Corp. vs. United Insurance Co. Johnson, *N. Y. Supreme Court Reports* v. 8.

The attitude of the American courts toward these various commercial regulations is interesting. The owner of the nankeens in the *Hero's* cargo, attempted to recover their value by legal action from the insurance company, on the ground that the voyage had been defeated by a "restraint of princes," a hazard which was included in his policy. In this however, he was unsuccessful. In the Supreme Court of the State of New York, where the case was ultimately settled, Justice Van Ness gave the opinion of the court. The fear of loss, he said was not the loss itself. Therefore the warning of the British cruiser was no reason for turning away from Leghorn. Nor was the apprehension of seizure and confiscation at Leghorn under the Milan Decree a sufficient reason for deviating from the voyage. There was no evidence that Leghorn was blockaded or neutral trade with that port interdicted. The *Hero* could probably have entered and discharged her cargo there, for she had not "submitted to be searched" within any just and equitable construction of the Milan Decree. Finally the vessel was not under "restraint of princes" at Gibraltar. The captain could have returned to America without a clearance. The warning of capture by British cruisers was a mere threat, without legal authority to support it.[96]

Similarly the captain of the ship *Amiable Matilda* from New York to Barcelona, after being visited by a British cruiser, and then hearing of the renewed hostilities of the Algerines, and the issue of the Milan Decree, broke up his voyage and returned to New York. In this case also the owner attempted to recover from the insurance company. At the trial an American captain who had been at Algeciras in January, 1808, testified as to conditions in the Mediterranean. It appeared that while there were a number of French and Spanish cruisers there, American vessels might escape them by seeking the protection of one of the British convoys, which frequently passed Gibraltar and went up the Mediterranean. Privateers, which generally kept in shore, were most dangerous off Algeciras and in the Gut of Gibraltar. Under the circumstances of the *Amiable Matilda*,

---

[96] *Ibid.*

French Revolution and Napoleon, 1793-1812   121

this witness testified that he would have proceeded to Barcelona, and certainly if he could have gone with a British convoy. The decision of the court was adverse to the owner. The breaking up of the voyage was not justified, because the captain had neglected to make use of the British convoy, and because the Milan Decree would not have applied to his vessel, he having been merely stopped and warned, but not searched.[97]

Another voyage which illustrated the perplexities and dangers of masters who found themselves in the neighborhood of Gibraltar at this period is that of the brig *Industry*. This vessel sailed from New York, November 1, 1807, bound for Barcelona with a cargo of flour, and pipe staves. During the prosecution of the voyage she fell in on December 4th, with His Majesty's ship of war *Hazard*, the commander of which informed the master of the *Industry* of the general blockade, and notified the same upon his ship's papers and also told him he must proceed to a port in England, or Gibraltar or Malta. Upon this notification, the master of the *Industry* changed the course of the brig for Gibraltar, with the intention of touching there, but when close off the harbor, he was chased by several Spanish gunboats. The vessel stood over toward the Barbary shore, in order to avoid these enemies, and the wind failing during the night, she drifted about fifteen miles to the eastward of Ceuta. Fearing the gunboats, the master changed his course for Malta, and was beating up to windward as far as Malaga, when she was captured December 25th, by His Majesty's ship of war *Grasshopper*, and carried into Gibraltar. The case which reached the Lords of Appeal in July, 1810, was decided in favor of the captors.[98]

The ship *Meridian* started from Boston to Rotterdam, November, 1807 but was stopped, and told that under the recent orders, she could not proceed to Rotterdam, except by way of British port. The captain therefore put into Plymouth where a severe storm crippled his vessel. Here he heard of the French decree penalizing American vessels which had been boarded

---

[97] Craig vs. United Ins. Co. *Ibid*, Vol. 6.
[98] Case of the *Industry, Appeals before Lords Comm. in Prize Causes*. New York Ships.

by British cruisers. As his cargo consisted in part of cotton, he could not obtain a clearance for Rotterdam,[99] and if he should unlade the cotton in England, that very fact of trading in a British port would lead to his seizure on the continent. He therefore sold his cargo as best he could in England. Here again the court refused to grant the owner insurance, on the ground that notice of blockade does not amount to detention.[100]

The ship *Neptune* sailed from Charleston September 1st, bound to Hamburg, if the blockade of that port had been raised; if not to Tonningen. October 4th, she was taken by a British vessel of war and carried into Plymouth, but liberated early in November. While the captain was conferring with the agent of the owner, as to how to shape his course, in view of the Orders in Council, he received a letter from the agent of the consignee in Hamburg, informing him that the French decree was rigidly enforced there and requesting him to proceed to Rotterdam, where it might be more easily evaded. But at London he heard from Lyon, the United States consul, that he had just received a letter from Forbes, at Hamburg, cautioning all Americans not to enter France, Holland, or Germany, after having been in a British port, and warning of the heavy penalties in case of false representation.[101] The captain seems to have been too prudent even to risk Tonningen, his ostensible destination, where he could probably have landed in safety. Experienced merchants and learned lawyers were consulted, all of whom concurred in the opinion that the voyage might be legally terminated in London, which was done. This action led to a lawsuit which resulted in the decision that freight had not been lost by any of the perils insured against, but altogether from the apprehension of peril, and the loss was not therefore chargeable to the underwriters.[102]

---

[99] By a law of April 4, 1808, export of cotton, wool from Great Britain was forbidden except under license and then only to the subjects of a state in amity with his Majesty.
[100] Lee vs. Gray, *Mass Reports*, Tyng, 7.
[101] See ant, p. 110-111.
[102] Tucker vs. United Marine and Fire Co., Tyng, *Mass. Supreme Court Reports*, Vol. 12. For similar verdicts, see Richardson vs. Marine Fire and Marine Ins. Co., *Ibid*, Vol. 6. Lee vs. Gray, *Ibid*, Vol. 7.

A voyage in which the captain suffered repeated annoyance from British cruisers, was that of the ship *Union*, which sailed from Philadelphia for Antwerp, September 13, 1807. On October 16th she was captured in the English Channel by the British ship *Resolution*, and taken into Plymouth, but the ship and cargo were soon returned, and the captain attempted to continue his voyage. When he arrived at Flushing Roads and reported himself from England, he was forbidden to land. According to the advice of his consignee, he then made for Rotterdam. But before he reached that port, he was captured by the British brig of war *Royalist*, and carried into the Downs. In spite of the November orders, the ship's papers were returned in a few days and on December 24th the captain was given permission to proceed to Rotterdam on payment of the captor's expenses, to which the master of the *Union* agreed, to avoid delay. Before he reached the Dutch port, however, he heard of the "decree of Holland" forbidding entry to all vessels that had been in England. He therefore proceeded to London and deposited his cargo.[103]

The encounters with British cruisers were not always offensive, and conducive to resentment on the part of the Americans. Many captains reported polite visits and courteous wishes for a prosperous voyage when the ships papers were in order and there was no ground of detention.[104] But when an attempt was made to have the British commanders omit the writing of the word "searched" on the ship's register, after their visit, the British ministry replied that they would make no relaxation in their procedure.[105] The possibility of denying the British visit and so escaping the operation of the Milan Decree was thereby defeated.

Some American vessels conformed to the orders by procuring licenses to continue their voyage from British ports. One of these was the ship *Hamlet* of Philadelphia which started from Philadelphia for Amsterdam, early in November, 1807, with a cargo of colonial produce—sugar, coffee, gum, indigo, etc.

---

[103] Savage vs. Pleasants, Binney, *Penna. Supreme Court Reports*, Vol. V.
[104] *Columbian Centinel*, Feb. 13, 1808, Poulson, *Amer. Daily Advertiser*, March 2, 1808.

Boarded by His Majesty's ship *Plover* on December 10th, the captain of the *Hamlet* put into Falmouth, where the London agents of the principal shipper directed the captain to take a particular government clearance for Amsterdam, which would enable him to pass the British blockade. Kept back by bad weather, the captain later learned of the hostile decrees of the Emperor of France and the King of Holland, and gave up his plans. His unfortunate vessel was wrecked off the Downs, in April, 1808.[104]

The ship *Logan*, started from New York October 31st, with Havana sugar for Amsterdam. Her voyage was attended with unusual hindrances and delays, and in the end she failed to reach her destination. Off the Scilly Islands, she was met by the British ship *Minerva*, and her papers endorsed in the usual manner. Her captain proceeded to Cowes, where he learned from English newspapers that neutral vessels from England were liable to seizure on the continent. On the advice of the owner's correspondents in London, he prepared to continue to Amsterdam. Having paid duties on his cargo he took out a license for Amsterdam, to continue for four months from December 30, 1807. The license system does not seem to have worked very smoothly, for in spite of this safe conduct, his vessel was seized by an officer and boat's crew of the British ship of war *Pelter*, on February 13th, and the ship was libelled at Portsmouth. After more than a month's delay, the vessel was restored, but then there ensued another month's delay while waiting for convoy to the Downs. On May 1st, the captain finally started for Amsterdam. His license expired apparently with that date, and perhaps for that reason, the vessel was boarded by the British sloop of war *Zenobia*, and again libelled. It was restored on June 21st, but by that time the long suffering captain learned that the Berlin and Milan decrees were rigorously enforced in Holland. He therefore took his vessel to London and abandoned the voyage.[107] The license feature of the Orders in Council

---

[105] Columbian Centinel, March 5, 1808.
[106] Snowden and North, vs. Phoenix Ins. Co., Binney, *Penna. Supreme Court Reports*, Vol. 3.
[107] Ferguson vs. Phoenix Ins. Co., *Ibid*, Vol. V (Tried 1813).

was thus proved to be valueless, as Pinkney had prophesied.[108]

Some American vessels, however, succeeded in making their way across the ocean, and reaching their desired ports without meeting any of the watchful British cruisers. The *Shepherdess* and the *Sally* from Baltimore reached Amsterdam in December, 1807, in blissful ignorance of Napoleon's new enforcement policy for the Berlin Decree, and of the recent British orders. They were the only ones among a vast number, of ships that had been expected to make that port. Backer wrote to Taylor from Amsterdam that in view of the British and French regulations no trade whatever could be carried on in safety. All sorts of produce had gone up in price,[109] and would have gone higher, had not the merchants, with persistent optimism, deluded themselves with the expectation that their troubles were but temporary.

The Orders as an Economic Weapon

If the situation of British revenues and industry was so favorable prior to the November orders, and if those orders had the effect of seriously reducing her exports, we may ask what gain the British government hoped to secure, to counterbalance so great a loss. The truth is that the situation described by Erskine and the London Merchants told but one half of the story. While it is true that British goods were entering the continent under neutral flags, prior to November, 1807, yet on the other hand, the continent was freely receiving food and raw materials from her colonies and from the United States, and in return was selling her manufactured goods overseas. The British sea power availed nothing in the commercial war, so long as this continued. The application of the Rule of 1756, and the blockades were the only check which England had so far applied and these had not greatly hindered the neutral carrier. American vessels bringing their cargoes to Europe were likely more and more to take their payment in the continental manufactures rather than in exchange on London as heretofore.

---

[108] Pinkney to Madison, Nov. 23, 1807, *A. S. P.*, For. 3, p. 204.
[109] Backer to Taylor, Jan. 4, 1808, Taylor-Bourne Papers.

Thus after the enforcement of the Berlin decree began, goods from enemy colonies tended to crowd out British colonial goods on the continent, and the market for British manufactures was restricted in both the continental and the American markets. Exact statistics illustrating this tendency are not available.

According to the British Custom House Records, the exports to the United States for the year 1807, fell short of those of the previous year, by nearly a million pounds sterling.[110] (The Non-Importation act, it will be remembered, did not go into effect until the middle of December, 1807, and was suspended a month later, hence had no effect on these figures.) No official record was kept by the United States government at that period, of the total imports from any country, but from those paying ad valorem duties, which includes the greatest number of all imports, it would appear that the British imports to the United States increased during the period. The total for 1805 was over the 31 million, for 1806, over 35 million and for 1807, nearly 39 million. That there was also an increase of imports from the Hanse towns and from Holland, the following table compiled from A. S. P. Commerce and Navigation will show. (I have added the totals of goods paying ad valorem duties in American and foreign ships, which are listed separately.)

Imports paying ad valorem duties:[111]

	From Holland	From Hamburg and Bremen
1801	$1,303,912	$4,284,478
1802	982,556	3,444,704
1803	694,998	1,402,762
1804	1,472,859	548,898
1805	2,318,748	1,861,089
1806	1,673,928	2,305,836
1807	1,882,583	2,190,730

While England herself suffered in cutting off supplies from the continent, she calculated that for the sake of the greater

---

[110] Pitkin, p. 169.
[111] *A. S. P.*, Commerce and Finance, I, p. 512.

loss inflicted on her enemy, it was expedient to pay the price. France needed the neutral carrier. England did not. Therefore, as Captain Mahan has shown,[112] it was bad strategy for Napoleon to issue his Berlin Decree, hindering the neutrals. It was good strategy for England to attempt to break up neutral commerce with the continent, except as the handmaid of the British system. The English ministers judged correctly when they decided that they could stand a partial closure of their continental markets longer than the continent could stand the lack of American and colonial goods, and an outlet for its manufactures.

The Milan Decree

The British Orders in Council acted as another challenge to Napoleon. Little more than a month after their issue he stepped forward again as the professed upholder of the principle of the law of nations, which he declared were also the principles of justice and honor. The pretensions set forth by the British orders, if allowed to become established principles and consecrated by usage would, he contended, be an indelible stain, in the eyes of posterity upon the name of any country submissive to the system. Neutral vessels having had one course marked out for them by the British Privy Council, were now threatened with seizure and condemnation, if they complied in any respect with the British program.

By the decree issued from Milan, December 17, 1807, every ship which had either been searched[113] by a British vessel, or paid any tax to the British government, was declared to be good prize. The blockade of the British Isles was reiterated. Any ship proceeding from the ports of the British Isles, or the British colonies, or countries occupied by British troops, or any ship proceeding to these places was to be good prize to French ships.[114]

---

[112] Mahan, *The Influence of Sea Power upon the French Revolution and Empire*, Vol. II, p. 353.
[113] It is to be noted that the word searched in the Milan Decree does not mean having the cargo searched for contraband goods, but really means visited, that is, having had the ship's papers examined.
[114] Milan Decree, *A. S. P.*, For. III, p. 289.

This decree was denounced in the United States as another violation of our treaty with France. It was pointed out that American vessels on voyages to Europe were forbidden by the laws of their country to arm, consequently they could not resist visits by British cruisers. In fact the law of nations compelled them to submit to such visits and searches, and made resistance to them a ground of condemnation if later captured. But Napoleon's decree now made such unavoidable visits a cause of confiscation.

Additional privateers were fitted out in French ports, to make prizes under the new decree.[115] So zealous were these hunters of the sea that they took vessels which had left the United States before the Milan Decree was known, and even vessels which had been visited by British cruisers on a previous voyage.[116]

The ship *Charleston Packet* after a regular entry at Bordeaux, was about to start on her return voyage and even had a permit to leave when she was obliged to put back, and was seized and sequestered on the ground that she had been visited by the English on October 9th, and December 3rd, the first date being 50 days, and the later 14 days, before the issue of the decree.[117]

The *Mercury* set sail from Boston for Alicant, October 27, 1807. She was stopped by an English vessel but the commander considering the impossibility of the Order in Councils having been known before the *Mercury* had left the United States, did not detain her. Still less could the captain have known of the Milan Decree. Nevertheless when the French privateer *La Josephine* came up with her, the French captain had no such scruples but seized her on the ground of Napoleon's recent pronouncement.[118]

It is a rule of war, to do the opposite of what the enemy desires to have done. But Napoleon was so anxious to arouse American resistance to the British orders, that he acted with British cruisers to deter American vessels from entering French ports. Many vessels bringing needed colonial produce and

---

[115] Lee to Madison, Consular Letters Bordeaux, Jan. 9, 1808.
[116] *Columbian Centinel*, April 2, 1808.
[117] Fr. For. Office, *Etats Unis* Cor. Pol., 1808.
[118] L. Goldsmith, *Exposition of the Conduct of France toward America* pp. 56–57.

prepared to take French goods as return cargoes were seized after they had run the gauntlet of British cruisers and finally reached French ports in safety. Thus the *Two Marys*, with cotton, and sugar bound for Nantes, was twice warned by British vessels not to enter a French port. In spite of this she persisted, only to find herself seized on her arrival.[119]

The ship *Peace and Plenty* with a cargo of sugar, pepper, cotton, indigo and salt fish, left Beverly, Mass., for Marseilles and was taken only half a league from her destination by a boat from the customs.[120]

The ship *Calliope* left New York, November 29, 1807, for Bordeaux with sugar, cotton, salt fish, campeachy wood and coffee. She had on board dispatches from the American government, from the French minister at Washington and an agent on board from the colonial prefect of Guadeloupe, bearing letters for the French government. Nevertheless, these did not save her. Forced to seek the port of L'Orient, after a visit from a British frigate, she was seized and later condemned, although her cargo was for French account.[121]

The *Sally* and the *Tario* were also seized on their arrival in the harbor of Bordeaux. The ship *James Madison* was stopped after she had taken on her cargo.[121] Consul Lee reported that the seamen from these vessels and others seized in near-by Spanish ports flocked to the consulate and sought return passage to America, creating a difficult problem for him.

Vessels were seized in the port of Calais and six of these were condemned under the Milan Decree at a single session of the court in July.[123]

At La Rochelle the ship *Three Apprentices* arrived from New York. She had been boarded on the French coast and several French prisoners had been put on board from the British vessel. After having taken on a return cargo, she was seized.[124]

---

[119] *Ibid*, also Watson vs. Marine Ins. Co., *Johnson N. Y. Reports*, Vol. VII.
[120] Goldsmith, p. 58–59.
[121] *Ibid*, pp. 60–61, also Jumel and Desobrey to Perry, Nov. 11, 1808, Letter Book, *Jumel and Desobrey*.
[122] Lee to Madison, Feb. 13, 1808, Consular Letters to Bordeaux.
[123] Letter to Bourne, July 10, 1808, from Calais, Taylor Papers.
[124] *Ibid*.

Armstrong indeed was told in a note from Champagny of January 15, 1808, that these seizures were to act as detentions merely, until the disposition of the United States in regard to the Orders in Council should be known. But this proved to be only a mockery. Many of these seized ships were condemned and sold, and the owners could obtain no redress.

One of these owners was John Purviance of Baltimore, American agent in London. His experiences in trying to redeem his ship give a good idea of the irregular proceedings in connection with the neutral seizures at this time. The ship in question had been condemned and sold at Leghorn. Mr. Purviance was told that the papers had been sent to Paris, to the office of Maret, Secretary of State. On applying there, he was told that no ship's papers were sent to that department, but the Minister of Marine would certainly know something about them. At the Marine they could not be found, but he was referred to another bureau. "In short, he went around to all the government offices in Paris, but no papers could he get, nor were they at the Council of Prizes, where they ought to have been, as the ship and cargo were already sold." A member of the Council of Prizes shed light on the situation. "There are many sequestered ships and cargoes sold in the different ports of France of which I have not the least knowledge. . . . Sometimes the Minister of Marine, sometimes the Grand Judge, or the Ministers of Interior or Police are in correspondence with the different constituted authorities in ports where ships and cargoes are sold, and the affair is arranged among themselves, and we who are the only competent persons to make the final arrangements, know no more of it than you do. I have often been applied to by persons making similar claims to that which you are now making, and I could not give them the necessary information, and they have not been more successful than you are."[125]

In order to procure condemnation in doubtful cases, each member of the crew was examined separately, with the hope of securing incriminating testimony, which was sometimes elicited by bribes.

---

[125] Goldsmith, p. 48.

The ship *Grace* from Boston to Leghorn, not having spoken or been visited by any British ship was carried into the Island of Elba by a French vessel. At the examination two of the crew, tempted by a reward of one-third of the cargo, swore that the vessel had been visited. Besides the loss of the vessel and cargo, in such an instance, the captain and mate were liable to fine and imprisonment.[126]

Lee reported on February 13, 1808, that by that time already thirty vessels seized under the French decrees were lying in French ports.[127]

---

[126] *Columbian Centinel*, April 6, 1808. See also same journal, April 2, 1808 for other seizures under Milan Decree.
[127] Lee to Madison, Feb. 13, 1808. Consular Letters, Bordeaux.

IV

Jefferson's Policy of Non-violent Coercion—American Commerce on the Eve of the Embargo—Jefferson adopts the policy of non-violent coercion—The embargo in Operation—The Embargo Abroad—The Embargo as a Diplomatic Weapon.

JEFFERSON'S POLICY OF NON-VIOLENT COERCION

American Commerce on the Eve of the Embargo

The American trade which was now about to receive a sudden and unexpected check, had reached unexampled proportions. The apprehension felt by shippers at the Essex Decision, had proved needless. As one American writer phrased it, "the bark of the British courts was worse than their bite."

The traffic in colonial goods as Table I, Chapter II shows, went on unimpaired. The export of coffee, which had reached the high mark of over 97 million lbs. in 1801, rose to the enormous amount of 145 million lbs. in 1806, and was but two million less in 1807. The amount of sugar sent out of the country in 1805 was about 47 million lbs., and an equal amount was re-exported in 1806, while for 1807 the amount was 42 million lbs. Cocoa reached its maximum in 1807, the amount exported in that year being 8 million lbs. Goods paying ad valorem duties, mostly European manufactures transported to the West Indies, were carried to the value of 19 million in 1806, and 18 million in 1807.[1]

The amount of duties remitted in drawbacks on imported goods which were re-exported, had risen to 8 million in 1805, rose to $9\frac{3}{4}$ million in 1806, and to nearly 10 million in 1807. We may see how practically negligible the Essex Decision was in checking the carrying trade, from the fact that in 1804 the amount of drawbacks was something over five million, but in 1807, the amount was nearly twice as large.[2]

---

[1] Pitkin *Statistical View*, p. 146.
[2] *Ibid.*, p. 333.

Staple American products were also exported in large amounts in 1807, particularly flour, lumber, and pot and pearl ashes. A new and valuable product had entered the list of native exports—cotton. In 1791 less than 200,000 lbs. had been exported, but ten years later, thanks to Whitney's clever invention, the amount had risen to 20 million lbs. In 1805 and 1806, the total export was thirty-seven million but in 1807 it had risen to 64 million lbs., the lion's share of which went to Great Britain.[3]

Imports were naturally in proportion, and the public revenue steadily rose. In 1805 it had been nearly fifteen millions, but in 1806 and 1807, it was more than sixteen million.[4]

Thomas Appleton, American consul at Leghorn, reported that from January 1 to June 30, 1807, 90 American vessels had arrived at that port, "a number to which our trade to this place has never before attained." They came mostly direct from America with coffee, sugar, and other colonial products, and brought back silk, olive oil, wines, and soap, or returned in ballast.[5]

Goods from Russia, and China and from the East and West Indies came in as usual, as well as the customary lines of manufactured articles from England,[6] and articles of luxury and elegance from France and Italy.

All contemporary observers remarked upon the growing wealth and prosperity of every class. A Boston Loyalist who returned for a visit in 1808, wrote, "The great number of new and elegant buildings which have been erected in this town within the last years strike the eye with astonishment and prove the rapid manner in which the people have been acquiring wealth."[7]

"What have twenty years of peace and government made us?" wrote a popular pamphleteer. "A nation—rich in all that constitutes national riches, a nation which is truly the admiration, if not the envy of the world. From being some thirty

---

[3] *Ibid.*, pp. 111–112.
[4] *Ibid.*, p. 333.
[5] Consular Letters, Leghorn.
[6] The Non-Importation Act, had been suspended until July 1, 1807.
[7] John Howe to Prevost, May 5, 1808, *American Hist. Review*, 17 p. 78.

years since the colonies, we have become as by enchantment, the successful rival of the greatest commercial nation on earth."[8]

The dangers to which commerce was exposed, failed to deter adventurous shippers, as one observer remarked: "the hazard was great, but subject to average." As the risks increased, new insurance companies entered the field,[9] and shippers frequently distributed their insurance among three or four companies.

Jefferson Adopts the Policy of Non-Violent Coercion

After his vivid description of the far-flung carrying trade of the United States as it went on during 1805, Dr. McMaster remarks that this splendid trade was marked for destruction,[10] implying that the fatal blow was given by the Essex Decision. The trade was indeed brought to an end, but the blow was struck by Jefferson and Congress at the close of 1807, not by the decisions of the English Admiralty courts, two and a half years before.

The laying of the "long embargo" by Congress in December of 1808, was a project which originated in the mind of Jefferson. No petitions of merchants from the coast cities for protection against the belligerents were spurring the administration to action at this particular time. Business men on the other hand were asking for wider opportunities for trade, and leniency toward England. The merchants of Philadelphia and Boston were pleading for the setting aside of the Non-Importation Act, passed, as we have seen, in retaliation for the Essex Decision. The enforcement of the Berlin Decree was barely known, and was certainly not accepted by the merchants as the settled policy of France. The orders in council had not been officially communicated. Nevertheless, in view of the increasing dangers which beset American commerce, Jefferson recommended to the legislature "an inhibition of the departure of our vessels from

---

[8] James Cheetham, *Peace or War*, p. 20.
[9] Fowler, *Hist. of Insurance in Philadelphia*, p. 78. See letter of Gibbs and Channing to John Parker and Son, Oct. 22, 1805, showing insurance in four companies for each of two vessels. *Gibbs and Channing Letter Book*.
[10] McMaster, *Hist. of U. S.*, III, p. 225.

the ports of the United States," for the protection of American vessels, seamen and merchandise.[11] Within four days, Congress passed, and the president signed the Embargo law (December 22, 1807).

This famous measure laid a sudden and complete interdict, indefinite as to time, upon the foreign commerce of the United States. Vessels of other nations already loaded might depart, but American registered and sea letter vessels had to give bonds to the amount of double the value of the vessel and cargo, if bound on a coasting voyage.[12]

The moment shippers in the sea ports received an inkling of the news from Washington, there was a wild scramble to get ships off, even those but half loaded, and without clearances. McMaster gives a vivid picture of the excitement and bustle along the waterfront in New York, in the last days of December.[13] Philadelphia did not receive the official news until January 4, 1808, but rumors had reached the city two days before, giving many vessels a chance to leave. Of these, however, more than twenty were stopped by revenue officers in the lower Delaware, and ignominiously forced to return.[14] The collector at New Orleans cleared forty-two vessels, even after the embargo was known because he had no official copy of it, even as late as January 28th.[15]

Various supplementary laws regulating the coasting trade, and placing heavy penalties for the evasion of the embargo

---

[11] Richardson, *Messages*, I, p. 433.
[12] *U. S. Statutes at Large*, 2, pp. 451–452.
[13] *Hist. of U. S.*, III, p. 229.
[14] McMaster, *Life of Girard*, II, p. 65. Some owners were able to reimburse themselves for their lost profits by insurance. The ship *Rover* cleared out from Wilmington, N. C. Jan. 1, 1808, but owing to contrary winds did not reach further than Fort Johnson on the Cape Fear River, thirty miles below the city, by Jan. 5th. Brought to by the firing of a gun from the fort, the captain was informed of the act of Dec. 22, and revenue officers took away his ship's papers, and stopped the voyage. In the suit against the Insurance Company brought by the owner of the cargo, the lawyers for the defendant held that the law of Dec. 1807, was not really an embargo, which they held occurred only in connection with war, as a measure of reprisal and partial hostility. The court however decided against this view. The embargo was held to be one of the contingencies insured against and the insurance was ordered to be paid. McBride vs. Marine Inc. Co., *N. Y. Supreme Court Reports*, Johnson 5. Same decision Walden vs. Phoenix Ins. Co., *Ibid*.
[15] Gallatin to Jefferson, Feb. 29, 1808, *Gallatin Works*.

were enacted during the following months.[16] Thinking that the tangled European situation might be cleared before their next meeting, Congress authorized the president to act in the meantime. In case of peace between the two great antagonists, or such a modification of their policy as would render it advisable the embargo might be wholly or partially suspended.[17]

Operation of the Embargo

The original embargo law required goods loaded and cleared for a coasting voyage to be landed in an American port, "dangers of the sea excepted." This furnished a loophole of which unscrupulous shippers did not fail to avail themselves. A typical attempt of this kind was made by the captain of the brig *James Wells*, which started from New York with a cargo of more than 1200 bbls. of flour, February 26, 1808, on a clearance to St. Mary's in the State of Georgia. On account of stress of weather and the leaky condition of his boat, the supercargo, who was also the owner declared that he was obliged to put into the port of Gustavia, on the Swedish island of St. Bartholomew. There he declared he was obliged to land his cargo because it was damaged, and afterward, since the governor of the island had forbidden the export of provisions, he was obliged to sell his flour there, most opportunely for him, at a very high price. The owner of the *James Wells* was prosecuted under the law and the case finally came before the Supreme Court. The evidence showed that the leak in the vessel was confined to the upper part of the works, the stress of weather was not very great, and no effort had apparently been made to reach an American port, and the vessel was therefore condemned.[18]

"There is one species of evasions," wrote Gallatin in May of 1808, "against which there can be no guard but in the watchfulness of our collectors and offices. I mean departing without a clearance."[19] Such an evasion, of which Gallatin had perhaps

---

[16] *U. S. Statutes at Large*, 2, pp. 499–501; pp. 473–474.
[17] *U. S. Statutes at Large*, 2, p. 490, April 22, 1808.
[18] Brig James Wells vs. U. S., Feb. 1812, Cranch 7.
[19] Gallatin to Jefferson, May 23, 1808, *Writings*, Vol. I, p. 391.

learned, had occurred in the case of the *John*, two weeks before he wrote these words.

This vessel, had taken on a crew secretly, and had slipped out of the harbor of Baltimore early on the morning of Sunday, May 8, 1808. Starting in ballast, she made her way to LaGuaira, in Venezuela, where she loaded with a cargo of 200,000 lbs. of coffee and 10,000 lbs. of the finest indigo, and on August 19th, she entered the harbor of Leghorn. Here the cargo, if it could have been unladed and sold immediately would have brought her consignees $1,250,000. But the vessel was sequestered by the French authorities and Appleton, the American consul, reported the case to Madison. The captain of the *John* had, of course, no proper ship's papers, and told Appleton that he knew he ran serious risks from American frigates as well as British cruisers and even Algerine pirates, for he had no Mediterranean pass, but he relied wholly on the swiftness of his vessel.[20] He declared that several other vessels had left Baltimore under similar circumstances at about the same time. Further investigations pointed to collusion on the part of certain customs officers in Baltimore. In July, 1810, the vessel and cargo were still under sequestration in Leghorn. The owner of the *John* had meanwhile been indicted in Baltimore, on the strength of the facts furnished by the American consul at Leghorn.[21]

Among successful embargo breakers during the fall of 1808, one or two examples may be given. One of the most suspicious cases which the court nevertheless finally exonerated was the brig *Short Staple*. This brig with another named the *Wm. King* was in the harbor of Boston, about the beginning of September, at the same time that a certain small British privateer, the *Ino*, was in the same port. The *Short Staple* and the *Wm. King* then proceeded to Baltimore, where they took on cargoes of flour, and their owners having given the necessary bonds, they cleared for Boston, on November 1st. The *Ino* had by this time

---

[20] Appleton to Armstrong, Sept. 6, 1808, Consular Dispatches, Leghorn.
[21] Consular Letters, Leghorn, Aug.-Dec., 1808. This case is also referred to in the letter of Armstong to Madison, Oct. 20, 1808. Madison Papers, Library of Congress.

furnished herself abundantly with provisions at Boston, under the plea of going to the Cape of Good Hope, and had now turned south and put into Hampton Roads, for the purpose of some slight repairs. No sooner had the American brigs set out on their coasting voyage, than the *Ino* started in pursuit. Although her crew was small, she captured both vessels, put two men on board each, and ordered them for St. Nicholas Mole in Santo Domingo. The prize masters started for that port. When a British ship of war hove in sight, the *Ino* took her prize crews out of the two brigs, and slipped away, because she feared the impressment of some of her men. Nevertheless, the two brigs made for the port to which they had been directed, without attempting to escape. Thither the *Ino* also came, but the captain made no effort to claim his prizes. Instead the captain of the *Short Staple* was allowed to sell his cargo to the heads of the negro government for the handsome price of $35 per bbl. The cargo of the *Wm. King* was sold by her captain in Jamaica. Both vessels then returned to American ports. Suits were brought against their owners for the violation of the embargo.

The case of the *Short Staple*, which was condemned in the District Court of Massachusetts, was appealed to the Circuit Court. There Justice Joseph Story affirmed the decision, on account of suspicious circumstances. The ground of the *Ino's* seizure of the brigs was declared to be frivolous—their carrying of French property, or being bound to the French West Indies. The fact that the captor did not take his prizes to any British court of vice admiralty, where he would pretty certainly have been decreed costs, if not condemnation, was highly suspicious. Story pronounced the capture not real—but evidently "an amicable arrangement in which a good market and not a good prize was the primary interest of the parties." The New York District Court pronounced the same judgment in the case of the *Wm. King*, which was likewise affirmed by the Circuit Court.[22]

The case of the *Short Staple* however, was appealed to the Supreme Court. The opinion of the Court was delivered by John Marshall. He declared that although the circumstances

---

[22] The *Wm. King*, Wheaton, Supreme Court Cases 2, 148—160.

appeared suspicious, every point had been fairly explained. After the prize masters had been removed, the captains of the brigs were under no obligation to return to American ports, for in case of recapture, such action might insure their condemnation. The judgment of the lower court was therefore reversed, and the *Short Staple* returned to her owners. From this verdict Story and one other justice dissented.[23]

The Embargo Abroad

When the news of the embargo reached England there was at first a slight rise in the price of American products, particularly cotton. This was succeeded by a period of speculation, which had pretty well declined by March of 1808. There was no dearth of American products in the country when the blow first fell. With tobacco, especially, the British market was fully stocked, there being a year's supply on hand, because the sales to the continent had been so largely prevented. Lumber and staves from America were in request in England throughout the period, the supplies through the Prussian ports being cut off, but when the manufacturing towns became dull, there was less demand from that quarter, and supplies were arriving from British North America. For flour and especially wheat, there was a constant demand, through the year, for the harvest of 1807 had been considerably injured by the unusual heat.[24]

The withholding of American naval stores also was a deprivation to the British market, a considerable part of these necessary commodities having for many years, come from the United States.[25]

On the whole, the rise in prices during the early months of 1808 occasioned by the cessation of American exports was less marked than one might expect. This was explained partly by the fact that the embargo was expected to be of short duration, and partly because peace was expected with France.

---

[23] The *Short Staple*, Cranch 9.
[24] Heathcote to Ellis and Allan, May 4, 1808, Ellis and Allan Papers. Also same to same, June 2, 1808, *Ibid.*
[25] Printed circular of Worrall and Williamson to Noah Scovil, Jan. 9, 1808, Scovil Mss.

By May, on account of the news of the failure of Rose's mission, the commercial world believed that the embargo would be continued for some time. Prices of American produce therefore mounted higher, but British merchants reminded their American correspondents that these would immediately fall, in case of the resumption of American shipments.[26]

Although no cargoes could come from America in payment, British merchants sent on at least a part of the stocks of coarse woolens annually imported[27] by their regular customers.

In June wheat and cotton prices continued to advance, but one firm wrote that the American shippers should not calculate on more than common prices, if trade were renewed, for, they wrote, "we have been so long without arrivals that the people of this country will be inclined to inure themselves to privations."[28] This probably refers to the use of tobacco, the rising price of which, in spite of the quantity on hand, was evidently lifting it out of the reach of the poorer people, in England, as in France.

While the English government, and some of the English merchants protested that the restrictive measures of the American government did not seriously affect their country, there was considerable anxiety on that side of the water, during the fall of 1808, for the resumption of trade.

The wheat crop of 1808 was reported as one-third below the average. While there was no real scarcity, the quality in many

---

[26] Heathcote to Ellis and Allan, May 4, 1808, Ellis and Allan Papers.

[27] *Ibid*, May 7, 1808. The following table shows that the exports from Great Britain to the United States were diminished by only a little more than one half, during the year 1808. This is partly explained by the fact that the twelve-months' period in the table includes some months before the embargo was in force.

Exports from Great Britain to the United States:

1805	11,011,409
1806	12,389,466
1807	11,846,513
1808	5,241,739
1809	7,258,500
1810	10,920,752

P. Colquhoun, *Treatise on Wealth, Power, and Resources of British Empire*, p. 99.

[28] Sugden and Fearon's letter, June 30, 1808, Ellis and Allan Papers.

districts was affected by blight and mildew.²⁹ The need was frequently expressed, for good sound American wheat, free from garlic, to mix with the English product. American exporters were advised to send wheat as soon as shipment could be resumed. "I wish your embargo was taken off," wrote a correspondent in London to Wm. Bayard of New York, November 3, 1808, that we might have a little of your flour, to reduce that necessary article, bread. The quarters loaf is this day raised to. fifteen pence ha'penny."³⁰ "Keep this article (wheat) in mind," wrote Conway Davidson of Liverpool to Wm. Taylor of Baltimore, "and if the embargo ceases during the winter or spring, your shipments to this country cannot be too extensive, because all surplus grain will not at all affect our prices."³¹

In August there began to be some small demand in England for tobacco from Spain, Gibraltar, and Sweden. Prices therefore rose, until in November, they were reported as "run madly up," by speculators.³²

Cotton also was increasingly in demand, because of the new markets in Spain and Portugal and their colonies, opened to British manufactured goods.³³

By February of 1809, embargo breakers had reached England in such numbers that the brisk bidding for American produce ceased, and the market was represented as stagnant.³⁴ Some idea of the cargoes, and the further operation of these American vessels, may be gathered from a Liverpool correspondent of Ellis and Allan. Under date of March 21, 1809, he wrote, "Except the *Sally* from City Point, we have had no embargo breakers with tobacco, but a considerable number from New York, Savannah, etc., chiefly with cotton and a little naval stores, which last article holds out great temptation, the cost being small, and the price very high here, and likely to continue, particularly as to turpentine. The ships that come in this way

---

²⁹ Report of Scott Harris & Co., quoted by Heathcote, Aug. 3, 1808, Ellis and Allan Papers.
³⁰ C. Roberts to Bayard, Nov. 3, 1808, LeRoy Bayard and McEwen Papers.
³¹ Letter, Oct. 28, 1808, Taylor-Bourne Papers.
³² Heathcote to Ellis and Allan, Ellis and Allan Papers.
³³ J. Robinson and Sons to Taylor, Oct. 8, 1808, Taylor-Bourne Papers
³⁴ Letter to Taylor, Feb. 11, *Ibid*.

find capital employment in the Baltic trade, in which they get extraordinary freights."[35]

This trading to the Baltic was not the only advantage reaped by British commerce from American vessels during the period. Besides these embargo breakers whose captains had no desire to see American shores for a while, there were the vessels of the United States abroad at the time, when the ban was laid, which had not returned to their home ports. These created a problem for the American consuls.

The fact that there were American vessels still at large, with genuine ships papers, played into the hands of unscrupulous British shippers. There was now another sort of "fraud of the neutral flags," but this time it was Great Britain and not her enemy, who profited by the deception. British vessels as we have seen gained entrance to continental ports, under the American flag, with American papers, the forgery of which had become a business in London.

"I have long been in expectation," wrote Lee from Bordeaux, "that the President would have instructed the consuls to detain in their hands the papers of all American vessels found in their districts after the embargo, unless they were bound directly to the United States. A determination of this nature would have done but little or no injury to our merchants, and put a stop to the nefarious practice of the English, who send shoals of American vessels from their ports, whose owners never saw America, and whose papers are manufactured in London. Ten vessels suspected of having been expedited in this way from London lately arrived in the River Charente, as coming from Norway and were admitted by the custom house." After giving an account of his investigation of some of these cases, Lee added, "It is proper however to state to you that our vessels' papers with all their private marks, are so completely copied in London that it is almost impossible to detect them."[36]

While British vessels were thus protecting themselves under American flags and papers, American vessels on the other

---

[35] Logan Lenox to Ellis and Allan, March 21, 1809, Ellis and Allan Papers
[36] Lee to Madison, Nov. 1, 1808, Consular Letters, Bordeaux.

hand were disguising themselves under the flag of France, or of European neutrals. They thus entered French ports, and escaped possible capture under the Bayonne decree, a measure of Napoleon's which we shall explain later. Lee reported a number of such cases to Madison in November of 1808. "We are led here to believe," he wrote, "by the arrival of several American built schooners, under American and French colors that violations of the embargo are more frequent than you are aware of. The pilot boat schooner *Ant*, built at Baltimore, came from Guadeloupe, under Danish colors, expedited, it is said from the United States." Six other vessels were listed entering under French or Danish colors, but belonging to American firms.[37]

The limit of ingenuity in avoiding obstacles was probably reached by the owners of such vessels as the American ship *Eliza*. This vessel had been a regular trader between New York and the small port of Auray in Brittany, and now retained her American captain and crew. She had however, been sold to an English house in Bordeaux, and her name changed to *Constant*. She continued her voyages between France and America, entering the ports of those countries under French colors. While at sea, however, she escaped capture from British cruisers, by her American papers, still carefully preserved, and by a British license. Lee urged that this vessel be intercepted when she next reached America. Other vessels followed the same tactics.[38]

Lee refused to assist these voyages by giving official clearances, both on account of their illegality, and for fear of the displeasure of the French authorities. Those same authorities however, were not so scrupulous. "These double expeditions," wrote Lee, have become much the fashion, and I am led to believe that this government winks at them. I have seen a permission from the Minister of Marine for the ships *Amity* and *Cincinnatus*, two certificated vessels to put to sea, loaded for the United States under French colors, but I shall withhold their papers." Lee also refused papers to certain other vessels posing as Ameri-

---

[37] Lee to Madison, Nov. 1, 1808, *Ibid*.
[38] Lee to Madison, Dec. 7, 1808, *Ibid*.

cans, which had received permission from the French authorities to sail. These were really French vessels bound for England."³⁹

In December of 1808 Lee reported fourteen American vessels at Bordeaux, six of which had been sequestered. Five of the fourteen had come from other ports within the Empire—Nantes, Morlaix, Amsterdam.⁴⁰ Thus it is apparent that the Bayonne decree was not universally applied, nor were the British cruisers successful in preventing entirely the trading of neutrals from port to port of France.

Some months later, Lee gave an interesting side light on Jefferson's policy of non-violent resistance as viewed by liberal minds in Europe. "The means of the government of the United States to secure their independence and to avoid being involved in the contest are the constant theme of the enlightened part of Europe, who regard them as the greatest specimens of human wisdom."⁴¹

The Embargo as a Diplomatic Weapon

The embargo was announced to Armstrong in a letter of February 8th. Madison described it as a measure of precaution which could not give offense to any nation. It was hoped however that the inconveniences resulting from it would lead to a change of conduct on the part of the belligerents. France would suffer from it, Madison predicted, and still more would some of her allies.⁴²

With announcement of the embargo to Champagny, Armstrong presented a protest against the Berlin decree, as formulated by the American department of state. Although the Council of the Administration of the Interior urged a modification of the decrees in favor of the Americans,⁴³ the Emperor refused to give way. He wished to force the United States into the attitude either of an open ally or an open enemy.

In consonance with this sentiment was the decision of the Emperor at this time condemning two American vessels for

---

³⁹ Same to same, Dec. 7, 1808, *Ibid*.
⁴⁰ Same to same, Dec. 17, 1808, *Ibid*.
⁴¹ Same to same, March 17, 1809, *Ibid*.
⁴² *A. S. P.*, For. III. pp. 249–250.
⁴³ *Ibid*., p. 250.

irregularities in their papers. These two belonged to a batch of one hundred and sixty cases of neutral vessels, chiefly Swedes, Danes, and Americans, awaiting the Emperor's decision. Their combined value exceeded one hundred million francs.[44]

While Napoleon commended the laying of the embargo, on the ground that it was a measure of retaliation against England,[45] he used the law as a justification for the sequestration of those American vessels recently seized, and all those which should come within his grasp in the next few months. By the so-called Bayonne decree, he declared that all American vessels coming to the ports of the Empire were to be seized. For, he declared, since the American embargo was now in force, they could not have come from their own country, but must have come from England.[46]

The offer to suspend the embargo on condition of the withdrawal of the decrees, brought no response. Instead of yielding, there came news of a new outrage. Four American vessels on a voyage from the West Indies, encountered several French cruisers on their voyage. After the transfer of their crews to safety, the vessels were burned, at sea, by the order of Rear Admiral Baudin.[47]

The sequestration of American ships was to continue, because, as Napoleon charged, they brought English goods to Holland and elsewhere. "This," he declared, "I will not suffer." Armstrong therefore, wrote to Madison (August, 1808) that further discussion with Champagny over these issues would be useless. "We had overrated," he declared, "our means of coercion upon the belligerents." The repeal of the embargo was urged by Armstrong, and the substitution of armed commerce.[49]

---

[44] *A. S. P.*, For. III, p. 250.
[45] Napoleon to Champagny, July 11, 1808, *Corr. Nap.*, 17, p. 364. Also 18, p. 1485.
[46] Napoleon to Gaudin, April 17, 1808, *Corr. Nap.*, 17. Also *A. S. P.*, For. III, p. 291.
[47] Armstrong to Champagny, Oct. 20, 1808. *Desp. France*, v. 11. The vessels were the *Brutus* and the *Dromo*. The reason given for the burning of the latter was that it had neither captain nor papers.
[48] Armstrong to Jefferson, July 28, 1808, Jefferson Mss., quoted by Adams.
[49] *A. S. P.*, For. III, p. 256.

During the summer of 1808, Pinkney was busy in London, with a task similar to that of Armstrong in Paris. He was attempting to bargain for the repeal of the orders, by the promise of the repeal of the embargo.

In his interviews with Canning, Pinkney urged that if this was done, non-intercourse between America and France would still be in force, the very object which Canning's government professed to have in mind. The prohibition to American vessels to trade with France would then be brought about, not by the command of the British government, but by the regulation of their own. This would operate, Pinkney urged, far more efficaciously to gain the end of the British government, and would open the way for complete understanding with the United States.[50]

One reason why Pinkney hoped for a favorable reply was the public criticism both in and out of Parliament, of the Government system. A petition of the merchants of Liverpool, presented March 3, 1808, declared that that city was the seat of three quarters of the American trade, and feared serious suffering if the orders in council and American retaliation were kept up.[51] Opposition to the orders was widespread and persistent. The petition from the merchants of London and Liverpool presented March 10, 1808, expressed the sentiments of many Englishmen. The opinion that the orders would prove beneficial to the commercial interests of the country, the petitioners believed, was founded in error. The great danger of the system was that it was likely to interrupt peace with the United States, "our intercourse with which, at all times valuable, is infinitely more so, since we are excluded from the continent of Europe." The valuable American market for British manufactures exceeded 10 million sterling, and as British consumption of American products fell far short of this, the only means of paying for

---

[50] *A. S. P.*, For. III, pp. 225–226.
[51] Hansard X, p. 889.
[52] Speech of Henry Brougham, April 1, 1808, before House of Commons, in support of petitioners from London, Liverpool, and Manchester. This speech was published as a pamphlet. See *Political Hist. of U. S.*, Vol. I, 1808. Gilpin Library, Penna. Hist. Soc.

these British goods was by the consumption of the produce of America in other countries, which the operation of the orders in council must interrupt. The petitioners declared that they could prove that the neutrality of America had been the means of circulating to a large amount, the products and manufacture of Great Britain in the dominions of her enemies.[52]

While Pinkney was laboring to convince Canning of the desirability of joint repeal, however, an enemy was sowing tares in the field. Senator Pickering of Massachusetts, and his friends were taking good care to have it thought in England that the embargo was a failure, opposition to Jefferson's policy rampant, and separate action by the New England states a possibility. Why then should Canning risk his iron-clad scheme of commercial warfare, for the sake of the removal of the embargo, which was soon to fall anyway, according to the New England Federalists.

Canning therefore refused any concession lest it be considered by the enemy a sign of weakness in his government.[53]

An order had already been issued, earlier in the year (April, 1808), providing that neutral (that is American) vessels laden with lumber and provisions, for ports in the West Indies and South America should not be molested no matter how deficient their ship's papers. This was practical notice to embargo breakers, that they had nothing to fear from British cruisers. Naturally, it was deeply resented by the American government.[54]

Thus, at both Paris and London, the embargo had proved a worthless pawn in the diplomatic game.

---

[53] *A. S. P.*, For. III, p. 232.
[54] Madison to Pinkney, *A. S. P.*, For. III, p. 224.

V

Repeal of the Embargo—Passage of Non-Intercourse Law—Trade with England—June-August, 1809 (suspension of non-intercourse) Trade under the non-intercourse law—Holland, North Germany, and Denmark—Danish Seizures — 1809–1810 — Trade to Spain 1809, Smuggled French goods exported through ports of Northern Spain—Trading to the "out ports" after Madison's Proclamation of August 10, 1809—Napoleon's Reprisal for the Non-Intercourse Law—Seizure of American vessels in Spain and Naples—Licenses proposed for American trade.

REPEAL OF THE EMBARGO—PASSAGE OF NON-INTERCOURSE LAW, MARCH, 1809

When the Ninth Congress convened, in November, 1808, the whole subject of the restrictive system and its effects, at home and abroad, as well as possible, substitutes in case of its repeal, were fully discussed.

Since there were still many evasions of the embargo, a more drastic force law was adopted January 9, 1809. This required a permit for the lading of every vessel. A joint bond given by master and owner, of six times the value of vessel and cargo, was required for every coasting voyage. The president was authorized to employ thirty armed vessels to enforce the law, and in addition, if necessary, land forces and militia.[1]

In New England, the existing opposition to the embargo, was fanned to fever heat by this new law. With no recognition of the difficulty and perplexity of the administration, scores of New England towns now passed resolutions denouncing the government's policy and even counselling resistance.[2] The General Court of Massachusetts forwarded a remonstrance to Congress, and nullified the law of January 9th. The Governor

---

[1] Laws of U. S., 2, pp. 506–511.
[2] H. Adams, *Hist. of U. S.*, IV, pp. 411–413, *New England Palladium*, Feb. 24, 1809.
[3] *Annals, 10 Cong.*, 2, pp. 444–450, Quoted, Morrison, *Life of H. G. Otis*, II, p. 12.

of Connecticut, Jonathan Trumbull, refused to appoint militia offices, to cooperate with the collectors of the ports, in enforcing the embargo. As the weeks passed, it became evident that public sentiment would no longer support the embargo. On March 1, 1809, it was therefore repealed, and the non-intercourse law substituted.

This measure repealed the non-importation law, the embargo, and all its enforcing acts. Instead of the partial exclusion of British goods, there was to be a total exclusion of all the products and merchandise of both England and France, and of their colonies, and dependencies. Owners of outgoing vessels were to give a double bond that they would not touch at English or French ports. Neither the public vessels nor the merchant marine of the two offending nations were to be admitted to our ports. The law was to continue in effect until the next session of Congress, but in the meantime if either of the belligerents repealed her decrees, the President was authorized to remove the ban against her.[3] Although the penalties for violation were severe, the impossibility of enforcing the law was freely predicted in Congress.[4]

The weakness of the non-intercourse law was thus recognized by the very men who enacted it. Ostensibly the pressure on the two belligerents was to be kept up. Practically, it was admitted, England would secure American supplies in a round about way.[5]

Soon after the passage of this law, occurred the discussions in Washington between Erskine and Smith, which seemed to promise a settlement of the outstanding difficulties with England. This settlement, so soon to be repudiated by Canning, led Madison to announce the suspension of the non-intercourse with England (April 19th) to take effect on the following June 2nd. On July 21st however, the news of the disavowal of Erskine's settlement by the British government reached Washington.

The administration was now confronted with a dilemma—how

---

[4] Speech of Taylor, *Annals, 10th Cong.* 2, p. 1514.
[5] *Ibid.*

to restore non-intercourse with England. It was solved by Madison's issue of a proclamation, on August 9th announcing that "the trade, renewable on the event of the orders being withdrawn, was to be considered as under the operation of the several acts by which such trade is suspended."

The step described in this awkward locution was not taken without serious misgivings by Madison. Adversaries, he admitted, would assail it because "the power given to the executive by the non-intercourse law was exhausted by the first exercise of it." But Madison argued that the proclamation of April 9th reopening the trade, had been void from the start, because the British government had never, in fact, repealed its edicts. Later decisions of the American courts proved Madison's misgivings to have been justified. In his proclamation of August 9th, he was declared by these decisions, to have exceeded his authority.

Trade with Great Britain June 10-August, 1809
(Suspension of Non-Intercourse)

When Madison's proclamation reopened the trade to Great Britain, American shippers eagerly proposed to resume their customary routes. So anxious were some of them to reach British ports that they started out before June 10th, for other ostensible destinations, with the understanding that the captain would take the vessel to a British port instead, after the appointed date.[6] Thus the five shippers who chartered the vessel *Missouri* from Baltimore signed an agreement that the captain, although he was to clear for Gothenburg in Sweden, should actually reach England by June 10th. Many shippers, however, boldly anticipated the date. American vessels laden with cotton, rice and tobacco were reported from England as arriving daily,

---

[6] "The sight was grand and sublime this morning, to view the number of vessels starting out of the port of Norfolk, destined to the various ports of the world, principally West India men" letter of March 16, 1809 Ellis and Allan Papers, Lawarson and Fowle to Henry and Alex Ladd, March 10, 1809, Lawarson and Fowle Corres.

[7] Agreement signed by Hollingsworth-Worthington, and four other firms, May 9, 1809, Taylor Bourne Papers. The Secretary of State had given his opinion in writing, that such voyages would be legal. Allan to Ellis, April 29, 1809, Ellis and Allan Papers.

French Revolution and Napoleon, 1793-1812   151

direct from the United States, during the latter part of May. Owing to the changed relations between the two countries, these shippers trusted that their bonds would not be forfeited.

By that time, however, the news of Erskine's blunder had reached England, and the government had disavowed his promises. A deputation of merchants trading to the continent called upon the ministers to learn what the attitude of the government would be to the American trade under these circumstances. They were told that all vessels that should clear from American ports, between June 10th and August 9th would be permitted to proceed to such ports as they were allowed to enter by the laws of their own country. Thus the Orders in Council were declared suspended for the period in question. The spirit of the ministers as one British merchant wrote was "to consider themselves bound to the acts of their minister until ample time has been allowed for a knowledge of their refusal to ratify his assurances to arrive in America."[7a]

Some of the American vessels which had gone to ports in Spain and Portugal, expecting to trans-ship their cargoes for England, now turned away from those ports, as we have seen, without breaking bulk and proceeded to British ports. Thus the ship *Charles* with tobacco, which had just reached Cadiz, was ordered by Mr. Charles Ellis, then in that city, to proceed to Liverpool. It was necessary, however, to promise to indemnify the captain, who professed doubts as to the legality of the voyage, for any possible loss of his bond in the United States.[8]

When the tenth of June arrived, there were, it was said, six hundred vessels in American harbors, ready to start for British ports. During the week of June 16–23, more American cotton was landed in Liverpool than had come throughout the year 1807.[9] Robert Hart, a shipper, arriving at London from Baltimore in July, found the docks so crowded that he was obliged to discharge his cargo in lighters. The many vessels returning

---

[7a] Heathcote to Charles Ellis, May 25, 1809, *Ibid*.
[8] Arbitration agreement between Charles Ellis and Capt. Story of the Charles, June 9, 1809. Ellis and Allan Papers.
[9] Heckscher, *The Continental System*, p. 138.

to the United States made it difficult for him to procure a return cargo.[10]

A glut of American goods naturally occurred very soon in the British markets, although the brief opening of the Dutch ports during the summer kept the prices up to a certain extent. The tobacco of Ellis and Allan was sold at a good price for the market was "extremely bare" and there was considerable demand.[11] Wheat and flour also found a good market, on account of the shortage of the British harvest. Although three months licenses had been issued to import French wheat, and Russian, Swedish, Prussian and Hamburg vessels were also bringing this grain in, good flour from America continued to bring a high price.[12]

On the whole, however, the quantity of American goods capable of being absorbed by the British markets was far less than usual, for in spite of smuggling, the British merchants describe the continent as closed to exports from Great Britain.

The announcement of the renewal of non-intercourse between the United States and Great Britain by Madison's proclamation of August 10th, caused "a number of long faces on 'change" as Robert Hart wrote to William Taylor, and sent the price of American goods up. By September, the prices offered for tobacco were "enormous" reaching 11d or 12d per lb. A speculation fever in American goods, especially tobacco developed;[13] driving that commodity to prices which according to prudent men of business "were not warranted by either a scarcity of the article, or any prospect that the future supply would not be thrice as abundant" as the wants of the country.[14]

During the two months intercourse with England, there was ample time to ship the fall supply of British goods. Woolens,

---

[10] Robert Hart to Taylor, July 12, 1809, Taylor-Bourne Papers. A correspondent of Christopher Champlin's wrote from Liverpool on July 22, that 84 American vessels had reached that city in the last fortnight, while from June 11 to July 22, the number was 226. The insurance premium on voyages to and from the United States at this time was only 2 per cent. Champlin Papers, R. I. Hist. Soc.
[11] Heathcote to Chas. Ellis, Sept. 4, 1809, Ellis and Allan Papers.
[12] Letter to Allan from London, Oct. 4, 1809, *Ibid.*
[13] Heathcote to Ellis and Allan, Sept. 11, 1809, *Ibid.*
[14] Heathcote to Charles Ellis, Sept. 14, 1809, *Ibid.*

hardware, and glassware therefore were ordered as usual, and shipped before Madison's proclamation burst the bubble. The quantities ordered, however, were not so large as in other years. Of cheaper woolens, especially a smaller amount was ordered. The Americans were making these for themselves. "Fewer will answer our purpose," wrote Allan to Ellis, "than we have ever had before. Keep in view the vast quantities of cloth that will be manufactured in farmers' and planters' families."[15]

With the closing of the direct trade, the indirect routes were again made use of, but non-intercourse evaders also arrived in British ports.[16] These lowered the prices of American goods considerably.

The hopes felt for a speedy settlement of the difficulties between the two countries, and the resumption of the trade, were dashed by the failure of Jackson's mission. Prices then rose again. Charles Ellis, who was at that time in England, commented upon the unreasonable tremors of the British merchants. "The smallest event," he wrote, "either one way or the other, changes markets. The man with good information and sound judgment cannot but make money out of them."[17] Prices for tobacco remained so good that Ellis, early in 1810, urged Allan, the more cautious member of the firm, to continue buying and shipping to the "out ports," resting assured that the firm could not lose, and might profit greatly. Richmond leaf was selling in London at 11–15c per lb. and stemmed tobacco at 13–15c.[18]

That these prices were the result of speculation, and not of actual demand, may be seen from the estimates of one British importer, that the quantity of tobacco then in transit, added to what was in the warehouses, was sufficient to supply English consumption for two years.[19]

The tone of the President's message of November 29, 1809, lacking as it did any hopeful note, place American produce in

---

[15] Allan to Ellis, May 4, 1809, *Ibid*.
[16] Logan Lenox to Ellis and Allan, Dec. 24, 1809, *Ibid*.
[17] Ellis to Allan, Dec. 22, 1809, *Ibid*.
[18] Same to same, Feb. 7, 1810, *Ibid*.
[19] Letter to Murdock of Liverpool, Sept. 10, 1810, Taylor-Bourne Papers.

a state of uncommon activity. The circuitous shipment of cargoes continued, but apprehensions were felt, lest the American government should cut off this trade. Pot and pearl ashes, turpentine and all kinds of lumber were "on the rise" in the British market.[20] American wheat, however, could not, at this time be sold at a profit, as great quantities of wheat were arriving from France, in spite of the complaints of many that such purchases were draining away the specie of the country to the enemy.[21]

Trade Under the Non-Intercourse Law—Trade with Holland

American shippers prepared to resume trade with Holland after the repeal of the embargo, particularly after they understood that British cruisers would no longer hinder their entrance to Dutch ports. "Numbers of American vessels are making ready from our ports to yours," wrote Jumel and Desobrey to a Dutch firm (May, 1809), "where they expect your government to admit them."[22]

In Holland, the outlook for the renewal of trade was not bright. From December 6, 1808 to March 4, 1809, not a single American vessel had entered or left the Dutch ports.[23] On March 31st, however, King Louis gave permission for the departure of American vessels either in ballast, or with the produce of the country. He also announced permission for the importation of certain articles, including tobacco from neutral countries, provided the vessel had not been visited by a British cruiser on her voyage.[24] The hazards of a voyage to the Dutch ports at this period may be inferred from the following extract from a letter of Backer to Taylor. "It strikes me that if you could bring it about to combine with Messrs. Mayer and Brants, and some of my other friends to buy or charter a ship of little

---

[20] Worral and Williamson, Liverpool, to Noah Scoville, Scoville Papers.
[21] Ellis to Allan, Feb. 10, Jan. 1, 1810, Ellis and Allan Papers.
[22] Jumel and Desobrey to Conderc and Brants, May 22, 1809, *Jumel and Desobrey Letter Book.*
[23] Letter from a Dutch correspondent to Wm. Bayard, April 14, 1809, Bayard Papers.
[24] For full particulars of the decree, see Hoekstra, *Op. cit.*, pp. 76–77.

French Revolution and Napoleon, 1793-1812   155

value, and send her out with a cargo of tobacco only, north about for this port, that you might fully succeed in getting her in here. The captain ought to have a set of papers whereby he could prove in case of visitation that he was bound for England, and in case of need he might go there, and write me, and wait till he heard from me, and I might probably find means to get admission when opportunity offers."[25]

At the end of June, Louis issued a decree allowing the admission for three months of certain other goods from America and from Dutch colonies. American vessels were admitted, and such goods as they brought, were if admissable, given up to the consignees. The forbidden goods were at first placed in the public stores, and afterward sold, "for the benefit of whoever may hereafter be entitled to the proceeds." Cargoes of cotton and other goods which entered in this brief interval of liberty won for their consignees handsome profits.[26]

Even this hampered trade was not to be allowed to continue, for only a month after the relaxation in favor of the admission of more goods such admission was withdrawn by Napoleon's order. The provisions of the decree of March 31st, just mentioned still held, however, by which tobacco pot and pearl ashes, whale oil and medicinal drugs were still allowed. Vessels which arrived laden wholly or in part with forbidden goods, were fortunately ordered to leave, instead of being seized and detained as in France.[27]

Besides the danger from British cruisers and the uncertainty of admission into Dutch ports, there was added the danger of seizure by the French.

The American vessel *Resort* left New York in June, 1809, bound for Bremen with a cargo of coffee. The captain was authorized, however, to seek a Dutch port, if he deemed it safe. Arriving off the coast of Holland, he fell in with two Dutch boats from whom he learned that Amsterdam was not blockaded, and that he might enter without fear of molestation from British

---

[25] Backer to Taylor, April 15, 1809, Taylor-Bourne Papers.
[26] Same to same, Sept. 14, 1809, *Ibid*. See also letter of Hughes and Duncan to Christopher Champlin, July 22, 1809, Champlin Papers, R. I. Hist. Soc.
[27] Backer to Taylor, Aug. 25, 1809, Taylor-Bourne Papers.

cruisers. As he was proceeding to the Texel, however, he was captured by the French privateer *Hebe*, and taken into Amsterdam. The vessel and cargo were afterward condemned by the Court of Prizes at Paris,[28] evidently on the ground that the coffee was the product of a British colony.

Napoleon soon announced a new pretext for seizure. In the Altenburg letter of August 22nd, Champagny informed Armstrong that the Emperor would tolerate no discrimination, as provided in the American Non-Intercourse Law, against France, and in favor of Holland.[29] If American vessels were forbidden to trade to French ports, the privateers of France would seize them, if they attempted to enter the ports of Holland.

During the summer of 1809, the American government appears to have sent the schooner *Enterprize* to cruise off the Texel for information. This was evidently with a view of furnishing the latest information on the ground to such American vessels as were attempting to reach ports in Holland and Germany and other parts of Northern Europe.[30]

The extent to which American trade to Holland was crippled in this period, we may judge from the shipments of tobacco and cotton. Of tobacco, something over 2,000 hhd. were shipped, in 1809, but in 1806 the amount had been 29,000.[31] Of cotton, slightly over 1,000,000 lbs. were shipped, whereas the amount in 1806 and 1807 had been over 3,000,000 lbs.[32]

A persistent American trader of this period was Richard Cleveland. He has left us a vivid account of his entry into Holland, in the summer of 1809, to procure a cargo for the United States. Although he applauded the embargo as the lesser of the two evils confronting the American government, he by no means allowed it to check his commercial activities.

---

[28] Duerhagen vs. U. S. Insurance Co., *Sergeant and Rawle Penna. Reports*, Vol. II.

[29] *A. S. P.*, For. III, p. 325.

[30] May 24, 1809, Schooner *Enterprise* was in New York Harbor officered, victualled, completely repaired and nearly ready for this service. She carried 12 guns, *A. S. P. Naval Af.*, I, pp. 193–202; Jumel and Desobrey to L. Clapin, July 24, 1809. Same to J. R. Skiddy, August 3, 1809.

[31] Pitkin, pp. 131–132.

[32] *Ibid.*, pp. 135–136, the amounts for the years 1806 and 1807 were far above the average.

He took passage for England, by way of Halifax, in the fall of 1808, in order to "place himself in the current of business" and seize favorable opportunities. Arriving in London, he projected a voyage to the Isle of France, with a cargo of French wines, purchased from the prizes brought in by the English, and another to the Baltic to secure Russian goods for the American market. Both of these plans fell through, and Cleveland finally decided to make his way to Holland.

The adventure is thus described by his son: "The difficulty was in getting from England to Holland at the time when all the continental powers had been compelled by Napoleon to unite in cutting off all intercourse with Great Britain. It was impossible openly to evade such a restriction, and the risk was of course, very great in attempting it secretly, but perhaps for that very reason, all the more tempting to one of such adventurous disposition. With his usual caution he refrained from mentioning in his letters, anything that could afford a clue to his real design. In company with a friend . . . he embarked on board a fishing smack, the master of which had agreed to land them on the coast of Holland. Approaching the shore on a still night, they were landed between eleven and twelve o'clock, among the sand dunes of the coast near the Brielle. The skipper had given them careful instructions as to the course, and they made their way towards the town, till they could hear the clocks striking, and then waited for daylight in a hollow of the hills of sand. At dawn they were aroused by a trampling which they were apprehensive might be the patrol, but which proved to be only a herd of cows, driven by a boy. He directed them to an inn, where they were cordially welcomed by the host and hostess, who had no sympathy with the rigorous exclusion of strangers. After careful instruction from the landlord, they went with a crowd of passengers, on board a canal boat, and proceeded without molestation to Amsterdam. They found at once that their expectation of large profits on the exports of Holland to the United States would be realized, if they could succeed in dispatching a cargo before July 1, 1809, when the English government had given notice that a blockade would commence. With the aid of an influential mercantile house this was accomplished. A ship was chartered, loaded and dispatched to New York, before the blockade began. She arrived safely and the results of the voyage were equal to expectations." Cleveland planned further large operations, but they had to be abandoned, "on account of the invasion of the Scheldt by a formidable force under Lord Chatham, and a general embargo in Holland."[33]

Trade with Hamburg and Bremen

The spring of the year 1809 found several American vessels in the port of Bremen, held there by the Bayonne Decree.[34] The order of February 25, 1809,[35] allowing the departure of American vessels if they carried out the produce of the country and sailed directly to the United States, was extended to the port of Bremen, also, and three vessels availed themselves of this permission. Others for various reasons did not leave, and some of these were detained in Bremen for more than a year.

The effect of the milder regulations permitting the departure of American vessels in various ports under French control, was to send down the prices of sugars, tobacco and cotton in the Hamburg market.[36] American goods, however, continued to be rigorously excluded from Hamburg, for American captains arriving at the mouths of the Elbe and the Weser turned away, having gathered from the news that they were able to pick up, that seizure awaited them in those north German ports.[37]

Forbes describes these vessels as in danger of seizure under the Bayonne Decree, predicated, as he remarked, upon the embargo. Here he was in error. As we know, the seizure of American vessels after the repeal of the embargo, was carried on in reprisals for Non-Intercourse Law, with its two-fold discrimination against France.

The turning back of these ships, however, did not mean that the markets of Hamburg and Bremen were not supplied with goods carried by American vessels. Far from it.

---

[33] W. S. Cleveland, *Voyages of a Merchant Navigator*, pp. 125–132, passim.
[34] Wichelhausen to R. Smith, Feb. 15, 1810, Consular Letters, Bremen.
[35] Consular Letters, Bordeaux II.
[36] J. Pitcairn to Sylvanus Bourne, April 21, 1809, Taylor-Bourne Mss.
[37] Wichelhausen to R. Smith, July 18, 1809, Consular Letters, Bremen.

Non-Intercourse—Tonningen

In the southern part of the peninsula of Jutland, in the province of Schleswig, the small river Eyder flows westward into the North Sea. At the mouth of this river is the little port of Tonningen. To this harbor flocked the American vessels during the years 1809 and 1810. In ordinary times few ocean going vessels sought this small harbor, although, as we have seen, Americans had begun to use it in 1806. In summer of the 1809, over ninety American vessels brought thier cargoes hither. The channel was dangerous, especially for large vessels, and the pilotage charges heavy, but this did not deter the Americans. Forbes left the city of the Elbe, and came to this Danish port, for as he wrote, the traffic to Tonningen was only the "distorted trade of Hamburg."[40] Agents of the leading Hamburg merchants, also moved to this place. After paying a heavy duty to the Danish government the goods were shipped to Altona and places in the vicinity, and thence in small quantities to Hamburg and other places in Germany. There was no molestation to entrance from British cruisers, as the port, by the orders of April, 1809 was not blockaded.[41]

Many American captains who started for Amsterdam turned aside when they heard of the prohibition laid, as we have seen on so many articles of import into Holland. These ships likewise sought the mouth of the Eyder. The vessels arriving at Tonningen brought coffee, tobacco, cotton, logwood, gum, and other articles of colonial produce.

The tobacco imported in Denmark and Norway from the United States which had amounted to something over 1500 hhd. in 1804, and in 1807, and reached over 2000 hhd. in 1805, rose to nearly ten thousand hhd. in 1809, and to 18,000 the following year, while exports to Holland and Hamburg declined. 288,000 lbs. of cotton was imported into Denmark and Norway in 1804, but in 1809, 2,000,000 lbs., and in 1810 over 14,000,000 lbs.[42]

---

[38] Forbes to R. Smith, Sept. 29, 1809, Consular Letters, Hamburg.
[39] Forbes to R. Smith, Sept. 29, 1809, Consular Letters, Hamburg.
[40] Forbes to Graham, Private Secretary to Madison, Nov. 21, 1809. *Ibid.*
[41] Wichelhausen to R. Smith, Feb. 1810, Consular Letters, Bremen.
[42] Pitkin *Statistical View*, pp. 131–136.

A good example of the nature of the trade is found in a letter from the New York firm of Jumel and Desobrey, to J. Skiddy, master of their ship *Eliza*, which started for the Danish port in August of 1809. The directions to Skiddy are, in part, as follows:

"As soon as you are admitted to Tonningen to an entry, the first step you are to take is to inform yourself whether an agent of the firm of Johan Gerhard Groesel of Hamburg is on the spot. If so you will not lose a moment to see him, and advise together as to what will be best to be done respecting the disposal of your cargo. If no such agent is on the spot, we think it will be very advisable to take post and repair yourself immediately to Hamburg and deliver the letter of recommendation which you have for him. . . . Purchase return cargo as per memorandum. . . . We give you no directions as to place where goods can be procured. We only suppose that in Tonningen you will not find anything worth buying. The place then, must be Hamburg, where we are led to believe that most of the goods mentioned in our memorandum will be found.[43] It will not be a hard matter to transport them from there to Tonningen, as it may be done in different ways, but we recommend you the safest one, as we are unwilling to run any risk for the sake of sparing some expenses."

The insurance policy covering the venture described the voyage as from "New York to Tonningen, with liberty to speak to the American government schooner *Enterprize*;[44] if turned away to have liberty to go to a near port, where the vessel may be admitted."

Many captains who aimed to reach unsafe ports in Europe at this period, were given Tonningen as an alternative. The ship *Governor Gilman* started in December, 1809, for St. Sebastians, but if warned by a British cruiser, the captain was ordered to

---

[43] These goods were eventually shipped to Charleston, since the New York market was overun with German goods. The captain was enjoined not to part with them at less than 70 per cent advance on the cost, which after all expenses were paid "would only yield a common profit". Letter of Jumel and Desobrey to John A. Skiddy, Master of Ship *Eliza*, Aug. 3, 1809, Letter Book, Jumel and Desobrey.

[44] *Ibid*, March 20 and 22, 1810.

an open port of Northern Europe without the Baltic. In the end, he turned to Tonningen.[45]

Kiel, a port of Holstein on the other side of the peninsula of Jutland, was preferred by the Hamburg merchants next after Tonningen, because it was possible to transfer goods easily from there to Wismar and Rostock, the Baltic ports to the eastward. Goods were admitted to these ports, if accompanied by a certificate of origin signed by a French consul.[46]

Near the mouth of the Elbe, forty miles from Hamburg, was the port of Glückstadt in Holstein. At this Danish port several American vessels succeeded in landing their cargoes in the fall of 1809.[47]

Varel on the Jahde was a port aimed at by some captains, but in November there was issued a new decree by the French government, ordering the confiscation of all vessels and cargoes entering the Jahde, the Weser and the Elbe.[48] Insurance to these ports now rose in London to impossible heights. To Varel on the Jahde, the rate was now 25 guineas per cent. "No freight," wrote a Dutch merchant to his American correspondent, "will bear this premium."[49]

The ports of Schleswig and Holstein therefore, continued to be the entrance gates for goods for Germany and Holland. A letter from Amsterdam of September 14, 1809, speaks of "vast numbers" of arrivals of American vessels at Tonningen, but adds than "the cost of transport of goods from there to the interior of Germany is very considerable and this keeps prices up."[50] In November a Hamburg correspondent wrote that the transportation of goods from Altona was attended with much difficulty on account of the French decrees. Sugar, however, could be transported under certain restrictions. The import of this commodity, and that of coffee, into the Hamburg market was so extensive as to supply all purchasers, while the supplies

---

[45] Bayard to Prest. Comm'l. Ins. Co., Dec. 4, 1809 Bayard Papers.
[46] Swift to Taylor, June 5, 1810, Taylor-Bourne Papers.
[47] Wonhengerke to Taylor, Nov. 1, 1809, Taylor Mss.
[48] Hoyte vs. Gilman, *Mass. Reports*, 8.
[49] *Ibid.*
[50] Letter of Conway and Davis to Wm. Taylor—Taylor-Bourne Papers.

of cotton and of teas were if anything, in excess of the demand.[51] These conditions, however, were not destined to continue.

Danish Seizures, 1809–1810

Trouble was brewing for the American shippers seeking the harbors of Schleswig and Holstein. Since the high handed seizure of her fleet by the English, Denmark had ranged herself on the side of the French. English goods were therefore excluded from her ports. But the facility afforded the vessels of the United States led British[52] shippers to assume the American character. This created a serious problem for Forbes.

The ship *Anna* was one of the first of such offenders. She was known to have left Boston June 10, 1809, with a cargo of pot and pearl ashes, but she arrived at Tonningen with a cargo of gum, procured in England. Her captain carried a forged sea letter, which he admitted to Forbes had been procured from the notorious Van Sander[53] in London. Fearing that the denunciation of the vessel to the Danish authorities would mean the confiscation of the "immense stocks of American goods which was then in Holstein," Forbes contented himself with the withholding of the incriminating paper, and reported the case to Secretary Smith. As a check, the abuse, he advocated the printing of American sea letters on special water marked paper.[54]

The following month, however, four vessels appeared under the same circumstances. Forbes then called a meeting of the American merchants in Tonningen, and laid the matter before them. They agreed that these vessels should be denounced to the Danish government. Forbes therefore wrote to the king, demanding the seizure of these ships, which were violating the laws of both their own country and of Denmark. He pledged himself "to discriminate the fair and permitted trade" of his

---

[51] Letter to Taylor from Hamburg, Nov. 8, 1809, *Ibid*.

[52] Cf. Petition of London and Liverpool merchants to Parliament, March 10, 1808 "the neutrality of America has been the means of circulating to a large extent articles of the production and manufactures of this country, in the dominion of our numerous enemies." Hansard X, pp. 1056–58.

[53] This man kept a shop where forged documents of this kind could be bought. J. Q. Adams, *Writings*, III, p. 363.

[54] Forbes to Madison, No. 7, 1809, Consular Letters, Hamburg.

[55] Forbes to King of Denmark, Dec. 12, 1809, *Ibid*.

countrymen, "from that detestable and poisonous fruit of collusive and contraband trade."⁵⁵ Out of 130 ships entering, Forbes claimed that at least 120 were innocent.

At first the Danish authorities were inclined to trust American ships papers, when the cargoes consisted of undoubted American products such as tobacco, rice and cotton, and such colonial products as sugar, dyewood, cacao and indigo, but it was ordered that in future the signature of a Danish chargé d'affaires or his agent should attest the origin of the cargo. In the winter of 1809, however, the Tonningen-Altona-Hamburg trade was menaced by a double blow. First, the Danish government ordered the sequestration of all West India produce in their ports, for the sake of ascertaining its origin;⁵⁶ secondly, the route to Hamburg was barred. As early as September, it had been rumored that the French had sent a host of their customs officers into the northern ports and rivers, and had drawn a cordon from Wismar on the Baltic to Antwerp, a distance of over two hundred miles, to prevent the introduction of any merchandise into the interior of Germany and France.⁵⁷

This was undoubtedly the forerunner of the decree concerted between the French and Danish governments, under date of November 20, 1809, forbidding the carrying of colonial produce to or from the city of Hamburg.⁵⁸

The route of this trade, and the change produced by these regulations, may be learned from a letter of Pitcairn, American chargé at Hamburg, to George Joy, a London broker who had volunteered to represent American trade interests at Copenhagen.⁵⁹ Cargoes truly American had been arriving at Tonningen.

---

⁵⁶ Forbes to R. Smith, Dec. 7, 1809, Consular Letters, Hamburg; Baring Brothers to Wm. Taylor, Dec. 5, 1809, Taylor-Bourne Papers; see also McMaster, *Life of Girard*, 2, p. 114.

⁵⁷ Bayard Sampson and Sharp, Sept. 4, 1809 to LeRoy, Bayard and McEvers Bayard Papers.

⁵⁸ Forbes to Robert Smith, Dec. 7, 1809, Consular Letters, Hamburg. Forbes to Armstrong, Dec. 15, 1809. Disp. Fr. II refers to the carrying out of this order.

⁵⁹ Joy, at the time American consul at Rotterdam appears to have been acting in this matter under the authorization of Pinkney and J. Q. Adams. Armstrong did not think favorably of Joy's volunteer mission to Denmark. His advocacy of American interests, Armstrong held was prima facie evidence that the property in question was English. Forbes to Armstrong Nov. 11, 1809, Armstrong to Forbes, Dec. 3, 1809, Desp. Fr. 11.

There they had been examined, been duly entered, and paid the duties. They were then transported, as we have seen, through the country at great expense, to Altona, under the magistrates certificate, and with permission for re-exportation. From there the goods were transported to Hamburg: linen, glassware, etc., up to the whole value of the cargo being given in exchange. These outward cargoes also benefitted the Danes by the land carriage and by the duties they paid in Tonningen. The Danish courts had given it as their opinion that the trade was legal and would suffer no interference. Yet now the whole property was at once laid under arrest.[60]

The trouble came not only from renegade Americans who brought in British goods under false American ships papers but from smugglers along the coast. By February, 1810, however, owing to Forbes's exertions with the government at Copenhagen, most of the American property had been adjudged innocent, and had been given up.

During the first six months of 1810, American vessels continued to arrive at Tonningen. The country, however, was coming more and more "under the command of France." Decrees forbidding the transport of goods from one Danish town to another were beginning to make this corner of the world a poor market.[61] The warehouses at Altona were glutted with colonial and American goods.

Forbes memorialized the king, for the purpose of securing permission for the reexportation of these goods, at least of cotton. Public opinion in Denmark admitted the demands of Forbes to be reasonable, and the trade highly profitable to Denmark, but the recent victories of France at Eckmühl and Wagram and the Austrian marriage had made Napoleon all powerful on the continent, so the Danish authorities rejected the petition of the American consul.[62] Concerned for the many

---

[60] J. Pitcairn to George Joy, Dec. 22, 1809, Consular Letters, Hamburg. de Blome, the Danish minister at the court of Russia, told J. Q. Adams that these transit duties were the only source of revenue left to Denmark. J. Q. Adams, *Writings*, III, p. 383.

[61] A. Ellerman to Esterbrook, Heligoland, March 31, 1810, Taylor-Bourne Papers.

[62] Melvin, p. 232, states that Denmark was allowed secretly to export colonial goods into Hamburg.

rich cargoes of American shippers then on their way to Tonningen, Forbes pointed out to the state department at Washington, the desirability of having some swift boats at the disposal of American agents in Europe, to warn merchantmen of danger in such a case.[63]

As late as July, 1810, a correspondent from Bremen advised shipment of American goods to that port via Tonningen, entailing, he added about 12 per cent extra charges.[64] But in that very month, the port was closed to Americans.

The news was conveyed to the secretary of state in a letter of Forbes from Tonningen dated July 12th. He wrote as follows: "An order has been received from the King of Denmark to shut this port and Husum to our flag. The motive, of this order, to prevent smuggling from Heligoland, is not justified by any single occurrence under our flag. "The measure had been forced on His Majesty's government," Forbes declared, by foreign influence, and this pretext taken to conceal any appearance of hostility to the United States. The island of Sylt was closed at the same time. Forbes expected that Sir James Saumerez would permit American vessels to proceed into the Baltic without British licenses, and to reach Flensburg, Kiel, and the other Danish ports within the Belts.[65] He himself closed the American consulate in Tonningen in September, and proceeded to that region to establish agencies, although he had received no authority to do so.

While in the southwestern corner of Denmark, American commerce had been comparatively unmolested until July of 1810, the ships which had attempted to pass the sound and enter the Baltic had fared very badly.

Ever since the fall of 1807, privateers had been authorized by the Danish government, operating under a very wide range of powers. Besides all vessels belonging to British subjects, they were empowered to seize such ships as were lacking sea pass,

---

[63] Forbes to Smith, March 17, 1810, Consular Letters, Hamburg.
[64] Widow, John Lang and Co. to Chas. Ellis, Bremen, July 12, 1810, Ellis and Allan Papers.
[65] Forbes to Smith, July 12, 1810, Consular Letters, Hamburg.
[66] *A. S. P.*, For. III, pp. 327-328.

muster roll, register, clearance, charter party, and even proof of the carpenter as to the building of the vessel.[66] Captains who had passed the sound were required to show a clearance from Elsinore. Irregularity in any of these documents would subject the vessel to seizure.

As soon as American shippers, relieved from the embargo, began their voyages to northern Europe in the spring of 1809, they began to feel the force of these regulations. They suffered for the irregularities of their countrymen, carried on since the beginning of the year 1808. Unscrupulous Americans, as we have seen, had then begun to carry on the trade of the English to the Baltic and to Archangel. As in the case of the Americans seized at Tonningen, they had used false American papers, procured in London. The ship *Romulus* of Boston, was a conspicuous example of such practices. She was condemned by the Danish government in May of 1809. It was even said that English ships were built to resemble those of the Americans, so as to facilitate the deception.[67]

Christiansand, on the south coast of Norway, was the port to which many captured Americans were carried. In July, 1809, the captains and supercargoes of the American vessels detained there drew up a memorial which they forwarded to President Madison. These memorialists declared that they had started from the United States equipped with all the documents required by the laws of their country and on perfectly legal voyages. They complained that they had been seized for the most trifling inaccuracy of their papers, and that members of their crew had been tempted by bribes to give false testimony. The American captains were given no copies of the charges against them, and the trials were conducted altogether in the Danish language. Some of the captured vessels had already been detained as long as three months and the support of the sailors was a serious loss to the shippers.

As the United States government had no consul or commercial agent in Norway, the Americans had presented their

---

[67] Memorial of American Captains at Christiansand, July 19, 1809. *A. S. P.*, For. III, p. 329.

case to Mr. Saabye, the American consul at Copenhagen, who had, however, not been able to help them. In their distress, they had then applied to Peter Isaacson, a Danish merchant of Christiansand to take charge of their interests. He was a man of substance and respectability, and had shown a disposition to demand justice for the unfortunate Americans.[68]

The captains at Christiansand appealed to President Madison for some remedy for their situation. They reminded him that since there was a strict blockade from the Weser to Bayonne, American vessels destined for places in Holland would probably try for ports in Sweden and the Baltic, and sail straight into the clutches of the Danes.[69]

Isaacson himself wrote to President Madison, under date of August 11, 1809, reporting on his efforts to assist the innocent Americans. While he was convinced of the neutrality of the United States, he had, as a loyal Dane, no sympathy with violations of the Berlin Decree. Those neutrals who by fictitious and counterfeit papers favored the commerce of Great Britain, and carried thither the objects of which she was most in need, were, in his opinion, enemies of Denmark. It was "nearly adopted as a common principle," he declared, not to respect the colors of any nation on the ocean, since flags as well as documents might be fictitious. Several of the Americans condemned, Isaacson reported, had been provided not only with double sets of papers, but with British licenses.

Twenty-six American vessels had been brought into Christiansand, of which by July of 1809 eighteen had undergone trial. Eight of these had been cleared and ten condemned but the privateers had appealed the former cases, and the Americans the latter, to the High Admiralty Court at Christiania.

Since the privateers, being mostly poor pilots and fishermen, could not, in the cases in which they had appealed, he required to furnish bonds against the delay suffered by the vessels in question, Isaacson had proposed to the government that such

---

[68] Wm. Adgate to Stephen Girard, McMaster, *Life of Girard*, Vol. II, p. 93.
[69] Memorial, *A. S. P.*, For. III, p. 329.

vessels be allowed to proceed on their voyages. In this he had not been successful.[70]

Among the vessels detained at Christiansand were two belonging to Stephen Girard. These were the *Good Friends* and the *Helvetius*, laden with cotton and bound to Gothenburg in Sweden. The Danish authorities in Norway professed ignorance of the repeal of the American embargo. Hence they claimed that these vessels were British, masquerading as Americans.

Girard's captains complained bitterly of the proceedings against them. According to them, everyone in Norway was interested in privateering which the government appeared to encourage, for a time at least, by "wholesale condemnations." The *Good Friends* was captured in May, 1809, and was detained for more than a year. After an appeal to the High Court of Admiralty at Christiania, the vessel was finally liberated, but not until over six thousand dollars had been paid to the captors.[71] The *Helvetius* was liberated, after a detention of two months, and the payment of eight hundred dollars.[72]

In such cases it was the custom for the European correspondents of the American merchants to interest themselves in the matter, and try to extricate the property of their customers from its difficulties. In the present instance Girard was much disappointed that the house of Hope and Co. and other Amsterdam firms did nothing to aid in the freeing of his vessels.[73]

John Quincy Adams, who was proceeding to St. Petersburg as minister to Russia, stopped at Christiansand and Elsinore in September, 1809, and learned the plight of his countrymen. During his short stay on the island of Zealand, he went to Copenhagen and attempted to secure some redress for the Americans, but was unable to accomplish anything.[74]

According to the report of Saabye to the State Department, made October 16, 1809, there had been a total of fifty-one American vessels brought in to Copenhagen, Christiansand, and

---

[70] Letter from Peter Isaacson to President Madison, July 19, 1809, *A. S. P.*, For. pp. 330–331.
[71] McMaster, *Life of Girard*, Vol. II, pp. 78–87.
[72] *Ibid.*, pp. 97–98.
[73] *Ibid.*, pp. 119–120.
[74] J. Q. Adams, *Memoirs*, II, pp. 30–36.

other ports in Norway. He inclosed a list of these vessels, which showed that fifteen had been cleared, but the majority were awaiting a final decision before the High Admiralty Court.[75] The Danish government was said to have prohibited further privateering except about Heligoland.[76]

Shippers in the United States naturally protested against the Danish seizures. In Philadelphia the merchants and insurance men were so aroused over their losses that in October, 1809 they petitioned Congress to send a public vessel and a special envoy to obtain redress.[77]

Before any such action could be taken, however, many of the sequestrations were removed, and the cargoes placed at the disposal of the proprietors. Commissioners were appointed in Altona, Tonningen, Frederickstadt and Husum, to examine the papers of the ships which had been held, and those found in order were released.[78] The king of Denmark issued a decree directing privateers not to detain any property unless on strong grounds of suspicion.[79]

In the latter part of 1809, a new privateering ordinance was issued by the Danish government providing that all vessels which accepted British convoy in the Baltic should by reason of that fact be considered good prize. By June 1st of the following year twenty American vessels had been seized under this ordinance. Some of these were directly from the United States and were taken after having passed Elsineur and paid their Sound dues there. Many of these were liberated on the payment of considerable sums, but others were condemned.[80]

Adams at St. Petersburg attempted to secure some redress for these cases through Baron de Blome, the Danish minister at the court of Russia. de Blome turned the matter off by expressing regrets that there was no authorized officer of the United States at the court of Denmark, but Adams concluded

---

[75] T. H. Backer to Taylor, Elsineur, Sept. 1809, Taylor-Bourne Papers.
[76] *A. S. P.*, For. III, p. 332.
[77] *Ibid.*
[78] McMaster, *Life of Girard*, 2, p. 114.
[79] That is that the American vessel was either carrying British or Colonial goods.
[80] Poulson, *Amer. Daily Advertiser*, April 11, 1810.

that the profits of privateering and the influence of France were too strong to be resisted.[81]

In spite of these seizures, many American shippers were convinced that the real disposition of the Danish government was friendly. After the closing of the North Sea ports of that country, they prepared, as we have seen, to continue to pass through the Sound and the Belts to Danish and other ports in the Baltic.

Non-Intercourse—Spain, 1809

In addition to the regular American trade to Spain and Portugal there was, in 1809, through the ports of those countries, an indirect trade to England. There was also through the northern ports of the Bay of Biscay, a certain amount of indirect trade with France.

Many American vessels laden for the British market on the removal of the embargo started for the port of Cadiz. The shippers were in some doubt as to the advisability of these voyages, however. Should the Spanish be in control there all would be well, but if the French had captured the city, the vessels would be in danger of seizure. Captains were therefore enjoined, in the latter case, to proceed to Gothenburg or to call at Falmouth for orders. In the event of landing safely at Cadiz, however, the captain was to charter a British vessel, to transship the cargo to England. Ellis and Allan, sending a ship load of tobacco to Cadiz, wrote their London correspondent, "that we intend her cargo for the British market, but that we are bound under double the value of the vessel and cargo, that she should not deliver her cargo in Great Britain, or France, nor in their dependencies."[82]

In spite of the defeat of the British at Coruna, American shippers knew that the British still maintained themselves in southern Spain, and therefore continued to ship to Cadiz. Arriving there, however, American captains found a great

---

[81] J. Q. Adams, *Writings*, III, p. 453. Poulson, *Amer. Daily Advertiser*, March 30, 1810.

[82] Wm. Galt to Ellis and Allan, April 14, 1809, Ellis and Allan Papers.

influx of goods from their country, and much difficulty in procuring freight for British ports, the vessels in the place having been requisitioned by the armies of Spain, Portugal and England.[83]

Some of these American vessels on arriving in Spain, evidently landed their cargoes and procured a certificate of such landing signed by the American consul. They then reloaded with the same cargo and started for England.[84]

The President's proclamation of April, 1809, made the indirect route unnecessary. Many captains learning of this, on reaching the shores of Spain, turned their prows northward and made English ports without breaking bulk.[85]

The Spanish ports, however, continued to be a good market, especially for flour, for the French had burned the fields of grain, in their retreat from the neighborhood of Cadiz, and the large British army which entered Spain was to draw its supplies from that port. Fortunately for American shippers, the vexatious quarantine law was altered so as to shorten the period of detention to about ten days during the summer months and the duties were taken off flour, rice and other grains.[86]

After August of 1809, the indirect trade had to be resumed. Cargoes for England kept arriving in the ports of Cadiz and Lisbon until the removal of the non-intercourse. Meade, writing in December of 1809, spoke of the large quantities of tobacco which had left for England, and the ease of trans-shipments. He recommended the port, under the then prevailing regulations "before any in Europe," as an entrepôt. The goods were best moved quickly, however, for the unsettled state of the country made it hazardous to hold the property there long.[87]

The freight rates were high, but the good prices received for flour and tobacco in London enabled the shippers to meet

---

[83] Ellis to Allan, May 5, 1809, *Ibid*.
[84] Wm. Galt to Ellis and Allan, April 14, 1809, *Ibid*.
[85] The ships, *Charles* and *Georgiana*, laden with tobacco, were sent to Cadiz, where their cargoes were to be trans-shipped to England. They proceeded to Liverpool and Cork, respectively, without unloading at Cadiz. Letters of Charles Ellis, May 24, 1809 and following, *Ibid*.
[86] R. W. Meade to Ellis and Allan, July 20, 1809, *Ibid*.
[87] Chas. Pollard to Ellis and Allan, Dec. 27, 1809, *Ibid*.

them. Ellis and Allan paid a freight of six guineas per hhd. for tobacco from Richmond to Lisbon, and an additional four or five pounds to English ports.[88]

Some shippers saved themselves this extra expense by defying the law, as we have seen, and sending their vessels directly to London. Some of these made a pretext of being driven there in distress, but it was possible to obtain insurance at Lloyd's on vessels from Virginia direct to London.[89]

Voyages to the northern ports of Spain, as we have stated, offered means for circumventing the non-intercourse law, by procuring French goods. The operations of the New York firm of Jumel and Desobrey furnished a good illustration of such trade. In May of 1809 they wrote to their correspondent at St. Sebastian stating that while prices of American and colonial merchandise at that port were very tempting, they hesitated about making voyages, fearing seizure by the French, who controlled the Spanish ports on the Bay of Biscay. The signal of the firm was a red flag with two half moons, and a J in the middle in white. If a vessel with such a signal should appear off shore toward the end of July, they requested the St. Sebastian house to send a message to the captain by a pilot from the shore. The word was to tell whether an incoming American vessel would be seized by the government, if it had been visited by British cruisers, and if so, what was the nearest open port.[90]

Soon after this the firm dispatched the ship *Eliza* for St. Sebastian with a cargo of Carracas cocoa, indigo, and hides, valued at $15,000. They took the precaution, however, to have the usual clause in the insurance policy altered, by which the insurance company was freed from any loss or damage arising from seizure or detention in any illicit or prohibited trade. They made instead the proviso that if the vessel should be seized because she had entered a port prohibited to American vessels, the whole risk of such seizure should be for account of the underwriters.[91]

---

[88] Charter Party of Hovey and Sizer, to Ellis and Allan, Dec. 8, 1809, *Ibid*.
[89] Ellis to Allan, Dec. 11, 1809, *Ibid*.
[90] Jumel and Desobrey to Pedro Queheille, May 31, 1809, *Jumel and Desobrey Letter Book*.
[91] Jumel and Desobrey to Lewis Clapier, July 7, 1809.

If the captain should be deflected from his course by belligerent cruisers, he was to make for the nearest permitted port. Upon arriving in port and landing his cargo he was to secure a certificate attesting the landing, in order that the firm might discharge its debenture bond at the custom house in New York, as provided by the non-intercourse law. Half of the proceeds was to be invested in a return cargo. This, however, was not to consist of Spanish goods of St. Sebastian, where there was nothing for sale which tempted the American merchant. Instead the goods were to be procured from Bordeaux. Mr. John Perry, the correspondent of Jumel and Desobrey in that city, was requested to procure the goods, and the following explanation was sent to Mr. Pedro Queheille, the consignee in St. Sebastian:

"By a law enforced here at present it is forbidden to trade with France. In sending merchandise to you from here, that is not breaking this law, because you are not in France, and that is why it is permitted to our vessels to go to your ports, but we fear to meet difficulties on the return of the vessel here, if the merchandise which it would bring could be proved to come from France, or be of French manufacture. Nevertheless it is for those that we are asking Mr. Perry. In consequence it will be very important to arrange things in such a way as to elude the *chicanery*,[92] in case the custom house of our city seizes them. By letter enclosed which you are to send to Mr. Perry without delay, we trace the course which he must follow to keep us regular. He will have to make a change in the labels of the manufactures so that the names, the measurements and all the rest of the inside covering of the merchandise shall be in the Spanish language. This done, he will send them to you, and it is there that your part will begin.

"See then what you must do very minutely at the departure from France into your territory. It is the custom to place seals (plombs) on the cases and the bales, and you take care that these seals are exactly taken off before the goods are sent on board. According to the invoice which Perry will send you, you will draw one up in Spanish in which, in place of francs

---

[92] My own italics, *Ibid.*, A. C. C.

and centimes, you will reduce the price exactly to reals and marvedis, in place of aunage, you say vares and in place of French names you give the same names in Spanish, so that absolutely nothing French shall appear there. Finally to complete our plan, you will take care in your letter to say some word on the subject of your manufactures from whence you have drawn the said merchandise, and finally you will take equal care to accompany the whole with one or more certificates to prove that each case or bale has been purchased in Spain. We think that will be able to obtain from one of your friends. The certificates furthermore are indispensable and you must leave nothing undone to get them.

"There is another precaution which we recommend to you as very essential. It is to see that excepting you, your clerks and Captain Ducasse, no one, and especially the ship's crew, shall know that the merchandise comes from France. On the contrary, it is necessary to act, speak, and do everything you think proper to make them think the merchandise Spanish."[93]

To Perry a letter of similar tenor was sent, the method of changing the labels and measurements being described in detail. "Everything we wish," wrote Jumel, "can, we believe, be purchased at Bordeaux, but if not, send to Lyons. The ribbons especially are essential, white sarcanets and black crepes are also wanted."[94]

These elaborate deceptions were in this case never carried out. The *Eliza* was apparently lost at sea and never reached St. Sebastian. But other vessels attempted the same trade. Jumel and Desobrey recommended Queheilla to other shippers, and the *Camelia*, the *Northern Liberties* and the *Ft. Tamany* proceeded to St. Sebastian in the fall of 1809. The latter, however, was warned off by British cruisers, and went to a port of Northern Europe instead.

The volume of French goods brought to America by these vessels was not large, for although, if we may trust the custom house records, the value of the fabrics procured from Spain

---

[93] Jumel and Desobrey to Pedro Queheille, Oct. 6, 1807, *Jumel and Desobrey Letter Book*.
[94] Same to John Perry, Oct. 6, 1809, *Ibid*.

in 1810 was three times as large as that in 1809, the total value of the duties did not exceed $50,000.

The trade was soon cut off by the strict enforcement, of the unpublished decree of August 4th, already noted, whereby Napoleon ordered the seizure of American vessels in the harbors of Spain, France and Italy, in retaliation for the Non-Intercourse Law.

The schooner *Prosper*, the second venture of Jumel and Desobrey to St. Sebastian, fell a victim to this decree. The shippers thoroughly realized their danger, but planned to avoid it. They wrote to their consignee, requesting that a signal be hoisted at a prominent point on the mainland, to inform the captain whether or not it would be safe for him to enter. A red and white flag was to be the signal for danger, a white one for safety. In case the captain was warned by British cruisers, or was turned away by a danger signal from the land, he was to proceed to Tonningen or Gothenburg.

The *Prosper* carried sugar and cocoa, cotton from Surinam, Guadeloupe and Cayenne, and gum from Senegal. The return cargo was to consist in part as before, of French goods with Spanish labels, ostensibly procured "from manufacturers in the interior of Spain." In addition, 150 pipes of Bordeaux brandy was to be sent, enclosed in Spanish containers, narrow at the ends and bulging at the center. "We should be lost," wrote Jumel, "if the word cognac were to appear on them."[95]

Weeks passed by, and no word came from the *Prosper*. At last, from the newspapers Jumel learned of the seizure of his vessel by the French immediately on her arrival. He expected the seizure to be but temporary, and for the purpose of ascertaining whether any enemy property was involved, but finally in November, 1810, he wrote to the three insurance companies concerned that "a total loss having ensued by reason of the perils insured against," the vessel was abandoned, and the full insurance claimed.[96]

---

[95] Jumel and Desobrey to John Perry, Dec. 9, 1809, *Ibid*.
[96] Same to Walter Brown, President Phoenix Ins. Co., Nov. 9, 1810, *Ibid*

Trading to the "Out Ports" after the President's Proclamation of August 10, 1809

As soon as news arrived in American ports of the reestablishment of the non-intercourse with England, the indirect channels were again used. Thus, in September, 1809, Ellis and Allan dispatched 50 hhd. of tobacco in the *Romulus* to Lisbon, whence it was to be reshipped to London.[97]

The ship *Andrew* was sent to Madeira in December of 1809 by the firm of Jumel and Desobrey of New York. "On arrival at Fayal," so ran their instructions to the captain, "go to Messrs. Thomas Hazard and Co., who should have in port a vessel, an English one in preference, ready to take in our flour and staves with the least possible expense for transporting the same immediately to the port of London, which is their ultimate and exclusive place of destination.[98] Since vast quantities of American produce had been pouring in to English ports even before the President's proclamation,[99] prices were low.

Madeira and the Western Islands (Azores) were less favored for ports of transshipment in the fall of 1809, as the approaching winter rendered those harbors dangerous, although Fayal was sought by some shippers, early in 1810, who on account of the uncertainties of the military situation feared seizure in the ports of Spain and Portugal.[100]

A captain who reached Fayal in January, 1810, with a cargo of flour, reported the harbor bad and the market for American produce worse. There were forty sails of American vessels there, chiefly ships with full cargoes, and but one English brig. There appeared to be no possibility of transshipment from that port.[101]

Amelia Island, off the northern coast of Florida, was the destination of many British ships which started from London or Liverpool to pick up American cargoes. By the close of the

---

[97] Allan to Charles Ellis, Sept. 7, 1809, Ellis and Allan Papers.
[98] Jumel and Desobrey, to Braker, Captain of the *Andrew*, Dec., 1809, Jumel and Desobrey Letter Book.
[99] Olieveira and Sons to Ellis and Allan, Aug. 24, 1809, Ellis and Allan Papers.
[100] Logan and Lenox to Ellis and Allan, Sept. 15, 1809, *Ibid.*
[101] David Snow to Ellis and Allan, Jan. 15, 1810, *Ibid.*

year there were said to be one hundred such vessels at that place.[102]

Havana was another of these focal points of trade. In February of 1810, this market was reported glutted, not only with goods brought from Great Britain and the United States, but with those from Spain and Germany as well, so that nearly every voyage there entailed a loss. British vessels, although they made "ruinous voyages," returned to Havana for fresh cargoes.[103]

The entry of these goods into England was facilitated by the action of the British government. Licenses were granted for the import of all articles of American produce from all these ports of deposit in British ships or those of countries in amity with her.[104]

Napoleon's Reprisal for the Non-Intercourse Law

The pressure exerted by European neutrals, as well as the protests of the American government against the drastic anti-commercial policy of Napoleon began to have some effect, by the beginning of 1809. In February of that year, the Emperor issued a decree, permitting American vessels detained in the ports of France and Holland under the Bayonne decree, to depart, provided that they carried out cargoes of the country's production, in each case, and gave bonds to proceed direct to the United States.[105] This permission was also extended to the port of Bremen.

In spite of Champagny's efforts to convince the Emperor of the value of the neutral carrier, to the industries of France,[106] Napoleon refused further concessions. He declared that the United States must actively resent Great Britain's practice of visit and search of American vessels. Non-intercourse with France, as established by the law of 1809, applied only to

---

[102] Taylor in House, *Annals 11th Cong.*, 1st Session, p. 1164.
[103] Grey and Martaris, Feb. 28, 1810 to Wm. Taylor, Taylor-Bourne Papers.
[104] Allan to Ellis, Oct. 4, 1809, Ellis and Allan Papers.
[105] Wichelhausen to R. Smith, July 18, 1809, Consular Letters, Bremen. Armstrong to Lee, Feb. 23. 1809, contains copy of decree of Feb. 25, Consular Letters, Bordeaux, Vol. II.
[106] Champagny to Napoleon, quoted by H. Adams, *Hist. of U. S. V.*, p.138.

France proper. It permitted trade with Holland and other neighboring states under French influence. The Emperor resented this. Champagny therefore warned Armstrong that the ports of Holland, Italy, and North Germany were to enjoy no advantage which France did not share. Their ports were all to be either opened or shut at the same time.[107]

Seizure of American Vessels in Spain and Italy

There was now an additional excuse for the seizure of American ships, furnished by the action of the American government itself. That clause of the non-intercourse law which decreed confiscation for French venturing into American ports was of course an empty threat, as no French merchant vessels were at sea. But Napoleon was not the man to miss so good a chance for retaliation. The non-intercourse law now took the place of the embargo, as a justification for the seizure of the ships of the United States.

An American vessel which had reached the port of San Sebastian in Spain in May of 1809, without any visit and search from the English was the first one to be declared forfeited under this rule. By a special order of August 4th this vessel was declared good prize.[108] Other ships reaching the French domains were to suffer a similar fate.

"Every American ship which shall enter the ports of France, Spain or Italy will be equally seized and confiscated, as long as the same measures shall continue to be executed in regard to French vessels in the harbors of the United States."[109] So ran the Emperor's order. Seizures were soon made wherever possible. In December of 1809, Napoleon ordered Berthier to seize all American vessels in Spanish ports under French control, both vessels and cargoes to be considered good prize.[110]

By the spring of 1810, forty-six American vessels were reported sequestered in the ports of Biscay. Many of their cargoes

---

[107] Champagny to Armstrong, Aug. 22, 1809, *A. S. P.*, For. III, pp. 325–6.
[108] H. Adams, *Hist. of U. S. V.*, p. 143.
[109] Decrét Imperial; Archives des affaires éstrangés, Mss. États Unis, quoted by H. Adams, *Hist. of U. S. V.*, p. 144.
[110] Napoleon to Prince of Neufchâtel (Berthier) Corr. XX, p. 78.

had been sent to Bayonne by the French authorities and sold. The stranded American sailors appealed to Lee at Bordeaux for aid, and two hundred and fifty of these men were sent home by him in one vessel.[111] Confiscation was the fate even of such American vessels as were on their way to other continental ports, and were driven into French harbors in distress.[112]

A few American vessels which had ventured into French ports were allowed to leave, carrying the products of the country. Lee reported that in the latter half of 1809, two left Bordeaux for Tonningen with flour, and three left for St. Eustatius, Riga, and Marona, respectively, with wine, fruit and brandy.[113]

A "non-intercourse breaker" of this period reported by Lee was the ship *Franklin*, which had made two voyages from Boston to Bordeaux. This vessel sailed as an American at sea, but became a French bottom when she reached the Garonne. Such an arrangement was made possible by the daring spirit of her owner, and the interested motives of influential men at Paris. Other Americans emboldened by this example but not similarly protected, attempted similar operations, and thus placed themselves in jeopardy.[114]

Armstrong registered a formal protest against the seizure of American vessels in ports under French control, in a notable letter March 10, 1810.[115] This letter was hailed by liberal opinion in Europe as a fine show of spirit on the part of the United States,[116] but beyond that it had no appreciable effect.

---

[111] Lee to R. Smith, March 30, 1810, Consular Letters, Bordeaux.
[112] Rice vs. Homer, Mass. Cases, Vol. XII.
[113] Lee Report, July 1 to Dec. 31, 1809, Consular Dispatches, Bordeaux.
[114] *Ibid.* It was probably some such scheme to which the firm of Jumel and Desobrey refer in the following letter written under date of Sept. 6, 1809, to their correspondent John Perry of Bordeaux; "If we have not attempted any operation of the kind of which your letter of Feb. 17 speaks, it is not the fault of our not having knowledge of it. We also know well that it would leave us a great chance to gain much, but they are always repugnant to us, in that they (the operations proposed) are in contravention of our laws, and that all those who have given themselves to them, even with all the cunning possible, have been discovered, with consequences most disagreeable and will remain known for an infraction which their future transactions must feel," *Letter Book, Jumel and Desobrey*. This firm, however, had no compunctions, as we have seen, in violating the non-intercourse law.
[115] Armstrong to Cadore, March 10, 1810, *A. S. P.*, For. III, pp. 381–82.
[116] *Writings to J. Q. Adams*, IV, p. 258.

All hope, indeed, of changing the Emperor's decision was blighted at the news of the decree sent forth by Napoleon from Rambouillet, March 23, 1810. This was the formal retaliatory decree for the American Non-Intercourse law, a measure which had been in force for the previous eleven months, but which was to expire with the life of the Congress, then in session at Washington. By the decree of Rambouillet all American vessels which had entered the ports of France of countries occupied by French arms, since May 20, 1809, were to be seized, and the product of the sales was to be deposited in the surplus fund.[117] The vessels which had been seized months before, had up to this time been declared by Cadore to be merely sequestered. Now their fate was sealed.

Although the effect of this decree would, of course, be to keep American vessels from the ports of France and her dependents. Napoleon hoped to induce a certain number of such ships to bring to his shores the particular articles which the industries of France required. He proposed a system of licensed trade.

On July 5, 1810, a decree was issued which set forth the elaborate scheme for this permitted trade to the Americans. Thirty vessels were to be admitted from the United States, bringing cotton, fish oil, codfish, logwood, hides and peltries. The return cargoes were to consist of wines, brandies, silks, linens, cloths, jewelry, household furniture, and other manufactured articles. The vessels were to come from the ports of New York and Charleston, and to discharge at Bordeaux, Nantes or Marseilles. The licenses authorizing this American trade were called permits, in order to soothe American sensibilities. They were to be issued by the French government, on application to the merchants who supplied the factories of France with raw materials, or to the manufacturers themselves. The French holders were to send them to the French consuls in the United States, who were to issue them to American shippers, after countersigning them. The American cargo must be accompanied by a certificate of origin signed by the consul,

---

[117] *A. S. P.*, For. III, p. 384.

and a letter from him, partly written in cipher.[118] New men were appointed to the consulships of New York and Charleston, to put the new system into effect.[119]

Napoleon must soon have concluded that the original number of permits would be insufficient. "When the thirty permits are exhausted," he wrote to Montalivet on July 16th, "issue thirty more, so as to have sixty or eighty persons licensed for the American trade." Other conditions were also to be relaxed. In the same letter he wrote, "If there should be any difficulty as to the necessary association with the factories, you can dispense with that. You may content yourself with the promise, which may or may not be worth anything."[120]

In the American commercial correspondence of the period, however, there is very little mention of the use of these licenses.[12]

---

[118] Melvin, *Napoleon's Navigation System*, p. 240–241; Melvin states that the brief version of the Decree in *A. S. P.*, For. III, p. 400 is incorrect.

[119] Armstrong to Madison, Aug. 5, 1810, Armstrong Letters, Madison Papers.

[120] Napoleon to Montalivet, New Letters of Napoleon, Lloyd, p. 192.

[121] Congress had considered the question of prohibiting the use of licenses in January, 1810. The following bill was then introduced: "Any person, a citizen of the United States, making use of a foreign license or permit purporting to be a permission to trade with any foreign and independent power, shall be guilty of a misdemeanor." It was argued however, that this would punish honest traders, and allow those who cared nothing for law to profit, that it would be impossible of enforcement and would interfere with the Baltic trade then carried on by means of licenses from Denmark, *Annals 11, Cong.*, I, pp. 1202–1205.

VI

THE MACON BILL AND ITS ENFORCEMENT AGAINST ENGLAND

Passage of the Macon Bill—Pretended Repeal of the Decrees of Berlin and Milan, by Cadore's letter of Aug. 5, 1810—The Trianon Decree—Confiscating American Vessels—Trianon Tariff—Baltic Trade 1810—Seizure of the New Orleans Packet—Madison's Proclamation reestablishing non-intercourse with Great Britain, Nov. 2, 1810.

When Congress assembled in November of 1809, the aspect of our foreign relations, according to Madison's message, was by no means reassuring. Neither Erskine or Jackson had been able to settle any of the points of disagreement with Great Britain. Non-intercourse had therefore been declared again in force with that country. From France also, there was nothing favorable to report.

Passage of the Macon Bill, May, 1810

Since the non-intercourse law was to expire with this session of Congress the whole question of the belligerents' restrictions upon our foreign trade had again to be aired. The non-intercourse law was declared a failure, operating only against Americans. Honest men were penalized by it, but evil men disregarded it. The brief opening of the trade with Great Britain and its closing again by the President's proclamation had given further opportunity for evasion. One of the district judges, declared Macon, had given an extra official opinion that the non-intercourse was not then in effect as to Great Britain.[1] English and French goods were plentiful on the counters of the merchants, but the treasury received not a cent by their admission, for they were smuggled. The farmers suffered by being forced to accept

---

[1] *Annals, 11th Cong.,* 2, p. 1635.

lower prices for their goods because the indirect carriage was expensive. Honest ship owners suffered because they could earn only a part of the transport charges. Many American owners transferred their vessels to the British flag, in order to continue in business. American underwriters would insure vessels sailing direct to British ports[2] and a similar insurance premium would guarantee the landing of cargoes of prohibited goods in Boston, New York or Philadelphia.[3]

After five months of discussion, Congress adopted a measure, May, 1810, usually known as Macon Bill, No. 2. This bill (drawn by Taylor of South Carolina and not by Macon) provided for the exclusion of the public ships of the two belligerents from American harbors, as before. Full commercial intercourse however was to be permitted, but each nation was offered an inducement to repeal her decrees. If either England or France did so, the United States would immediately cut off her intercourse with the other belligerent. Thus the United States government offered to become a contingent ally, as it were, with the belligerent which should repeal its hostile decrees.[4]

In view of the scant attention which both belligerents had so far given to the regulations of the American government this offer might well seem but a forlorn hope, representing no well defined policy. With the adoption of the Macon (Taylor) Bill on May 1, 1810, the policy of commercial restrain begun by the Non-Importation Act four years before, was finally abandoned. The President was again entrusted with a discretionary power of doubtful wisdom, in spite of the unfortunate outcome of similar experiment in the case of the non-intercourse. The result in the second case was, as events proved, to be even more disastrous than the first.

For the time being, however, the outlook was good. American shippers were naturally gratified at the removal of the restrictions of which they had complained. "Thank God," wrote Allan, from Richmond, "a merchant can now make some sober

---

[2] *Annals, 11th Cong.*, 2, p. 1320.
[3] *Ibid*, p. 1906.
[4] *Ibid.*, p. 1763. *U. S. Statutes at Large*, 2 p. 605-6.

calculations of his prices and that the gambling system is at an end."[5]

The challenge to Napoleon's government contained in the Macon Bill, was apparently accepted with promptness. On account of a mysterious rumor which gained currency in Paris in July of 1809, that Congress had declared war against France,[6] the Berlin and Milan decrees were suddenly declared revoked.

In the celebrated letter of Cadore to Armstrong (August 5, 1810), Napoleon accepted the offer of Madison with an alacrity and an absence of discussion which might well have aroused suspicion. The "repealing" clause of the letter ran as follows:

"In this new state of things (the passage of the Macon Bill) I am authorized to declare to you, sir, that the decrees of Berlin and Milan are revoked, and that after the 1st of November, they will cease to have effect; it being understood that, in consequence, of this declaration, the English shall revoke their orders in council and renounce the new "principles of blockade which they have wished to establish; or that the United States, conformable to the act you have just communicated, shall cause their rights to be respected by the English."[7]

This clause provided the chart and compass by which the American government steered its course for the next two years. Since the different interpretations drawn from it by the American and British Governments, respectively, were the prime cause of the final break between the two countries, it merits careful attention. In the first place the revocation of the British orders is, apparently, supposed to follow, as a result of "this declaration." That is, such revocation is not to be delayed until the actual carrying out by France of the promise at the future date. In the second place, the "new principles of blockade" upheld by Great Britain, were linked by Napoleon with the orders as a part of the British policy, the whole of which was to be withdrawn. In the third place, if such action was not taken by Great Britain, the United States was to cause her rights to

---

[5] Allen to Ellis, May 4, 1810, Ellis and Allan Papers.
[6] Armstrong to Madison Aug. 5, 1810, Madison Papers Lib. of Con. For. III, pp. 385–6.
[7] Cadore to Armstrong, Aug. 5, 1810, *Ibid*, pp. 386–7.

be respected by the English. Thus, in either eventuality, France hoped to profit. As Napoleon could have had no real expectation that Great Britain, would repeal her whole system, as a result of his offer, his real object was evidently to embroil the American government with his stubborn foe.

Pretended Repeal of the Decrees of Berlin and Milan by Cadore's Letter of August 5, 1810

Armstrong then pressed for an answer to several definite questions. First, he wished to know how American vessels which arrived before November 1st, would be received in France. Was the confiscating order of the preceding March—the Rambouillet Decree still in force? What was the nature of the licenses which neutral vessels leaving France must carry by Napoleon's decree of the preceding July? Finally what was to be the fate of the American property already seized by the French?[8]

In reply Armstrong was assured that the decree of Rambouillet had been repealed as soon as the lapsing of the American Non-Intercourse Law had been made known, but American vessels arriving in France would be subject to the decrees, until the date set for their revocation.

Trianon Decree, August 5, 1810—Confiscating American Vessels

The licenses were made out to be a great concession to the Americans. Theirs was said to be the only flag which had obtained them. For the cargoes confiscated, however, there was held out no hope. The principle of reprisal was to be rigorously applied.[9]

In fact, on the very day when Cadore wrote this letter, a decree was secretly issued by Napoleon, ordering the sale of the sequestered vessels and cargoes, and the deposit of the proceeds in the public treasury. This action was taken, the Emperor declared, in retaliation for the clause in the non-intercourse act

---

[8] Armstrong to Cadore, Sept. 7, 1810, *A. S. P.*, For. III, p. 388.
[9] Cadore to Armstrong, Sept. 12, 1810, *A. S. P.*, For. III, pp. 388–389.

of 1809, which ordered seizure for all French vessels which should come to the United States.

This decree was not communicated to Armstrong, but was kept secret. It was found by Albert Gallatin, eleven years later, when he was in Paris in 1821 to press for compensation for the damages resulting from its application. Gallatin stigmatized the enactment and concealment of the decree as "a glaring act of combined injustice, bad faith and meanness." "No one can suppose," he wrote, "that if it had been communicated or published at the same time (as issued) the United States, would with respect to the promised revocation of the Berlin and Milan decrees, have taken the ground which ultimately led to the war with Great Britain."[10]

Yet the American government could have expected nothing else, after Cadore's plain announcement that the principle of reprisal was to be maintained. Armstrong, however, seems not to have considered that decision as final.

Madison has in general been condemned by historians for accepting the letter of Cadore at its face value. Since he was dependent upon Armstrong for accounts of the actual animus of Napoleon's government toward the United States, the comments of the American minister on the revocation became especially interesting. Armstrong had desired to be relieved of his mission. His request was granted and in the fall of 1810 he returned to the United States. One of his last letters from France was one of September 29th to Pinkney. While this was an official communication, designed to hasten the action of the British ministers in following Napoleon's example, there is no reason to think that it represented anything but Armstrong's sincere opinion. According to the Pinkney letter, the decrees had been retracted in the most positive terms. Armstrong declared that this retraction did not call, as Wellesley insisted, for a contemporaneous cessation of the British Orders in Council and blockade system before the first of November. After that date had arrived, England was either to remove her

---

[10] *Adams Writings of Gallatin*, Vol. II, p. 197.

orders, or the United States should revive against her the appropriate sections of the non-intercourse law.[11]

It has been suggested that Armstrong may have proclaimed his faith in the repeal in order to magnify his own diplomatic success in gaining his point over Napoleon. If, however, he really believed that the repeal meant nothing, he would doubtless have been more anxious to show his own astuteness in seeing through the fraud, than to pretend to a success which time would soon show to be illusory. Armstrong had certainly had enough experience of Napoleon's duplicity to have been on his guard. Yet he seems to have taken the revocation in good faith.

The British ministry, however, refused to believe that Napoleon had really withdrawn his decrees. Until they had decisive proof of such withdrawal Wellesley wrote to Pinkney, that the Orders in Council would remain.[12]

Trianon Tariff

The prospects of American trade with France which were seriously threatened by Napoleon's permit system, received a further blow at the announcement of the new tariff, issued from Trianon in August.

Since in spite of the severity of the laws, British colonial goods filtered into the continent, by means of smuggling, it occurred to the French authorities that they might reap the smugglers' profits, by permitting the entrance of these goods at high duties. The smugglers would thus lose their gains, and the treasury would be enriched. Moreover, the high prices would keep down the consumption of the foreign products, and favor the use of the domestic substitutes.

The permits to American shippers were only a part of Napoleon's *Nouveau Système*. Licenses of many kinds were issued to French and other continental shippers to import the articles, hitherto absolutely barred, in theory at least. At the gates of the continent, these goods were stopped, and a huge toll levied.

---

[11] *A. S. P.*, For., III, p. 389.
[12] *Ibid.*, p. 366.

Licenses and the new high tariff duties thus went hand in hand. The scheme was all a part of that general reorganization of French industry projected during the year 1810.[13]

The rates of the Trianon tariff were far above the original cost of the articles. The rate on cotton was 60c per lb., on sugar, 30-40c; on coffee, 40c; on cocoa, $1, and on indigo, $2.[14] The rates on pepper, logwood, peruvian bark and other colonial articles were in proportion.

"The continental system," wrote Adams, "whatever may have been its original design, appears terminating in a mere tax, levied upon commerce by France, equal or more than equal to that which Great Britain has levied by the superiority of her naval power."[15]

Bavaria, Mecklenburg, Sweden, the Hanse towns, the Swiss cantons, all the lands allied with Napoleon, adopted the rates of the Trianon tariff, at the word of the Emperor, during the fall of 1810.[16]

The duties laid by this tariff, as Adams observed, amounted to prohibitions. Merchants who had cargoes on the ocean, on the way to Europe, feared that the whole would be "lost in the high duties."[17] With their customary sanguiness, merchants hoped for modifications. The only comfort they received was the announcement in December, that duties might be paid in goods. In that case little or nothing would be left to the owners.[18]

Armstrong, therefore, during the summer of 1810, had not only to discuss the terms of a new treaty, and strive for the release of the sequestered vessels, but also to protest against the *Nouveau Système* as it affected America, and present to Cadore the offer embodied in the Macon Bill.

Baltic Trade—1810

Driven by the relentless policy of Napoleon from the harbors of Schleswig and Holstein in the summer of 1810, American

---
[13] See *Melvin*, Chap. IX, Licensed Navigation.
[14] J. Q. Adams, *Writing*, III, p. 479.
[15] *Ibid*.
[16] Moniteur, Oct., Nov., 1810.
[17] McEwers to LeRoy and Bayard, Paris, Nov. 7, 1810, Bayard Papers.
[18] Forbes to Smith, Dec. 8, 1810, Consular Letters, Hamburg.

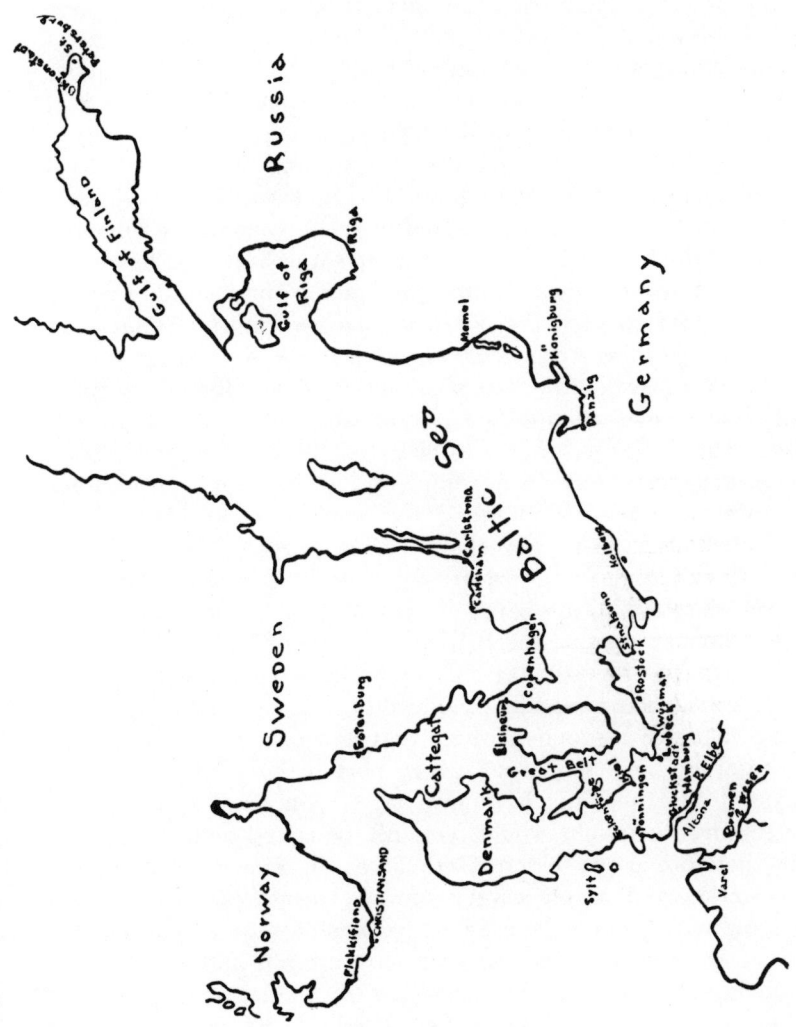

shippers persisted in seeking other ways of reaching continental markets. They aimed at ports still further to the northward and eastward. They tried the ports of Sweden, and when these failed, they found an entrance at Cronstadt in Russia.

The changes in the commercial regulations of these countries were so rapid and frequent that shippers from the other side of the Atlantic could plan for no definite port or market.

The gameness of the Americans in running the risk of British cruisers and French custom officers, and the high insurance rates involved, are well illustrated in the voyage of the schooner *Cremer* which sailed from Boston in March of 1810, with a cargo of Batavian sugar, coffee and spice. The insurance policy on the cargo covered the ocean voyage to a port of deposit in Europe, including blockaded ports, and the safe landing, and quiet possession in the hands of the consignee for thirty days. All risks of every name and nature were included except that the assured was to take the risks of the French and Dutch decrees against American commerce. The vessel cleared for Tonningen, but was intended for some port of Holland, or wherever else the master should deem proper. The premium was 25 per cent to return 10 per cent if from any cause the vessel should not discharge in Holland or a blockaded port. The schooner escaped the British blockade of Holland and went so far up the Maese that she might have gone to Rotterdam but as she was proceeding to that city, the master learned from the owner's correspondent there that he would not be permitted to enter or land his cargo at any port in Holland, and if discovered by the French guards or custom house officers his vessel and his freight would certainly be seized and confiscated. He therefore proceeded to Gothenburg in Sweden, but finding the market at that place very poor, he turned his prow toward the Baltic. But on June 22nd, he was captured by a Danish privateer, and later carried into Copenhagen and condemned, probably because the cargo consisted of colonial produce.[19]

The wide choice of ports permitted to the masters of the vessels destined for the north of Europe in the summer of 1810 is

---

[19] Coolidge vs. Gray, *Mass. Supreme Court Reports*, Vol. 8.

illustrated in the directions to Peter Wirgman, of the ship *William Wilson*. This vessel, leased by fourteen merchants of Baltimore, started from that city in May of 1810. Her cargo consisted of campeachy logwood, Nicaraugua dyewood, coffee and sugar. The master was ordered to proceed to the island of Sylt, and there to ascertain whether he might attempt the ports of Hamburg or Bremen.[20] If these were closed the cargo was to be landed at the Sylt, if that was permitted. If not he was to proceed to an open port in the North or Baltic Sea.[21] If the cargo was delivered in the Baltic, not higher than Kiel or Colberg, then there was to be an advance of 1 per cent over the freight money, if as high as Königsberg, an advance of 2 per cent. The vessel was ultimately seized in the Baltic by a Danish privateer and taken into the port of Flekkifiord in Norway. On his liberation, four months later, the captain decided that on account of the approach of the winter season, the danger from privateers, and the political situation in the north of Europe, there was no safety in the Baltic. He therefore took his vessel to Hull in England, where his cargo, sold in a poor market, brought only enough to cover cost and charges.[22]

The owners of the cargo were very much dissatisfied at this result. They brought suit against Peter Wirgman in the American courts, on the ground that he should have gone to some port in the Baltic and secured good prices for his cargo.

At the trial a number of captains were called to give their version of conditions in the Baltic in the winter of 1810. The sympathies of the reader are with the captain, when he reads the lengthy hypothetical question placed before these captains. It ran as follows:

"If you had been placed in the situation of Peter Wirgman in charge of the *William Wilson* and cargo in the latter part

---

[20] It is surprising that any American shippers would have considered these ports possible in May, 1810. Probably the lessees of the Wilson expected that Armstrong's negotiations would have proved successful, in lifting the ban against the Americans in the Hanse towns by the time of that vessels arrival.

[21] Directions to Peter Wirgman, Master of the *Wm. Wilson*, May 12, 1810. Taylor-Bourne Papers.

[22] Letters and Papers in regard to the *Wm. Wilson*, May, 1810, Jan., 1811, Taylor-Bourne Papers.

of December, 1810, lying in an exposed port of Norway, acquitted by their Admiralty Court, apprehensive of an appeal by the Danish privateers men, and watched by a French privateer, finding it impracticable, to obtain permission to land your cargo in the Danish dominions, lying at an anchorage from which by a positive order from the customs you were compelled to leave, the harbor above frozen up, and the ice threatening your ship with destruction, having sustained the loss of one anchor and cable, and finding it impossible to get another, the fear before you of a general seizure of American property, on the continent of Europe, a knowledge of new duties in Sweden amounting to a prohibition of your cargo, and a positive law in Prussia to prohibit all trade with the ports of that kingdom in colonial produce—In this situation of accumulated danger and distress, to what part of the world would you have directed your course?"

The captains, however, made deposition of the following successful voyages: Gideon Tucker of Salem, Mass.—The brig *Catherine* sailed from Salem, September 22, 1810, was taken and carried to Copenhagen and there detained about three weeks. She sailed from thence December 1st for Riga, and there sold her cargo of sugar, coffee and logwood without interference. Wm. Proctor, also of Salem, with his ship *Adelaide*, sailed March 10, 1810, with cargo of sugar, coffee, and logwood, and landed at Königsburg in Prussia, May, 1810, and sold cargo unmolested.[23]

Another voyage of this period, full of risk and uncertainty, but which finally terminated successfully was that of John Swift in the schooner *Matchless*. He started from Baltimore in May of 1810, for Gottenburg with a cargo of coffee. Arriving at that port, he found it so glutted with coffee that he planned to go to Stralsund, in Swedish Pomerania whence he calculated his goods could be transported to the Hamburg market.[24] He was the more confirmed in this determination, when he learned of Napoleon's Rambouillet Decree, which left Swedish Pomerania

---

[23] *Ibid.*
[24] Swift to Wm. Taylor, May 4, 1810, Taylor-Bourne Papers.

and Russia as the only safe coasts for Americans in the Baltic.

There were at that time over two hundred merchantment in the port of Gothenburg, many of them with forged papers and all with licenses. Many of these were evidently Americans. They left the Swedish port under the protection of some of the many British men of war which were proceeding to the Baltic and were willing to afford convoy to American vessels as far as the Belt.[25]

Swift started to make arrangements for convoy for his vessel, and waited upon the British consul, with the view of securing a license, modified to his situation. The reply was in the negative "unless the produce was exported from the United Kingdom and that one of the owners was a British subject."[26]

Soon after this Admiral Saumerez received notice from the British government to allow no Swedish vessel to proceed to any port hostile to Great Britain, unless in possession of a British license. This, in the opinion of Saumerez, also applied to American vessels, even those carrying the products of their own country to Baltic ports.[27] The news created consternation in the mind of Swift and the many other American captains in those waters. They faced seizure by the British cruisers which were very numerous from Gothenburg to the Belt. Swift had about decided to "take to his heels" when the news of the removal of the non-intercourse led Saumerez to lift the ban from the American vessels. Swift now gave up the idea of proceeding to Stralsund, having learned that the governor, acting under Napoleon's orders, intended to seize American property in that port. He considered going to Memel or St. Petersburg, or even leaving the Baltic and trying again for Tonningen or Sylt. He finally succeeded in landing his cargo safely at Rostock in Mecklenburg with the permission of the French minister to that government and by the middle of July the jubilant captain reported it all safely at Roitenburg,

---

[25] Same to same, May 28, 1810, *Ibid*.
[26] Same to same, May 26, 1810, Taylor-Bourne Papers.
[27] Saumerez to W. Smith, Br. Consul at Gothenburg, May 24, 1810, Taylor-Bourne Papers. J. Q. Adams to Secy. Smith, June 25, 1810, *Writings J. Q. Adams*.

in the heart of Germany; although the charges were considerable, the cargo sold for a good figure in shillings, Hambro banco. A return cargo of Hamburg linens and glassware was shipped from Kiel.[28]

By this time, however, orders were issued by the King of Prussia July 19, 1810, "for the more effectual preservation of the continental system . . . to close all his ports against American vessels, altogether without exception." Any vessel belonging to an American citizen, or coming from an American port, was to be turned away, on entering a Pussian harbor.[29] The injustice of the order becomes manifest, when we consider, that as in the case of the Hamburg trade described by Forbes, English vessels with English cargoes, entered Prussian ports, by fraud and the connivance of the custom officials. These officials did not receive similar bribes from American officials, and they and the Prussian merchants with English connections, were not loathe to place in execution this order, dictated by Napoleon. Nevertheless, American vessels, according to John Quincy Adams, were able to "approximate" the Prussian ports, sufficiently to discharge their cargoes, "on a proper explanation of circumstances to the French consuls."[30]

Ten days after the Prussian order, there was issued a similar order by the Duke of Mecklenburg-Schwerin, closing the ports of Wismar and Rostock.[31]

On August 13th, the remaining ports of Holstein, in addition to those of Tonningen and Husum, previously closed, were sealed by the King of Denmark.[32] Similarly, the long arm of Napoleon effected the closing of the ports of Sweden, to the Americans.[33]

A voyage frustrated by the two latter orders was that of the ship *Union*. This vessel started from Philadelphia, October 12, 1810, with a cargo of ginger, coffee, and cotton, bound for Eckenforde, a Danish port in Holstein. During the voyage the *Union* encountered storms which made her leaky. On De-

---

[28] Swift to Taylor, July 17, 1810, Taylor-Bourne Papers.
[29] Same to same, Aug. 17, 1810, *Ibid.*
[30] J. Q. Adams to Secy. Smith, Aug. 31, 1810, *Writings*, III, p. 478
[31] *Ibid.*, p. 477–478.
[32] *Ibid.*, p. 478.
[33] Corr. Napoleon, 20, pp. 19, 356, 372.

cember 8th she arrived on the quarantine grounds of Gottenburg, where her captain was informed of a decree of the King of Denmark of September 8, 1810, prohibiting entry of all vessels having on board cargoes of colonial produce, into the ports of his dominions, and directing them to be turned off on pain of confiscation.[34] The captain, therefore, attempted to land his cargo at Gothenburg, but the King of Sweden, having enacted a similar order, he was refused permission. The leaky condition of his vessel made it necessary to secure repairs, so the captain proceeded to Leith in Scotland, where he left the cotton in payment, and finding no place where the rest of his cargo could be landed, he brought it home to Philadelphia.[35]

Seizure of the New Orleans Packet

On the departure of Armstrong in October of 1810, American interests in France were temporarily left in the hands of a chargé d'affaires, Jonathan Russell. November the first was drawing near. On October 7th Pinkney had written Russell, asking that he be furnished with the most striking proof after that date, that the repeal of the French decrees had actually taken place. Russell waited until December 1st to make his report. Then he wrote that so far as he knew, no event had occurred, either before or since the date, to vary the very positive and precise assurance of the repeal of the 5th of August.

Only a few days later, however, this illusion was shaken. The ship *New Orleans Packet*, started from New York, July 25, 1810, with a cargo of provisions, including 300 bags of cocoa, having cleared for Lisbon, but actually intending to go to Gibraltar. On the voyage the vessel was boarded by an English frigate, and after a short detention, allowed to proceed. The captain after reaching Gibraltar, changed his plans, and started for the port of Bordeaux. On his arrival at Bordeaux, on December 3rd his vessel was there sequestered, for having been

---

[34] The decree of Aug. 3 of the same year, mentioned above, closing Danish ports to all American vessels, would have excluded the Union in any case.
[35] Krumbhar vs. Marine Ins. Co., Sergeant and Rawle, *Penna. Cases*, I, p. 281.

visited by a British man of war. The schooner *Friendship* of Baltimore suffered the same fate.[36]

About this time the news of the President's proclamation reached Paris. Seeing how eager the United States was to take them at their word, the French government was obliged to make some show of keeping its promises. Massa, the Minister of Justice, therefore issued an order to the President of the Tribunal of Prizes, declaring that since the non-intercourse was to be established between the United States and Great Britain, to all captures of American vessels made after November 1st, the Berlin and Milan decrees should not apply. These vessels should be sequestered until February 2nd of the next year. If by that time the United States had caused her rights to be respected by Great Britain, the American vessels and cargoes were to be restored to their proprietors.[37] At the same time, the Minister of Finance addressed to the Director General of Customs, a notice to the same effect.

By this time, the American government should have seen that Napoleon was beginning to retreat from his position. Loopholes were appearing by which the Emperor might evade the carrying out of his promises. Russell, however, maintained a hopeful attitude. He wrote to Pinkney announcing the release of the American schooner, *Grace Ann Green*, which had been seized on her arrival at Marseilles, because she came from Gibraltar. As she clearly came within the scope of the Berlin and Milan decrees, her release might be considered conclusive proof of their revocation.[38] Two or three other American ships which had been seized would doubtless be liberated, he thought, in accordance with the tenor of Massa's letter of December 26th. "I am willing to believe," he wrote, "that what this government has done, although it may not be entirely satisfactory to the United States, will at least be sufficient to procure from the British government a repeal of the orders in council, and the restoration of all American property taken

---

[36] Russell to Smith, June 9, 1811, *A. S. P.*, For. III, p. 502.
[37] Letter from Minister of Justice to President of Council of Prizes, Dec. 26, 1810, *A. S. P.*, For. III, p. 393.
[38] Russell to Pinkney, Dec. 30, 1810, *A. S. P.*, For. III, p. 417.

under them since November 1st. It is possible that the French cruisers may hereafter continue their depradations, but abuses of this kind are very distinct from the operation of the Berlin and Milan decrees, and cannot, by the most extravagant construction of the law of retortion, afford a pretext for the continuance of the British order."[39]

In London, therefore, Pinkney continued his attempts to convince the British ministers that both the manner and the terms of the French repeal were satisfactory. As to the practical effects of the repeal, Pinkney declared that American vessels bound to England were suffered to pass by French cruisers, so that the Berlin decree at least was not operative.[40] As for the Milan decree, the British were themselves interfering with the demonstration of its repeal, for British cruisers stopped American vessels proceeding to France, and carried them into England. An instance of this was the American vessel *Fox* which had been taken by a British man of war, on its voyage from Boston to Cherbourg.[41]

To this Wellesley replied that Napoleon's repeal appeared to be contingent upon Great Britain's repeal, before the preceding November 1st, of both her orders and her blockade system. If the repeal of the orders only had been specified, the British government would have been glad to comply, but so long as the French maintained their system of violence and injustice, the blockade system must be maintained by the English.[42] American vessels, therefore, continued to be seized under the Orders in Council. The protests of the American minister in the case of the two schooners laden with codfish, the *Polly* and the *Mary* bound from Marblehead to Bordeaux, therefore met with no response.[43] Pinkney was now utterly out of patience. Ill in body and harassed in mind, he saw no prospect of success.

---

[39] Russell to Pinkney, Dec. 27, 1810, *Ibid*.
[40] Pinkney to Wellesley, Dec. 10, 1810, *Ibid*., pp. 376–379.
[41] Pinkney to Wellesley, Dec. 8, 1810, *Ibid*., p. 376. British cruisers were thus carrying out the Orders in Council and seizing American vessels on their way to French ports, instead of merely "visiting" them and then allowing them to proceed to their destinations, and thus demonstrate the fact that the Milan Decree was revoked.
[42] Wellesley to Pinkney, Dec. 29, 1810, *A. S. P.*, For. III, pp. 376–379.
[43] Pinkney to Wellesley, Jan. 15, 1811, *Ibid*, p. 412.

He therefore followed the instructions of his government, and prepared to return home.

The formal protest of the American government against the new permit system of Napoleon was presented by Russell in January of 1811.[44] In May, Bassano, who had now succeeded Cadore as Minister of Foreign Affairs, notified Russell of a new regulation. There were at that time sixteen American vessels in French ports whose cargoes had been placed provisionally on deposit, pending a decision as to their entrance. These were now authorized to be admitted, but they were required to take back the value of their cargoes in French products, two-thirds of which was to be in silks.[45]

To this regulation Russell shortly filed a protest. He pointed out that the American merchant might better be left to choose for himself which among the many articles of French manufacture would find the best sale in the American market. If he were compelled to buy silks the French manufacturers would surely raise their prices for that commodity, and the American market would become overstocked with it. The American merchant, thus compelled to buy at a high price and sell at a low one, would soon cease to trade with France.[46] As Russell wrote to Monroe, "a trade which has to run the gauntlet of a British blockade, and is crushed with extravagant duties inward and shackled with this singular restriction outward, cannot continue."[47]

Russell was unable to secure any further concessions. Interest in the French negotiations had meanwhile been transferred to the other side of the Atlantic where Serrurier, the new French minister arrived in February, 1811.

Madison's Proclamation Reestablishing Non-Intercourse with Great Britain, November 2, 1810

When Madison received the copies of the letters of Armstrong to Pinkney, reporting without question the non-enforce-

---
[44] Russell to Cadore, Jan. 12, 1811, *A. S. P.*, For. III, p. 501.
[45] Bassano to Russell, May 14, 1811, *A. S. P.*, For. III, p. 505.
[46] Russell to Bassano, June 10, 1811, *Ibid.*
[47] *Ibid*, Russell to Secretary of State, July 15, 1811.

ment of the French decrees, he made haste to announce the fact to the American people. His famous proclamation of November 2, 1810, declared that it had officially been made known that the decrees had been repealed and that therefore, in accordance with the conditions laid down in the Macon Bill, the non-intercourse with England, would come into effect three months hence, that is on February 1st of the following year.

When Congress assembled in December, 1810, Madison, after reciting in his message the unpromising state of affairs with both England and France, pointed out that, in view of his recent proclamation, one of the tasks before Congress would be a decision as to just how far the law of May 1, 1810, was to be applied.

The chief topics which engaged attention at this session were the acquisition of Florida, and the Bank of the United States. By February 22nd, however, Congress took up in earnest the question of foreign commerce. Eppes, the chairman of the committee on Foreign Relations, had presented a bill two weeks before, designed to support the position of the President. This measure provided that if Great Britain should repeal her edicts, the President should issue a proclamation to that effect. In case no such announcement was made, the importation of British goods was to cease after February 2nd.[48]

Before the House had a chance to discuss this measure, however, the President received and communicated to Congress the news from Russell of the seizure of the *New Orelans Packet*, which had taken place early in December, 1810. Eppes' Bill was then withdrawn for further consideration.

The truth was that as February 2nd drew near, many men in Congress shrank from the drastic carrying out of Madison's program. It would entail hardship on scores of American merchants, for the goods which they had on shipboard, it was pointed out, were really their own property and not English.[49] Besides this, the inevitable falling of the revenues was a most distasteful prospect, for no one was anxious to propose internal

---

[48] *Annals 11th Cong.*, 3, pp. 547–551.
[49] Speech of Burwell, *Annals, Ibid.*, p. 872.

taxes. If the non-intercourse was established, American shippers would be driven from the ocean, for no cargo which they would send out, could bear the freight of the outward and the return voyage. The growers of hemp, cotton, tobacco and grain would be unable to export. The Southern planter would be without his coarse cloths, the farmer would be deprived of his plaster for fertilizer, and all would suffer from the lack of salt.[50]

Especially now when doubt was growing in regard to the good faith of Napoleon, it appeared that the United States would really, be punished herself by establishing non-intercourse and thus playing into the hands of the French, who had no intention of restoring the sequestered property. The valuable birthright of British trade, it seemed, was to be sold "for a mess of Gallic pottage." Many members therefore counselled delay in imposing the non-intercourse against England.

Randolph declared that since France had made a hostile retaliation for the non-intercourse law of 1809, any further concession to her should be out of the question. In order to cut the Gordian knot and yet save the face of the President, Randolph proposed the repeal of the Macon Bill. "I want, sir," he declared, "to relieve the Virginia planter, and not to settle questions of good or bad faith with the Emperor and his courtiers."[51]

Gardiner, of New York, also supported this view. If on December 6th, the French government by seizing the *New Orleans Packet* had not ceased to enforce her edicts, it was unfair to begin to punish England as early as February 2nd for that date was not three months from the time that France had kept her word. Even if the President felt obliged to take the words Cadore's latter in good faith, Gardiner held that the Americans could not expect Great Britain to do so.[52]

Another who supported the repeal of the law was Wheaton. Why, he asked, enforce a law against Great Britain so embarrassing to the country, since France continued to annoy us by

---

[50] Speech of Emott, *Ibid*, p. 932.
[51] *Ibid.*, 890.
[52] *Ibid.*, p. 875.

seizures, if not by the old decrees, then under new pretexts, meanwhile refusing to surrender the sequestered vessels.[53]

This view, however, was met by great opposition from many. The good faith of the country, they declared, was pledged to carry out the President's promise to France, and any proposal to repeal the law threatened a stain upon the national honor. To this Randolph replied that the law was not a pledge to either belligerent, but a rule of action for Congress. Quincy gave it as his opinion that supposing there had been a pledge, if the French decrees were not repealed by November 1st, we were absolved, and were now free to do as we pleased. In the end Randolph's motion for the repeal of the Macon Bill was lost.

On February 6th a bill was brought in by the committee on Foreign Relations, designed to give partial relief to American merchants from the blow which by the terms of the President's proclamation, was about to fall. It provided that any vessel or merchandise owned by American citizens which had left British ports before February 2nd, should not fall under the provisions of the law. The ground for this proposal was the pleas of the merchants that their orders for the spring consignments of 1811, had been sent out in the previous September or October, had been purchased with cash, and had actually been paid for before the President's proclamation was issued. This property could not be brought in before February 2nd, but it was bona fide American, and its seizure would tend to destroy our own resources, and produce no effect in Great Britain.[54]

Critics of the course of the Executive were not wanting. Among the most outspoken of these was Emmott of New York. He attacked Napoleon's "swindling decree" of March, 1810, issued in retaliation for an American law which had been repealed about fifteen months before, and had really never harmed France anyway. The members of Congress, Emmot declared, had been under the impression that the President, in issuing his proclamation, had had grounds for his action of which the outside world was ignorant. When it appeared that he had

---

[53] *Ibid.*, p. 888.
[54] Speech of Eppes, *Ibid.*, pp. 938–945.

only the letter of Cadore, the matter assumed a different aspect. In the opinion of Emmot, the wisdom of Madison's course was open to serious question. The lack of a formal decree of repeal was ominous. The withdrawal postulated by Cadore was conditional. Emmot therefore declared that the issuance of the proclamation was an "incautious act." Before the President had acted upon a proposition "so loose and general" he should have asked for explanations and particulars. Since the Emperor by his high tariffs, his prohibition of certain commodities, and his permit system virtually cut Americans off from the continent, why should our government harp upon the iniquity of the Orders in Council. "If the English by their orders and blockades, formerly kept us from the continent," declared Emmot, "the French have now taken their place."[55]

To meet this need, an amendment to the bill of the Foreign Relations Committee was produced by Eppes. Hoping against hope that the British decrees had already been repealed, the makers of the amendment provided for such a contingency. Vessels which had left England, before it could be ascertained whether Great Britain had actually repealed her orders on or before February 2nd, should be released after giving bonds. The object of this amendment was to relieve the courts of deciding whether the non-intercourse was in force or not. Vessels were daily arriving and the hapless collectors were liable to damage suits for alarming sums, in the prevailing state of uncertainty. In the end, Congress acted favorably upon this amendment, February 23, 1811.[56]

When the discussion over the commercial intercourse had begun, great hopes had been entertained that with the arrival of the new French minister, Serrurier, the question of the repeal would be definitely settled, one way or the other. By the end of February, however, Congress learned that Serrurier's instructions were a disappointment. He brought no new light, on the subject on which the country was most interested.

The opponents of the non-intercourse were thereupon

---

[55] *Ibid*, p. 910–932 passim.
[56] *Annals 11 Cong.*, 3 p. 1007.

strengthened. Quincy declared that against the whole system of restriction there were four counts: it was disadvantageous to the merchants and farmers, unprofitable to the treasury, not protective to the manufacturer, because of the uncertainty of its duration, and in the end, not competent to crush either belligerent. The Emperor's repeal was merely verbal, therefore no obligation resulted. We owed nothing, declared Quincy, to France or Great Britain, but everything to the American people.[57]

Bigelow, another member from Massachusetts, likewise opposed the non-intercourse against Great Britain. "Do you believe," he asked, "that your merchants, a great portion of whose property has been seized by foreign nations, when the remnant of their vessels, which have escaped, shall upon entering your own ports, be seized by your own custom house officers, that they will be satisfied to lose the remainder of their property in pursuance of your own laws. They will think it hard enough that millions of their property have been seized by France, by Denmark and by Sweden, without having the remainder seized on their return and confiscated by their own government. Surely, sir, they will require strong evidence of the fact, that your faith is pledged to France, before they will be satisfied with the measure you are about to adopt."[58]

In this and many other speeches on the subject, the opponents of the non-intercourse seemed to have the best of the argument, and to be in the majority. In the exhausting session of February 26th which lasted for eighteen hours, and did not close until 4.30 on the morning of the 27th, the majority of the speakers certainly depreciated the enforcement of the non-intercourse, and ridiculed the idea of a pledge owed to Napoleon. Nevertheless, on the next day the vote of the members upheld the administration. Eppes's bill was passed, providing for a change of front whenever Great Britain should yield her orders, but until that time, the non-intercourse was to go into effect.[59]

---

[57] *Ibid*, pp. 1011–1027.
[58] *Annals, 11th Cong.*, III, p. 1060.
[59] *Ibid*, pp. 1338–39.

While the Eleventh Congress supported Madison's position with regard to the two belligerents, the President himself was filled with misgivings as to Napoleon's intentions. He saw clearly that the Emperor's need of money was a constant factor, and he was not wide of the mark when he observed that the Emperor was ignorant of commerce. In a letter of March 18, 1811, to Jefferson, Madison admitted his belief that Napoleon distrusted the stability of the American pledge to enforce non-intercourse and wished to carry out his promise only at the same pace as America carried out hers. In this Madison declared, the folly of Napoleon was obvious. Folly, he meant, if he was really sincere in wishing a good understanding, with the United States.[60]

The communications of Serrurier, as we have seen, did nothing to clear up the mystery. He had nothing to bring forward except vague and general statements that the decrees were withdrawn. He urged that as a further evidence of good faith, an American minister should be sent to France.

James Monroe succeeded Robert Smith as the head of the State department on April 1, 1811. The new secretary was not inclined to acknowledge the repeal of the decrees. He was especially angered because the Emperor still authorized his consuls in America to grant licenses to vessels leaving the United States for France. Public sentiment supported him and opposed the sending of a new minister. In the end, however, Monroe was obliged to support the position of his chief. Unofficial news arrived that the Emperor had released American vessels kept in sequestration since the previous November, and admitted their cargo for sale. Without further ado, the new minister, who had already been selected, Joel Barlow, was given his instructions and departed.

Meanwhile Foster, the new British minister, had arrived bearing the word that his government refused to concede the repeal of the decrees. Madison was in a dilemma. As Henry Adams writes, the President was obliged in the morning solemnly to assure Foster that the decrees were repealed, and in the afternoon to rate Serrurier because they were still in force.

---

[60] Hunt, *Writings of James Madison*, Vol. VIII, pp. 133–135.

Finally in July, Serrurier had something definite to communicate. He made much of the announcement that the sixteen American vessels sequestered since the preceding November 2nd, had been freed. Some of them, he stated, had already left port, upon conforming to the municipal laws of the country, by exporting wine and silks of French manufacture. This, of course, was no concession. The vessels should never have been seized at all, if the letter of Cadore had meant anything. Indeed the freeing of the vessels was not attributed in Serrurier's note, to the keeping of the French pledges, but to the passage by Congress of the non-intercourse with England.

The objectionable commercial regulations of France were to continue. All American vessels arriving at French ports, bringing the products of their own country, would be required to carry certificates of origin. They would be obliged to pay the heavy duties to which these products were subject, and to take away wine, silk and other French manufactures, in accordance with the regulations. Coffee, sugar, cocoa, and other colonial products, could only be admitted by permit. Since the Emperor was encouraging the raising of substitutes for certain of these products in his own dominions he could not permit their indefinite importation. Tobacco having been made a state monopoly, the government would purchase only the quantity necessary for consumption, and whatever was landed beyond this amount, might be stored in warehouses and later transported to Germany and other parts of Europe as a market opened. These regulations Serrurier described as a disposition of the Emperor in favor of American commerce, of which he seemed to think the American government would be delighted to hear.[61]

Meanwhile Foster maintained his position that the decrees had not been repealed. This was proved, he maintained, by the Fauntainebleau Decree, the Report of the Minister of Foreign Affairs and the Minister of Justice to the Council of Prizes of December, 1810, as well as by Napoleon's speech to the Hanse deputies.[62] Even after word had been received from Russell of

---

[61] *A. S. P.*, For. III, pp. 508–509.
[62] *Ibid.*, p. 435.

the release of the *New Orleans Packet*, the *Grace Ann Green*, and three other American vessels, Foster refused to concede the withdrawal of the decrees, and urged the American government to withdraw the non-intercourse law against England.[63] He continued to maintain this position until the outbreak of hostilities.

[63] Foster to Monroe, Oct. 22, 1811, *Ibid.*, p. 449.

VII

REPEAL OF THE FRENCH DECREES AND BRITISH ORDERS

The Mission of Barlow—Petitions for Repeal of Orders—Phillimore's Pamphlet—Repeal of the Orders in Council.

The Mission of Barlow

Barlow, who arrived in Paris in the summer of 1811, was no stranger to France. He had been in Paris during the days of the Revolution, and had been an active participant on the popular side, in the stirring events of 1789.[1] His sympathy with the French people was strong. He believed that the two nations needed each others productions, and that the relationship between them was, at bottom, friendly.

The effect of the license and tariff regulations of the French government which had been adopted coincident with the putative repeal of the decrees, had made itself felt by the summer of 1811. These regulations were now perceived by the American government to be not temporary expedients, but a part of a permanent system of Napoleon's. The question, therefore, as to whether the decrees had really been repealed had by this time well nigh lost its point, because even if they had been withdrawn, the new regulations constituted a grievance quite as serious as the old one.

The first letter of Barlow to Bassano showed a careful study of the possibilities of commercial exchange between the two countries, as they appeared to the American minister. He seems to have accepted the success of Napoleon's system as already a fait accompli, for he assumed that the continent could duplicate in kinds and volume and cheapness the manufactures produced across the channel. He therefore pointed out to Bassano the

---

[1] Todd, *Life and Letters of Joel Barlow*, p. 86 ff.

feasibility of having the manufactures of France supplant those of England in the American markets, provided the French government would remove its hampering restrictions on American trade. Among these he specified the regulation that American vessels should bring back cargoes of French goods exclusively, and the enormous duties on colonial products. Such excluding regulations were not in the spirit of the removal of the decrees, nor could they have been contemplated in the act of Congress which invited such removal. "In depriving themselves of the commerce of England," wrote Barlow, "it was not their intention to be deprived, of that of all Europe." Because the United States was an agricultural country, the manufactures of Europe were absolutely necessary to the convenience of its people. Moreover, their system of finances, which they did not wish to change, called for continued importation of foreign goods. In years of active commerce, about seventeen million dollars was collected annually in revenue by the custom houses, while all other sources of taxation, yielded but one million.[2]

As a result of Bassano's replies Barlow was for a time encouraged. He believed in December of 1811, that Napoleon was really about to change his system, but by the close of the year, several checks had already appeared. Seizures of American vessels by French privateers in the Baltic and the Mediterranean continued. Napoleon flatly refused to permit the entrance of colonial produce without a special license.[3]

At the beginning of 1812, several events occurred which showed that far from becoming more accommodating France was perpetrating new injuries. One of these was the burning of four American vessels, seized at sea by a French squadron, the commander of which had orders from the Minister of Marine and Colonies authorizing his act. This incident will be more fully explained later. At the same time a decree was issued calling for the seizure by Napoleon's agents of all colonial products found in Swedish Pomerania.[4]

---

[2] Barlow to Bassano, Nov. 10, 1811. Desp. Fr. 13, only the concluding paragraphs of this letter are found in *A. S. P.*, For. III, p. 513.
[3] Bassano to Barlow, Dec. 27, 1811, *A. S. P.*, For. III, pp. 516–517.
[4] Nap. Corr., 20, pp. 356–372.

The time for reaching an agreement meanwhile was slipping away. By February of 1812, the Emperor was so busy with preparations for the Russian campaign, that he had no time for American affairs.

All that Barlow had been able to gain was a verbal notification to the Custom Houses directing the inviting of American vessels to the French market, and promising an amelioration of the regulations as to ownership and origin.

Meanwhile Russell was writing from London for proofs, proofs, and still more proofs of the repeal of the decrees, with which to confront Wellesley. Barlow promptly furnished them. Seven ships, he reported on March 2, 1812, had recently come into French ports and been freely received, all of which would in case of no revocation, have been subject to seizure by the French. Of these, however, three were bringing colonial goods to France, and were armed with licenses for that purpose. Two others had been seized by French cruisers, and taken into port, where they had been set free by the Emperor's order. This circumstance showed that the news of the repeal had not penetrated to the owners of privateers, nor to the French admiralty courts, but each case as it arose was carried to Napoleon.

Nevertheless, Barlow would confess to no flaw in his exhibit of Napoleon's good faith. Since his arrival in France, in the previous September, more than thirty American vessels had arrived, bringing the products of the United States, and all had been hospitably received, although all those bringing colonial goods were required to carry licenses.[5]

Two weeks later however, the American minister was seized with apprehension. Bassano's Report to the Emperor on Neutral Trade appeared. This document declared that so long as England's policy of blockade persisted, the decrees of Berlin and Milan must be enforced. No mention was made of the setting aside of the decrees in the case of the United States.[6] Certainly all was not well, if in a report on neutral trade a suspension in favor of the most prominent neutral was not mentioned.

---

[5] Barlow to Russell, March 2, 1812, *A. S. P.*, For. III, pp. 517–519.
[6] *A. S. P.*, For. III, pp. 457–59.

Still more sinister news now reached Barlow. A French squadron had started from Nantes in January, 1812, with orders to stop neutral vessels bound for Lisbon and Cadiz. It was evidently as a result of this order that the French cruisers *Medusa* and *Nymph* stopped two American vessels, the *Telegraph* and the *Dolly*, and burned them at sea.[7] The excuse for this outrage was that the American ships would have conveyed information to the enemy, as to the whereabout of the French cruisers. A particularly shameful circumstance was that a part of the *Telegraph's* cargo consisting of spices was smuggled on shore at Brest, and sold for the benefit of the crew of the *Medusa*.[8]

By April 21st, it became clear, in spite of all Barlow's "proofs," that the British government would not concede the repeal of the decrees, basing their refusal on Bassano's report of March. Thereupon Barlow applied again to that minister, asking the French government to make public "an authentic act declaring the Berlin and Milan decrees as related to the United States to have ceased November 1, 1810."[9]

To Barlow's surprise Bassano then quietly handed him a decree of repeal, signed by Napoleon, and dated more than a year earlier, April 28, 1811. This document declared that since Congress, by its act of March 2, 1811, had ordered the execution of the non-intercourse with England, and that this constituted an act of resistance to that power, the decrees of Berlin and Milan were definitely, considered as not to have existence in regard to American vessels, from the date November 1, 1810.[10]

Barlow was naturally non-plussed at the sight of this remarkable document. In reply to his question, Bassano admitted that it had never been published, but he coolly asserted that a copy had been sent to Barlow's predecessor, and another for-

---

[7] It appears that this squadron also burned the ship *Asia* and the brig *Gershom*, Jan. 17, 23, 1812 sailing from Duxbury, with cargoes of corn and flour. The crews of these vessels, thirty-seven in number were placed on board the American brig *Thames*, on Feb. 3d. *Annals 12 Cong.*, I Vol. 2, pp. 1234–35.

[8] *A. S. P.*, For. III, p. 520. Earlier cases of the burning of American ships by French commanders were the *Brutus*, 1808, Armstrong to Champagny, Oct. 20, 1808, Desp. Fr. 11; The *Jefferson*, 1809 *Columbian Centinel*, March 30, 1808; The *John*, Dec. 1809; *Poulson*, March 30, 1810.

[9] *A. S. P.*, For. III, p. 603.

[10] *Ibid*, p. 432.

warded to Serrurier. As Armstrong was not there to deny the fact and as it was easy to assume that Serrurier's copy had been "lost in the mails," Bassano apparently considered it safe to make such a statement.

This so-called decree was, therefore, evidently trumped up for the occasion. It was only produced because the French government wished to turn away the wrath of the United States from herself, and wished to fan the flame of discontent between United States and Great Britain.

As we shall see, however, the British ministers, in the summer of 1812, were seeking some convenient way by which they might withdraw their Orders in Council, while still "saving their face," and this bogus decree of April, 1811, furnished the excuse for such action.

Why, it may be asked, if the American government was to be given this official repeal in May, was no mention of the matter made in Bassano's report of March. From the letter written to Serrurier we may find the answer. Napoleon had not yet openly declared war on Russia. He therefore wished to keep his European allies strictly in line for the maintenance of his system, and any exception in favor of one neutral would encourage laxness of enforcement on the part of France's unwilling allies. Therefore "no exceptions" was the language of the Senatus Consultum.

But why give in to the United States now, if not earlier? Henry Adams has doubtless furnished the correct answer. "Bold and often rash, a diplomatist as Napoleon was, he still felt that at the moment of going to war with Russia, he could not entirely disregard the wishes of the United States. In appearance he gave way, and sacrificed the system so long and so tenaciously defended."[11]

This decree cynically disregarded the letter of Cadore, and the letters of the Grand Judge Massa to the President of the Council of Prizes and of the Minister of Finance to the Director General of Customs. According to this document the American government had been mistaken in taking Cadore's letter at its

---

[11] H. Adams, *Hist. of United States*, Vol. VI, pp. 257-258.

face value. The decrees had not really been repealed until six months later than November of 1810, and then as a result of the action of the American Congress in cutting off trade with England. This changed the whole situation. The British ministry had been right, and Madison had been wrong.

Deeply chagrined at the outcome, Madison wrote to Barlow that the action of the French government would be an everlasting reproach to it.[12] As Napoleon's government had so many everlasting reproaches upon its head, one more or less would trouble its authors very little. The President rightly surmised that the repeal would furnish Great Britain with a pretext for the withdrawal of her orders, but by the time the news of this reached America, the government of the United States had already declared war and was not disposed to retrace its steps.

Petitions for Repeal of the Orders in Council

While Foster in Washington was keeping up an uncompromising front to the very outbreak of hostilities, the government which he represented was steadily being compelled, by pressure from the United States, to reverse its decision.

It is true that for months after the departure of Pinkney, the outlook continued to be unpromising. In May of 1811, the judgment in the case of the *Fox* was handed down by Sir William Scott. This case involved all the captures made by the British cruisers since the previous November. The judgment was averse to the American position.

The *Fox* was an American vessel which had been seized on November 15, 1810, on a voyage from Boston to Cherbourg. The captors contended that under the Orders in Council of April 26, 1809, the ship and cargo were seizable, because destined to a port of France. The claimants, on the contrary averred that the Orders were extinct, because founded on measures which the French had retracted. According to the judgment of Sir William Scott, no retraction had been issued by the king, for there had been no public declaration of the repeal of the enemy decrees.

---

[12] Madison, *Writings*, 8, p. 208.

By this decision the seizure of the *Fox* and of twenty-five other vessels was upheld. Of these twenty-two had started from American ports, laden for the most part with fish, cotton, rice, tobacco, and colonial goods. In addition two American vessels had been seized, coming from Bordeaux, and two from Bayonne, laden with brandy and wine, and silk and other dry goods.[13]

"In adhering to these measures," wrote Smith, "which bear so hard upon us, the ministry has not only the support of the country, but also of that part of the mercantile interest, which is jealous of the commerce of the United States, and of the Navy, whose object must always be an increase to the number of prizes. I might perhaps safely add that calculations were also made on our forbearance, our divisions and our inability of active resistance."[14]

The closing of the American markets by the Non-Intercourse Act, however, was beginning to have disastrous effects in England. The whirring of the wheels in the factory districts was checked, and the labors of the craftsmen were interrupted. The merchants saw with dismay their best customers cut off.

Beginning with the spring of 1811, there began to appear in Parliament those revealing petitions from the factory operatives which give such a vivid picture of the misery caused by the closing of the American markets.[15] As unemployment increased, wages fell, but the price of provisions remained cruelly high.

The petitions all urged the revocation of the Orders in Council, in order to pave the way for the removal of the non-intercourse and non-importation acts lately passed by the Congress of the United States.

Samuel F. B. Morse, who was in England at this time, wrote to his parents in August of 1811: "I find I have arrived in England at a very critical state of affairs. If such a state continues much longer, England must fall. American measure affect this country more than you can have any idea of."[16]

---

[13] A. S. P., For. III, pp. 417–421. See also E. S. Roscoe, *Report of Prizes determined by High Court of Admiralty before Lord Commissioners of Appeals in Prize Cases*, II, p. 63.
[14] Smith to Monroe, Oct. 17, 1811, Desp. Eng. 17.
[15] Hansard, 20, pp. 342–43.
[16] S. F. B. Morse: *Letters and Journals*, Vol. I, p. 39.

The impulse toward the repeal of the Orders in Council was strengthened during the year of 1811, by the appearance of the pamphlet by Joseph Phillimore, entitled *Reflections on the Nature and Extent of the License Trade*. Phillimore was regius professor of Civil law at Oxford and was one of the greatest legal authorities in England. He argued for a repeal of the Orders. The license system by which Dutch and Danish and Hanseatic vessels carried British goods to the continent, was denounced because of its contravention of the navigation acts, and its tendency to promote dishonesty and deceit. Not only did the system strengthen England's enemies on the sea, but it was unjust to the United States, Phillimore pointed out.

As to the practical effect of the orders, Phillimore was in substantial agreement with the petitioners. "There is no one," he wrote, "in the slightest degree conversant with the actual state of mercantile affairs in this country, who is not aware that a renewal of the political relations between the two countries. . . . (Great Britain and the United States) would tend more to revive the drooping spirit of our manufacturers, would afford greater relief to the accumulated distresses of the mercantile part of the community, and would more effectually promote the valuable interests of Great Britain, than any other public measure which could possibly be adopted.[17]

The greatest opponent of the orders in the House was the brilliant lawyer, Henry Brougham. He declared that there were many who had not entirely disapproved of the system at its inception, who were now surprised at its unexpected results.[18] He, however, had opposed the new system from the beginning. He now stood forth as the champion of repeal, and it was largely owing to his exertions that the system was finally abandoned.

The government could not be insensible to the strain to which the nation was being subjected. The manufacturers had great orders from America, which they could not execute, and great stocks which they could not export, on account of the obstruction of the orders.

---

[17] J. Phillimore, *Reflections on the Nature and Extent of the License Trade*, Preface, p. 10.
[18] Hansard, 21, p. 1162.

From the port of Liverpool alone, during the year 1807, just prior to issue of the Orders of November, 480 American vessels had cleared out, laden almost entirely with British manufactures. In the six months of 1809, when the orders were thought to be suspended by Erskine's agreement, the number had been 336. Now this trade was at a standstill, and the shipwrights, rope makers, carpenters, porters, carters and laborers were reported to be "in a state of unexampled sufferings and distress." One-sixth of the population were in need of assistance.[19]

The Federalist newspapers in the United States maintained that the Non-Intercourse Law caused no inconvenience in England. Morse wrote from London (April 21, 1912) to his friends in America to disabuse their minds of this error. "You may be assured the effects are great and severe. I am myself an eye witness of the effects. The country is in a state of rebellion from literal starvation. Accounts are daily received which grow more and more alarming from the great manufacturing towns. Troops are in motion all over the country, and but last week measures were adopted by Parliament to prevent this metropolis from rising to rebellion, by ordering troops to be stationed round the city, to be ready at a moment's warning."[20]

Such was the state of affairs when the country was shaken by the news of the assassination of Percival. With the passing of the Prime Minister, the backbone of the support of the orders was broken.

Repeal of the Orders in Council

On June 16th, Brougham brought in the report of the committee for the investigation of the effect of the orders. Over a hundred witnesses from more than thirty manufacturing and commercial districts had been examined. The distress reported from all these centers was heartrending. Brougham warned the government that the refusal of the petitions would let loose upon the country thousands of desperate and hungry men, who must either find food or perish. The masters had exhausted

---

[19] Hansard 22, pp. 1058–1062.
[20] Morse, *Letters and Journals*, Vol. I, p. 70.

their money and credit in trying to keep their workmen employed. Furniture and clothing had been pawned by the operatives, until the pawn brokers would take no more. The landlord visiting the cottages to collect his rents, found the dwellings altered and stripped, the workers sitting down to a scanty meal of oatmeal and water, their only food in twenty-four hours. Such in the spring of 1812 was the plight of those whom the amiable gentlemen in Parliament habitually referred to as "the lower orders of the people." Yet it was to these workingmen, as Brougham reminded his hearers, that the nation owed its greatness. From a stubborn determination to maintain its so-called maritime rights, the nation was sacrificing the American market, a branch of trade in comparison with which, as Brougham pointed out, every other sunk into insignificance when one considered its extent, its certainty of payment, and its progressive increase.[21]

Finally on June 23rd, the government yielded, the edict of repeal was issued. The text of the document stated that since the American chargé had transmitted to the British Foreign Minister what purported to be a decree of the French government of April 18, 1811, repealing the decrees, the orders would be revoked as regards America, from the following August 1st. The orders thus withdrawn were those of November, 1807, and April, 1809.

With this action of the government an immense feeling of relief seemed to take possession of the leaders on both sides of the debate. All parties agreed that America would accept the revocation with alacrity, and all outstanding difficulties with that country would soon be solved.[22] In the manufacturing and commercial centers, all was bustle and activity, to hasten to fill the conditional orders, and to ship off the surplus stocks.

The news which arrived from America a few weeks later put a sobering check upon this general elation. Foster's mission had ended in failure, and Congress had declared war.

---

[21] Hansard 23, pp. 716–718.
[22] *Ibid.*

VIII

American Commerce, 1811–12—Trade to Russia—Trade to Spain—Trade to the West Indies—Meeting of 12th Congress—The Merchants and the War—Conclusion.

AMERICAN COMMERCE, 1811–1812

Trade to Russia

The Americans, during the summer of 1810 were, as we have seen, successively shut out of those countries bordering on the north and the Baltic Sea, which were under Napoleon's direct influence, they gradually converged upon the ports of Russia. Thus the ship *Hudson*, of New York, was ordered to go to any port in Europe not blockaded, with liberty to go to Gottenburg and wait for orders. The ship finally deposited her cargo at Riga, where she loaded a cargo of hemp, and returned home, October, 1810.[1]

American business ventures to Russia had, prior to the year 1808, not been very considerable in amount. But more than 150 American vessels entered Russian ports during the season of 1810. Sixteen spent the winter at Cronstadt, and several at Archangel.[2]

The Czar Alexander I had by letters to Madison, and in other ways, manifested a partiality for the United States and expressed the feeling that an American mission to Russia would be welcome. The chief reason for this was the cutting off of commercial relations between England and Russia, required by the Treaty of Tilsit. As Romanzoff, the Czar's Minister of Foreign Affairs, explained to Armstrong, "in dissolving our commercial connections with Great Britain, it became necessary to seek some other power in whom we might find a substitute; and on looking around, I could see none but the United States who

---

[1] Saltus vs. Comm'l. Ins. Co., *New York Supreme Court Records*, Johnson 10.
[2] J. Q. Adams, *Writings*, III, p. 325.

were at all competent to this object."[3] The Czar also was known to cherish liberal principles and policy with respect to the rights of the sea. As the policy of England in 1808 had continued unfavorable to American commerce Madison had wished to attempt to reach a common understanding with the great continental allies, France and Russia. The failure to reach any real understanding with France we have already seen. With Russia, however, there was a different story.

John Quincy Adams, the man chosen for the Russian mission, had by his support of the embargo rendered himself highly objectionable to the New England Federalists and by the same token, had recommended himself to the Republican administration.

Adams arrived, as American minister to Russia, in November, 1809. He was received with cordiality by the Emperor and Count Romanzoff, both of whom expressed the greatest friendliness toward the republic of the west. This was owing partly to the enlightened and progressive views of Alexander, and partly as explained, to the need felt by the Czar's government for replacing British commercial connections, with those of America.

Adams was able to secure the help of the Czar in securing the liberation of the American property still detained by the Danish government in Holstein. Since Russian products to a large amount had been ordered as return cargoes for these vessels, Adams argued that Russian business interests had considerable stake in the outcome.[4]

The sale of American cargoes in Russia had up to this time been handled by a small group of merchants who did a commission business and who were closely associated. Their tendency when American goods arrived was to depress the prices to be paid for the incoming goods and to raise the prices of the Russian commodities to be taken in exchange.[5] As the commerce be-

---

[3] *A. S. P.*, For, III. p. 299.
[4] J. Q. Adams, *Writings*, III, p. 381.
[5] J. Q. Adams, *Writings*, IV, p. 137. This account by Adams does not agree with the statement of Morison, *Maritime Hist. of Massachusetts*. From a study of some of the actual voyages, apparently Morison declares (p. 194) "Profits in this Russian trade were immense. The ship *Catherine* of Boston 281 tons, worth possibly $7,000, cleared $115,000 net in one voyage in 1809."

tween the two countries increased, responsible Americans came out, in some cases, to handle the business with the result that the trade became more profitable.[6]

Russia, as the ally of France, being at this time at war with England, the admission of English vessels, or those coming from English ports was strictly prohibited. The problem of Adams was, therefore, similar to that of Forbes in Holstein. Many bona fide American vessels were detained on the supposition of being English. At the same time some vessels arrived with false American papers, procured in London. For the real Americans Adams exerted himself to procure admission without delay. This was especially necessary for those arriving at Archangel. Many Americans, to avoid the Danish privateers which seized American vessels at the entrance to the Baltic, made the long voyage to this distant port on the White Sea, whence their imports were carried a thousand miles overland to Moscow. The port was open but four months of the year, and delay in admission would require the ships to remain over winter, and thus lose the profits of the voyage. Boards of inquiry known as Commissions of Neutrality had been appointed in the various Russian ports, to investigate the nationality of the incoming vessels.[7] There being no American consul at Archangel, inquiries had to be made from that distant port, to Adams and Harris, the consul general at St. Petersburg. This entailed great delay. Certain business interests concerned in the English trade attempted in various ways to prevent the entrance of the Americans, but the government, both in theory and practice, favored their admission. By applications to both Romanzoff and Campenhausen, Minister of Finance, Adams was successful in having all these cases favorably settled.

---

[6] Some of these Yankee shipmasters met with novel experiences when they spent their first winters in Russia. "Wintering in Riga", writes Morison, "in 1810–1811, they took part in the open handed social life of the Balt nobility; skating carnivals, sleigh rides at breakneck speed over the flat country, montagnes russes, brilliant balls and Gargantuan dinners." Those who were obliged to spend the winter at Archangel, found that experience rather exhausting, as the Russian merchants, after hibernating, expected their American customers to stay up and drink with them through the bright summer nights." Morison, Maritime History of Massachusetts, pp. 193–194.
[7] J. Q. Adams, *Writings*, III, p. 489.

Another matter which needed attention was the admission of American vessels from Portugal. The Russian government had recently placed a ban on vessels arriving from this country, now the ally of England. A number of American vessels, having left Lisbon and Oporto before this regulation was known, were seeking admission to Russian ports. For these cases also, Adams was able to secure favorable consideration.

While the Russian government admitted every American vessel recognized as such by the American minister or consul, there had been for a time, a check to the admission of these vessels, by the English, to the Baltic. In the summer of 1810, the British fleet held a strong position in the Baltic. There were twenty ships of the line, besides frigates and smaller vessels stationed at various passages giving entrance to that sea. Admiral Saumarez himself was before Gothenburg. He declared, as we have seen, that no vessel would be allowed to pass on to any port from which British vessels were excluded, unless it carried a British license. When three American captains sought an interview with Saumerez, as to how he would regard American vessels, he replied that he did not know that he should send out boats to bring in vessels coming directly from America but that he considered even them included in his orders.[8] As soon, however, as Saumerez learned of the repeal of the non-intercourse, he allowed American vessels to come and go freely in the Baltic.[9]

The efforts of Napoleon to exclude English commerce, under which he included that of America, from all northern Europe would after all prove ineffectual, if this trade was to be admitted to Russia. The crucial test came in the fall of 1810, when a great convoy of six hundred vessels, which had collected at Gottenburg under the protection of Saumerez' fleet, threatened to dump its cargoes upon the Russian shores. This possibility gave great concern to Napoleon, who held that whatever papers these vessels carried, they were really all English. He exhorted Alexander to disregard the complaints of the merchants, and to

---

[8] B. G. Baisely to Armstrong, June 4, 1810, Desp. Fr.
[9] J. Q. Adams, *Writings*, III, p. 501.

keep his ports closed to these ships. The Czar promised to do so.

As a matter of fact, however, the American vessels already admitted had been, for a time at least, a part of the Gottenburg convoy. Alexander did not propose to shut out the Americans. The terms of his agreement with Napoleon made no such stipulation.[10] The admission of the Americans would provide an outlet for the country's exports. Adams understood the situation. "The Russian system of exportation," he wrote, "is an object of such importance not only to the nation, but to the crown and to the nobility who compose the imperial councils and command in the armies that they can never consent to sacrifice it, nor would the sovereign himself, perhaps, be secure upon his throne, should he arrest entirely the circulation which feeds the source of his own revenue, and of the private fortunes of all the principal nobility."[11]

Caulaincourt, the French Ambassador, attempted to throw suspicion on the American cargoes, by questioning the origin of their colonial goods, especially sugar. It must, he claimed, be of English growth. Adams pointed out that sugar was produced within the limits of the United States, and that the Spanish and French West Indies were open to Americans.[12] The French Ambassador also raised the question of the certificates of origin. The *Moniteur* of July 10, 1810, had declared that all clearances and certificates of origin, purporting to be American, were false, for such documents were no longer granted by French consuls, according to His Majesty's order.[13] It was not until August 31, 1810, that Cadore's order forbidding French consuls to furnish certificates of origin (except to vessels bound to French ports), was sent out.[14] There was therefore no time for the vessels which left America in the summer of 1810, to have been affected by this order, and the assumption of the falsity of such papers carried by American vessels in the fall and winter of the same year was grossly unfair.

---

[10] Ibid III p. 552.
[11] J. Q. Adams, *Writings*, IV, p. 251.
[12] *Ibid.*, p. 10.
[13] See also Moniteur, Nov. 12, 1810.
[14] J. Q. Adams, *Writings*, IV, p. 49. Also *A. S. P.*, For. III, p. 400, letter of Turreau to Secy. of State.

The feeling in Russia toward her troublesome ally was beginning to cool, toward the close of 1810. Alexander, and, to a less extent Romanzoff, were therefore not especially concerned to please the French in commercial matters, and American vessels continued to be admitted freely. Those which came from ports where there was a Russian consul were expected to bring certificates from him, but this rule was set aside in the case of the Americans, by the express command of the Emperor.[15]

The tension between the French Emperor and his Russian ally was owing to the causes already given, and in addition to the French occupation of the Baltic, from Hanover to Courland, and to the new Russian tariff, which tended to exclude French luxuries. One of the objects of the tariff, Alexander wrote to Napoleon, was "to accord a certain facility to American commerce, as the sole commerce by sea which Russia is able to make use of to export her products, too extensive to be exported by land."[16]

When the shipping season of 1811 opened, American vessels started for the ports of northern Europe in Holstein, Prussia or Sweden to which they had formerly been admitted. This was because the shippers hoped either that the orders for the exclusion of Americans would not be strictly enforced, or that the ban might be lifted before the vessels arrived. These vessels nearly all found their way in the end to Russian ports. Adams expected his countrymen "in swarms" and he was not disappointed. By June 25th, forty American vessels had arrived at Cronstadt,[17] and a proportionate number at Riga and Archangel. Between June 21st, and July 21st, the number of American vessels, reaching Cronstadt was fifty,[18] and the total number for the year 1811 at that port was one hundred and thirty-nine.[19]

The cargoes of these vessels consisted altogether of five or six articles of colonial merchandise—sugar, coffee, cotton,

---

[15] J. Q. Adams, *Writings*, IV, p. 13.
[16] Tatischeff, S., Alexander Ier et Napoleon d'apres leur Correspondence inedité, p. 549.
[17] J. Q. Adams, *Writings*, IV, pp. 117 137.
[18] *Ibid.*, p. 142.
[19] *Ibid.*, p. 269.

indigo, and dye woods.[20] A typical cargo was that of the *Alfred* from Portsmouth, N. H., laden with 100 bales of Louisiana cotton, and 25 tons of logwood, destined "for one or more points of Europe north and east of the Elbe." The cargo was insured for $11,000, at a premium of 20 per cent. The goods finally reached St. Petersburg, and were sold there, although for low prices.[21]

The Russian ports were soon overstocked with these colonial goods. "Hitherto," wrote Adams, in June 25, 1811, "the American trade to this country has been an advantageous one to those of our merchants who have adventured in it. But this year they have already so completely glutted the market here, and are continually pouring in such profuse additional supplies, that most of them will find it altogether unprofitable, if not ruinous speculation. Indeed there are numbers of those daily arriving, which were not destined for this country, but which have been compelled to come as the only place where they could obtain admission. They continue to be received with every encouragement on the part of the government, and with a degree of favor enjoyed by no other nation."[22]

The arrival of the many Americans in Russian ports at this time was facilitated by conditions in the Baltic, which were more favorable than during the two preceding years. The depredations of the Danes had almost entirely ceased, and the English allowed unopposed passage through the Sound.[23]

The trade was so manifestly to the interest of the Russians, and the disposition of the government so friendly to the Ameri-

---

[20] In regard to the Baltic trade of the year 1811, it was estimated that the number of American vessels paying duty at Elsineur, Jan. 1–Dec. 1, was 102. Of the products of the United States carried; the largest item was cotton, then followed cotton twist, rice, tobacco, cheese, rum, beef, pork, bread and flour, to the value of $958,974.17. Of foreign goods, the largest item, was sugar, followed by coffee, indigo, dye woods, spices, cocoa, nankeens, hides, tea, etc., to the value of $2,173,517.10. Besides this there were about 80 cargoes that went through the Belts, either under British convoy or singly paying Sound Dues at Aayeborg. The lowest value of American produce that went through Baltic markets in 1811, was estimated at $5,000,000. Niles Register, May 23, 1812.
[21] Haven vs. Gray, *Mass. Reports*, 12.
[22] J. Q. Adams, *Writings*, Vol. IV, p. 117.
[23] *Ibid.*, p. 149.

cans, that the struggle of the French influence to exclude them gradually ceased.

Some of the Americans came in ballast. They were really from England, where they had been chartered at very high freight rates to carry back cargoes of hemp, which was then in great demand in England, for the use of the navy and the merchant marine.[24] These vessels had come through the Belts under British convoy. Two of them, the *Angerona* and the *Philadelphia Packet*, carried forged papers. They were detected by Harris, the consul at St. Petersburg and incurred the penalty for that offense.[25] The Russian government, however, did not concern itself about the nationality of these vessels. Gurieff, Minister of Finance, expressly told Adams, that if a vessel came empty, he did not care whence it came. The American minister naturally did not feel himself obliged to be more scrupulous than the Russian government. As these ships would be under British convoy, both going and coming, they would be in no danger of capture by French or Danish privateers. Adams therefore troubled himself no more about them. To check the abuse of false papers, Adams urged, however, further legislation against the sale of real American ships papers, with the ship or separately, in foreign ports.[26]

The fear of Adams that the Russian markets would be glutted with the colonial goods brought by the Americans, proved to be groundless. In the fall of the year 1811 an outlet for these goods was found toward the west. Some found their way into Prussian territory. They reached Vienna through Brody in Galicia, a little town in Austrian territory, near the Russian border. This town became the entrepôt for goods which entered the Black Sea, as well as from the Baltic. From here these goods were carried into Bavaria, South Germany and Switzerland and even smuggled into France.[27] It was probably to pay for goods thus imported into Germany that an effort was made

---

[24] J. Q. Adams, *Writings*, IV, p. 185.
[25] *Ibid.*, pp. 185–186.
[26] J. Q. Adams to Monroe, *Ibid.*, IV, p. 235.
[27] Heckscher, *Continental System*, pp. 232–233, J. Q. Adams, *Writings*, IV, p. 282.

to have Silesian linens admitted to Russia for re-export to America. The attempt, however, was unsuccessful.[28]

When the trading season of 1812 opened, the number of American vessels seeking ports in the north of Europe was smaller than for the preceding years. J. Pitcairn, acting consul at Hamburg, wrote that by the end of April several Americans had arrived in the first Cattegat ports, but did not venture up, until they heard from Mr. Barlow, or until the privateers were shut up in port from some other cause.[29] By the end of May only four Americans had passed by Gottenburg on their way up the Baltic,—"a puny representation of our former trade," wrote Pitcairn, "but in the present time a proof of the judgment and prudence of the traders. On the one hand lay delays, expenses, bad or already supplied markets, and often condemnations, on the other, remaining at home which I am persuaded, will, to the whole mass of the nation merchants and underwriters leave at the end of the year more profit than by voyages so unfavorably circumstanced."[30]

The plight of the American vessels overtaken by the war of 1812 in northern European waters is well illustrated by Girard's ship, the *Helvetius*. This vessel was dispatched for St. Petersburg, March, 1812, with a cargo costing over $80,000. The captain was directed to touch at Elsinore to pay Sound duties, and for orders. If that port was blockaded, Gothenburg was to be substituted. With his usual shrewdness, Girard directed the captain while at sea, to keep a sharp lookout, and to avoid as much as possible to meet or speak any vessel. The *Helvetius* carried several guns, not "for hostile purpose, but merely to protect the ship, crew and cargo." The vessel reached Cronstadt in safety, the cargo was quickly sold, and the return voyage begun, July 22nd, the captain intending to join the British convoy at Hano.

"On August 1," the captain wrote, "I got the captain of a New York Pilot boat on board the *Helvetius*, near Gotland, in the Baltic, who informed me that he was dispatched by the

---
[28] J. Q. Adams, *Memoirs*, II, p. 341.
[29] Pitcairn to Bourne, April 12, 1812, Taylor-Bourne Papers.
[30] *Ibid.*

house of Minturn and Champlin of that place on June 22nd, in ballast, with letters from several houses in New York, desiring their captains and supercargoes to put into the nearest and safest port, for America had declared war against England. In consequence I made up my mind to go to Carlscrona in Sweden, where I arrived safe with the *Helvetius* on August 3rd, in company with seven American vessels. The commander in chief there assured us he would protect our ships and cargoes while at Carlscrona, which is a good harbor and protected by two batteries and seven ships of the line."

Wishing to verify the information in regard to the war, the captain left his ship and proceeded to Copenhagen. There he read the declaration of war signed by the President. He conferred with Forbes and received the assurance that the King of Sweden would protect in his harbors those bona fide Americans who had paid their Sound dues, and had the receipts for them. Returning to Carlscrona, he hoped to hear of a reconciliation. Instead he learned on October 20th that the British government had issued letters of marque and reprisal against American vessels. "I hope to make myself contented," he wrote, "in this most miserable part of the world for this winter and the ship is now frozen up alongside of six American vessels that sailed from St. Petersburg in company, and got in here the same day with me, all of us have become housekeepers, and trying to make ourselves as comfortable as possible, at our owners expense."[31]

Trade to Spain

While trading with the British Isles was strictly prohibited after February 1, 1811, American shippers were doing a rushing business in selling cargoes of flour to the Commissary of the British armies in Spain and Portugal. This trade, as we have seen, had begun in 1809. The number of barrels of flour exported from the United States to Spain was more than three times as large in 1810 as in the previous year and in the following three

---

[31] McMaster, *Life of Girard*, Vol. II, pp. 209–211.

years, the increase was still greater.[32] On account of wet weather in the United States, the harvest of 1810 was not abundant. Prices were therefore high, and no surplus accumulated in the American markets. In December, 1810, $10 per bbl. was paid in Alexandria, Va.[33] and the price later rose. The price received in Lisbon and Oporto was extremely high,—$18, $19, even sometimes $20 per bbl.[34] The continuance of this good market, however, depended upon the success of Wellesley. Should the French armies occupy Lisbon and Cadiz, the market would immediately be lost to the Americans. The best business management favored leaving it to the captain, after he had reached the other side whether Lisbon, Oporto, or Cadiz would afford the best market for his cargo.

There was a competition among the shippers to buy up all the flour available in the American market. The New York firm of LeRoy, Bayard and McEwers sent one of their members quietly south to Georgetown and Richmond in February of 1811 to buy if possible 6000 bbl. at $8 per bbl. The price quoted at that time in Lisbon was $20.[35]

John Allan, writing from Lisbon on May 11, 1811, declared that no insurance was necessary on the vessels from America, at that time, as there was no fear of capture, and storms at the spring season were unusual. Twenty-seven vessels with flour had arrived at Lisbon the previous day. The market had therefore declined somewhat.[36] The flour was either sold to the British Commissary, or to the Spanish Government, or bought up by speculators who in vessels of light draft carried it to

---

[32] Pitkin, *Statistical View*, p. 150—Export of flour.
```
1809....................    40,047 bbl.
1810....................   144,436
1811....................   306,074
1812....................   381,726
1813....................   430,101
```
For a thorough discussion of the American Grain Trade to Spain and Portugal during this period, see W. F. Galpin, The American Grain Trade to the Spanish Peninsula, 1810–14, *Amer. Hist. Review*, Vol. 28, pp. 24–44.

[33] Letter of J. Noyes, Dec. 19, 1810, Lawarson and Fowle Letters.
[34] Letter from Cadiz, April 1812, Ellis and Allan Papers. F. and E. Motley, on Lisbon prices, Jan. 9, 1811, Lawarson and Fowle Letters.
[35] LeRoy to Bayard, Feb. 15, 1811, LeRoy, Bayard and McEwens, Papers.
[36] Letter from Lisbon, Ellis and Allan Papers.

whatever port along the coast the market was best.[37] With the arrivals of new British troops, the demand for flour became immense, as Allan wrote, but on account of the great quantity shipped, the price fell to $15.

The Philadelphia flour brought the best price.[38] That from Baltimore was almost as desirable. That from New Orleans did not carry well. But one cargo of this, even though sour on arrival, sold for a good sum. Another, even though infested with weevils and other insects was sold to the Spanish government for the use of the hapless soldiers departing for South America. The owner of this wretched stuff went strictly on the principle of caveat emptor, and furnished douceurs to the minor government officials, lest the flour should be rejected.[39]

We have the full details of one voyage, in the charter party of the ship *Orizimbo*, owned by David Estabrook of Baltimore. This fine vessel was chartered by Gilmore and Sons in March of 1811 to carry a full cargo of flour to Lisbon from that port, for the exclusive account of the British government. The master was instructed to procure information, before he entered the port, and if it was found in possession of the French, he was to take the flour to Cadiz, or Gibraltar and deliver it there. The shippers agreed to pay the owner 9s6d per bbl. for freight, with 5 per cent primage. Should the commander of the British blockading squadron think proper to order the ship to any other port such order should be received by the master of the ship in writing. If the port of discharge was to be England, an additional freight of half a Spanish dollar was to be paid. Thirty-five running days were to be allowed for waiting orders and discharging cargo. After that, the freighters were to pay 18s per day for any delay of the consignees. Each party to the transaction deposited a bond of $20,000 for the fulfillment of his obligations. The *Orizimbo* duly arrived at Lisbon in May, and delivered her cargo there, realizing 100 per cent profit for the freighters. This vessel made later trips of the same kind.[40]

---

[37] Letter of Allan from Oporto, *Ibid.*, May 12, 1811.
[38] Letter of John Allan, from Lisbon, May 24, 1811., *Ibid.*
[39] Letter of Taylor from Cadiz, Oct. 15, 1811, Taylor-Bourne Papers.
[40] Charter Party of the *Orizimbo*, March 15, 1811, and later letters, Taylor-Bourne Papers.

Yellow corn, corn meal, rye meal and flour were the principal articles for the Spanish market, but parcels of rice, white beans, salt pork and tobacco were sometimes sent. No other American articles found a sale there. The vessels returned in ballast, or brought back salt purchased at about 20c per bushel.[41]

By June of 1811, the flood of American flour to the Peninsular ports had depressed the price to $13,[42] and after the British Commissary had supplied his needs there remained 15,000 bbl. in the Lisbon market.[43] Nevertheless by October, the demand for flour in that port had again become brisk.[44] The total number of American vessels entering Lisbon from July 1st to December 31, 1811, was 284.

The trade continued up to and even after America's declaration of war. The need for the armies in Spain was so great that after July, 1812, the British authorities issued licenses protecting American vessels bearing flour to the Peninsula. The farmers and shippers professed to see nothing inconsistent in the trade so profitable to them. They argued that this commerce was with a neutral, not an enemy, but even if it was trading with the enemy, they declared in the spirit the old mercantilist theory, that it was enriching American citizens and draining Great Britain of her specie. Even Thomas Jefferson defended the trade on the latter ground! Not until May, 1813, was it possible, after repeated efforts to secure a majority for a bill in Congress forbidding American vessels to leave port with British licenses.[45]

Trade to the West Indies

During the whole of this period, trade from American ports to the West Indies continued active. One of the most extensive and lucrative lines of this commerce was that to Havana. In the early part of 1810, when the repeal of the non-intercourse and the substitution of other measures was pending in Congress,

---

[41] Letter of D. Esterbrook to Capt. Packard, April 22, 1811, *Ibid*.
[42] Josiah Allan to John Allan, June 17, 1811, Ellis and Allan Papers.
[43] Letter of W. Matlack, June 29, 1811, Ellis and Allan Papers.
[44] Letter of Brown, Reed, and Co. to Taylor, Oct. 6, 1811, Taylor Papers.
[45] House, *Journal*, July 16, 1813.

American merchants were not disposed to adventure largely in the Havana trade. They preferred to bring home the cargoes already owed, for the goods sent from the United States, and bide their time. "The times are restless," wrote Jumel to Desobrey, in trying to hurry home a shipment of coffee from Havana, "and the situation of the United States could before long become such that it would be very dangerous to have return here the property of which American merchants possess so much with you."[46] By May, however, this crisis was passed, and the word from Havana was reassuring. That port was open freely to commerce with both Great Britain and the United States, and on account of the preoccupation of the home government with the French invasion, not likely to be shut by orders from Spain.[47]

Any British island might theoretically be opened to American commerce for a period of six months, by a proclamation of the governor, whenever that official deemed it advisable to do so. But these islands were really open from the early part of 1810 to the close of 1811 by an Order in Council.[48] We find references among the merchants letters to voyages to Jamaica, Barbadoes, Trinidad, and the Windward and Leeward Islands.

The islands belonging to France and Holland had by 1810 all fallen into the hands of the British. These were also open to the Americans,[49] but they could not carry away the principal commodities, for example, molasses, sugar and coffee could be exported from Martinique only in British bottoms, and to British ports. Some American captains apparently attempted to violate this rule, and take sugar to American ports. Several of such vessels were seized at Tortola, and after that the British cruisers became more vigilant, so that the practice could not be continued.[50] In the fall of 1811 several American vessels

---

[46] Jumel and Desobrey, *Letter Book*, Feb. 1, 1810.
[47] Vincent Gray to Wm. Taylor, May 9, 1810, Taylor-Bourne Papers.
[48] Poulson, *Daily Advertiser*, April 18, 1810.
[49] The governor of Curaçoa issued a proclamation Dec. 6, 1811, allowing the importation "of dried or salted fish in American bottoms until July 12 next, and of all kinds of provisions" (except beef, pork and butter) until Dec. 31, 1812, *Ibid.*, Feb. 19, 1812.
[50] W. R. Swift to Elbers and Kraafts, St. Bartholomew, Dec. 10, 1811, Taylor-Bourne Papers.

were seized off La Guaira on the charge, it would appear, of illegal trading, but were later released by the order of the Admiral on the station.⁵¹

There was trading also to the Danish island of St. Thomas, the Swedish island of St. Bartholomew, and even to war torn Haiti. Here "King Henry" and Petion were carrying on a miserable struggle, each claiming to represent the authority of the French government, and each in control of a part of the island with separate custom houses and offices.⁵²

The most important commodity sold in the West India market was flour. It brought $18 per bbl. in May, 1810, at Havana, but this was not considered a good price on account of the heavy duties and other charges.⁵³ In the fall of that year the markets in the West Indies were reported as very good indeed. One letter advised captains to call first at Barbadoes, at which point the prices at the various islands might be learned. The captain might thus proceed to the most advantageous market. No certificates from either English or Spanish consuls were necessary at this time simply regular custom house clearances.⁵⁴ In January of 1811, the price of Kentucky flour in Havana was $17, while the finer grades brought $21.⁵⁵

The firm of Lewis and Lee of New Orleans, were among the merchants who engaged in this trade. They received large quantities of flour from the western country—as much as 2000 bbl. in a single day. In June of 1811 they sent a cargo of flour to the West Indies, evidently to any island in the English control, for the captain was instructed to dispose of his cargo, if possible, to the agents of the British Commissary General. Whether this was actually done, does not appear but the profits of this voyage amounted to six thousand dollars.⁵⁶

---

⁵¹ Jos. G. Arbuthnot to Wm. Taylor, Nov. 18, 1811, *Ibid.*
⁵² Sawyer vs. Maine Fire and Marine Ins. Co., *Mass. Supreme Court Reports*, 12.
⁵³ Letter to Wm. Taylor from Havana, May 21, 1810, Taylor-Bourne Papers.
⁵⁴ Daniel Higginbotham to Ellis and Allan, Oct. 27, 1810, Ellis and Allan Papers.
⁵⁵ Vincent Gray to Wm. Taylor, Jan. 8, 1811, Taylor-Bourne Papers.
⁵⁶ Lewis and Lee to Wm. Taylor, June 14, 1811. Same to Wm. Shute, June 21, *Ibid.*

In May of 1812, the price of flour was quoted at $22 per bbl. at Antigua, $26 at Grenada and St. Kitts, $30 at Trinidad and $31 at Montserret.[57] Just before the outbreak of the war, the highest price attained at any market of the period on either side of the Atlantic was reached at Trinidad, where those who were lucky enough to be on the spot might receive $35 per bbl.[58]

In the West India letters, occasional mention is made of the trade to the Spanish ports in Mexico. In May of 1810, William Taylor of Baltimore received this advance news from his correspondent in Havana: "The port of Campeachy is open for the admission of American vessels with corn free of duty, with liberty to export logwood from there, also free of duty. The quantity required by proclamation is 222,000 bbl., a quantity to raise the market in the United States as soon as the wants of those people are known."[59] In February of 1812, the royal assent was granted making "a free trade" to the port of Vera Cruz.[60]

Meeting of the Twelfth Congress

By the time of the meeting of the Twelfth Congress in November, 1811, the intentions of the British government had become more unmistakable. The course of the American government therefore became clearer. The possibility of armed resistance was imminent. We are here concerned not with the military and financial measures looking toward war, but with the part that commercial considerations played in the matter. The restrictive system of England was held by some as a justification for armed resistance, but in one of the discussions, Sheffey of Virginia raised the question as to the practical effect of the repeal of the Orders in Council. We furnished France, he pointed out with none of the great necessaries of life. Our principal trade was in the colonial products which by the Berlin decree and subsequent municipal regulations were totally excluded with the view to encourage their growth in French dominions,

---

[57] Wm. Shute to Wm. Taylor, May 16, 1812, *Ibid*.
[58] Same to same, June 7, 1812, *Ibid*.
[59] Letter to Wm. Taylor, May 21, 1810, *Ibid*.
[60] Letter to Wm. Taylor from Vera Cruz, Feb. 19, 1812, *Ibid*.

so that repeal of the Orders in Council would have very little practical effect.

Sheffey then reviewed the figures of the foreign commerce of the United States, for the year 1807, the year before the Orders in Council went into effect. In that year our exports to Great Britain and her dependencies in the four quarters of the globe amounted to twenty-eight million. To the French West Indies, the Isles of France and Bourbon, the Cape of Good Hope, and the Dutch possessions in Asia and Africa, our export of domestic products amounted to four millions. These places were now in the possession of Great Britain, so our trade was still permitted there, making a total of thirty-two million to Great Britain and her dependencies. At the same time the value of our foreign and domestic exports to France and Belgium amounted to but twelve million. Thirty-two million was almost two-thirds of the value of our whole foreign commerce. If we should open hostilities with Great Britain, we should abandon the great share of our foreign commerce, and actually contend for the less. If the Orders in Council were removed tomorrow our commerce to France would not be worth two millions. With true insight, Sheffey observed that the injuries to our commerce were not owing to the individual injustice of the rulers in either France or England, but to the general state of Europe. There could be no permanent security, until there should be a general peace.[61]

Clay, who spoke on December 30th, took the opposite view. If pecuniary considerations alone were to govern, he insisted, there was sufficient motive for war, for the Orders in Council were responsible for the fall in revenue from sixteen millions to six million. The real purpose British aggressions, Clay contended, was not to distress an enemy, but to destroy a rival. The sails of the American merchantmen, whitening every sea, and the growing body of American sailors—these filled old England with jealousy.[62]

The proposal of the Committee on Foreign Affairs for increasing the naval forces met with the same objections as did

---

[61] Annals 12, *Cong.* 1–1, pp. 619–635.
[62] *Ibid.*, pp. 596–602.

that for the increase of the land forces. It went against the old Republican grain to favor such policies.

The change in each case, was advocated by the new men in Congress, the young Republican element from the south and west. The opponents of the plans for an enlarged navy declared that it was impossible to protect our commerce anyway. To try to safeguard the carrying trade was foolish since that had largely been swept away since the French islands had been seized by Great Britain, and on the return of peace, France herself would not permit the trade. France, Spain and Holland combined in the Armed Neutrality could not protect their commerce against the large British fleets.[63]

Against all these objections, able arguments were offered by Clay, by Mitchill of New York and by Cheeves. The object of all government the latter reminded his hearers, was protection. Commerce being a legitimate and necessary activity of Americans it was entitled to be safeguarded by the national government. The desire to protect the interests of commerce had been a large factor in the formation of the union.[64]

On March 21st, Foster communicated the latest advices from his government. The Prince Regent would concede nothing. With no note of conciliation in its tone, the ministry declared itself unmoved by the hostile attitude of Congress.

The news from France was equally disheartening. On February 14th there had appeared in an American newspaper a list of American vessels captured by the French since November, 1810. Most of these had been seized during the year 1811. They included the *Washington* from Newburyport, and two other New England vessels carried by French privateers, into Copenhagen. The *Hesper* and the *James*, with combined cargoes valued at $200,000 had been condemned in July, 1811. The brig *Julian*, captured July 4, 1811, and taken into the port of Dantzig, had had her cargo of nankeens privately sold by the captors, before condemnation, and used to fit out the French garrison at that place with new nankeen trousers. The *Two Betsys*, Captain

---

[63] *Ibid.*, pp. 823–998 passim.
[64] *Annals 12, Cong.*, 1-1, pp. 803–816.

Hultz, had been burned on July 9, 1811. The schooner *Express*, bound for Philadelphia, on September 8th, was boarded by a French frigate, and robbed of 1500 specie, and of all her spare blocks, of tar, oil and paints, and beef and pork, and threatened with burning. The total number of vessels listed was seventeen, besides two others, but where the French vessels were obliged to desist, because English cruisers had appeared.[65] These vessels are in addition to the eight listed by Jonathan Russell in a note to Bassano of May 11, 1811.[66] If we add together the vessels of the two lists, the total is twenty-five. Of the seventeen vessels reported in February as captured, some had already been condemned, and there was little hope that any would be set free. Most of the captures were probably made upon the supposition that the American vessels were masked English merchantmen. It was not claimed that any were seized under the Berlin or Milan decrees, but that gave the Americans no comfort. All they knew was that France was continuing to harass their commerce. Whatever Napoleon had meant by his repeal of the decrees, his new policy was equally unfriendly to the Americans.

The following month, came the news of a series of fresh outrages perpetrated by the French. These incidents we have already noted, in the account of Barlow's mission.[67] It was the burning of four American vessels, by the French squadron which had set out from Nantes in January, 1812. It was therefore a debatable question, which antagonist had given greater cause for armed resistance.

The nearness of war was brought home to the hesitating legislators by the ominous message of the executive sent on April 1st. On that day Madison recommended as expedient under existing circumstances and prospects, that a general embargo be laid on all vessels then in port, or hereinafter arriving, for a period of 60 days. The mercantile groups viewed this step with disapproval. Quincy spoke for the shipping interests of Massachusetts, when he protested that of the total export for the previous year of forty-five million, seven-eighths had gone to

---

[65] Poulson, *Amer. Daily Advertiser*, Feb. 14, 1812.
[66] *A. S. P.*, For. III, p. 506.
[67] See ante chap., VII, pp. 238–239.

Great Britain, Spain and Portugal. It was questionable if under the existing circumstance, Great Britain would capture these vessels. If an embargo took place, and the goods remained at home, the loss of the owners of the property would be certain. If it went abroad the loss was only possible.[68] Clay, however, approved the proposal. Those who thought war could be avoided, he declared, were wilfully blinded. The embargo measure was finally passed by both houses, and signed by the President on April 4th.[69]

The scenes preceding the long embargo were now re-enacted. Every vessel at all fit for sea was hurried off. In New York fifty vessels loaded in one day. Men worked night and day. The price of produce and labor rose and freight rates went up 20 per cent. The cargoes thus hastily dispatched before the blow fell, were mostly flour from Spain and Portugal.[70]

Hardly had the embargo been adopted, when petitions for its repeal began to appear. While the farming and shipping interests opposed the Embargo, the commercial groups sought to secure the repeal, either partial or entire, of the non-importation law. The Boston merchants had presented a petition in November, 1811, asking for permission to import articles ordered before the issue of the President's proclamation of November, 1810.[71] The merchants of New York and Philadelphia also petitioned for suspension.[72] Early in 1812, the Secretary of War had proposed a suspension in order to allow the entrance of the supply of blankets used annually by the Indian Bureau.[73] On the 9th of April a bill was introduced into the House to suspend the law so far as to permit the entrance of such British products as had actually been contracted for prior to February 1, 1811. This repeal, it was claimed by Calhoun, would go far toward reconciling the mercantile class toward the government's war policy. Twenty to thirty million dollars worth of property would be withdrawn from the enemy,—the property of American

---

[68] *Annals 12, Cong.*, 1-2, pp. 1601-1605.
[69] *Ibid.*, 2266-67.
[70] *National Intelligencer*, April 9th and 14th, 1812.
[71] *Ibid.*, 1-1, p. 356.
[72] *Ibid.*, 1-2, p. 325.
[73] *Niles Register*, II, p. 7.

merchants which might otherwise be lost. Since British goods were entering the country anyway, honest men it was argued, should be allowed to handle the trade, rather than smugglers. The goods so admitted being liable to double duty,[74] would afford such a revenue as would obviate the necessity for direct or internal taxes.[75]

Those who opposed the repeal declared that by such a move we should abandon one of our most efficient weapons of annoyance to Great Britain. The articles which had been contracted for prior to February 1, 1811, it was declared to be impossible to ascertain. Another argument which carried not a little weight was that repeal would repress the exertions of American manufacturers, and check the prosperity of their rising establishments. Discussion of the matter continued until after the declaration of war. The vote on the matter, taken in the House on June 25th, actually resulted in a tie, but the measure was lost by the adverse vote of the Speaker.[76] Clay gleefully voted against it, as being incompatible with the state of war then existing. In France, as we know, the proposal for the repeal of non-intercourse furnished one more excuse for Napoleon to defer a favorable answer to Barlow.[77]

That the British government was sincere in its desire to come to terms with America was shown by the new proposal offered by Castlereagh, in April, that England should give up her system of licensed trade to the continent, and in its place should substitute a vigorous blockade.[78] But the American government refused to consider this as a satisfactory alternative to a repeal of the orders. The war party in Congress insisted that the honor of the country now demanded the final step.

On June 1st, therefore, the President sent to Congress a

---

[74] According to Gallatin's plan for new taxes, not yet enacted into law.
[75] *Annals 12, Cong.*, 1–2, 1536–38.
[76] *Annals 12, Cong.*, 1–2, p. 1546. Apparently however, the President granted special permission to merchants of standing, to send out vessels in ballast to bring home property from abroad. After May 5 Gallatin wrote to a Boston applicant that the President would grant no more such privileges. *Columbian Centinel,* June 3, 1812.
[77] Barlow to Monroe, *A. S. P.,* For. III, p. 519.
[78] Castlereagh to Foster, April 10, 1812, Papers, etc., 1813, p. 511, cited by Adams, *Hist. of U. S.,* VI, p. 221.

message calling, apparently, for an immediate declaration of war. In this communication Madison summed up the injuries of impressment, the hovering of British cruisers along the Atlantic coast, the "pretended blockades," and the Orders in Council. It had become certain, he declared, that Britain's grievance was not that we supplied her enemy with goods, but that we interfered with the profits which she coveted for her own commerce. The Fox blockade, which was assigned by the French as the cause of the Berlin decree, had not for a long time been maintained, by an adequate force, if indeed it had ever been so maintained. Yet the British government refused to withdraw it.

On June 3rd, the Committee on Foreign Affairs reported on the President's message. This report was the work of Monroe, Secretary of State. In summing up the grievances against England, Monroe, like Madison, stressed the blockade of May, 1806, from the Elbe to Brest. "Your committee think it just to remark," so ran the report, "that this act of the British Government does not appear to have been adopted in the sense in which it has since been construed. On consideration, the character of the distinguished statesman, who announced it, we are persuaded that it was conceived in a spirit of conciliation, and intended to lead to an accommodation of all differences between the United States and Great Britain.[79] His death disappointed that hope, and the act has since become subservient to other purposes. It has been made, by his successors, a pretext for that vast system of usurpation, which has so long oppressed and harassed our commerce."[80]

In regard to the Orders of November, 1807, the report observed that the exceptions made (permitting trade through British ports) were adopted not from a regard to neutral rights, but to promote the commerce of England. This order had virtually declared war on the United States. While the impressment of seamen continued, it was impossible to consider the United

---

[79] It will be remembered that Monroe had been our minister in London, when the blockade was first announced, and that he had at that time taken a similar view of the matter. See ante, p. 58.
[80] *Annals, 12 Cong.*, 1–2, pp. 1546–54.

States a free nation. The report concluded with the statement that the hostility of Great Britain had made it manifest that the United States were considered by it, as the commercial rival of Great Britain, and that their prosperity and growth were incompatible with her welfare. A contest for their sovereignty and independence was therefore forced upon the United States, and the committee, recommended an immediate appeal to arms. A bill declaring war against England was accordingly introduced by Calhoun, following this report.

The House had been discussing foreign affairs behind closed doors, on several occasions since April 1st. They had gone into secret session on the first of June to discuss the war message of the President. They did so, however, against the vigorous protest of those who opposed the war. This minority wished to postpone action, and secure full and free discussion of the momentous step. Failing in this, they gave up any further effort at discussion within the walls of Congress. The day following the presentation of the report from Calhoun's committee, June 4th, the vote on the declaration of war was taken in the House. Out of 128 votes cast, there were 79 in favor of the bill, but, 49 in opposition—a formidable minority.

Opposition having thus been smothered in the lower house, the Federalists looked to the Senate to check the madness of the young war Republicans. Such an attempt was indeed made, but the differences of opinion among those who opposed the war, prevented them from accomplishing anything. On the 17th of June, the declaration of war was passed by the Senate. On the following day, June 18th, the House concurred in the amendments and the bill was signed by the President.

Thus, practically without army or navy, without adequate defenses, or the imposition of new taxes, the country found itself at war with the greatest power in the world.

In spite of this, there was no public apprehension of danger. The war makers held the belief that Great Britain would attempt no invasion, that the eight million Americans had nothing to fear from the few hundred thousand in Canada, and that ships of war could not approach near the coast, except at the entrance of the great bays and rivers.[81]

One week after the declaration of war by the President and Congress, there appeared in the Federalist newspapers the protest of the minority of the House. The signers asserted that the difficulty of impressment could have been settled peaceably and that the British blockades of the northern coast of France in 1806 had never been a great cause of complaint from our government until May, 1810, when we had been prompted to such action by Napoleon.

Thus the Orders in Council alone were left as a casus belli. The writers of the address conceded that the British Orders and the French decrees were subversive of neutral rights, but since the belligerents justified them only on the ground of particular necessity, it appeared very unlikely that the United States by hostile operations could compel either party to abandon its position.

Since many lines of commerce could still be carried on, in spite of the restrictions, there seemed "as little wisdom as obligation to yield solid and concrete realities for unattainable pretensions."[82] So argued the Federalists in Congress against the War of 1812.

The Merchants and the War

The American commercial interests which, as we have seen, had begun by calling on their government for protection against foreign injuries in 1805, now found their pleas answered in a fashion little to their liking. They had expected of that government that which was impossible—to procure peaceful conditions by diplomatic protest. Every act of peaceful coercions attempted by the American government embargo, non-intercourse, and at last war, met with the disapproval of the merchants. Neutrality had been to them "a perpetual harvest." Their views were expressed in the protest of the minority in Congress which declared that "the field of commercial enterprise, after allowing

---

[81] *National Intelligencer*, April 14, 1812.
[82] *Annals, 12, Cong.*, 2, p. 1638.

to the decrees and orders their full practical effect, is still rich and extensive. . . . Notwithstanding the violence of the belligerents, were the restrictions of our own government removed, the commerce of the United States might be extensive and profitable."[83] There was still the valuable grain trade to the Peninsula, the newly opened commerce with Russia and Sweden, and if the non-importation were removed, the regular large volume of trade to Great Britain. As the Orders in Council were removed, the British merchants as we have seen, were preparing great cargoes for the American trade, in payment for which the Yankee shippers were preparing to send their accumulated stores of cotton, tobacco, grain and hemp.

"This war for commerce," declared Randolph, "is deprecated by all the commercial portion of our country, by New York and New England, the great holders of our navigation and capital."[84]

To a certain extent Randolph was right. A group of fifty-eight New York merchants and bankers and insurance men, when they found that war was imminent, petitioned for the continuation of embargo, and non-intercourse, as likely to produce all the benefits of war, and avoid its calamities. The distress of the British manufacturers would by that time compel their government to give in.[85] Similar petitions were presented in Congress from Philadelphia[86] and from Salem.[87] The petition from New Bedford[88] called for the removal of commercial restrictions as well as opposition to the war. From Baltimore,[89] Savannah, and Charleston, however, came addresses commending the government's action.

Bentley, of Salem, reports that the news of the probability of war was "vexatious to speculators of all parties." Concerning the past behavior of this group he observes, "The extent to which these men had evaded the law created an unfavorable view of

---

[83] *Niles Register*, Vol. 2–45.
[84] *Annals 12, Cong.*, 1–2, pp. 1461–62.
[85] *Ibid.*, 1–1, p. 254.
[86] *Ibid.*, Vol. 2, p. 1482.
[87] *Ibid.*, p. 1562.
[88] *Ibid.*, pp. 1483–1570.
[89] *Ibid.*, pp. 1479, 1487.

the mercantile character and proved how much gain predominated over the boasted patriotism of the speculators. When the actual declaration of war arrived, the merchants of both parties who had ships at sea were the most displeased and violent of all the people. These men," he added, "had been so accustomed to dictate to the constituted authorities that now they threatened the dissolution of the union."[90]

On the other hand, in the correspondence of the few business men preserved to us, naturally of the more conservative and reputable merchants, there is to be found no marked opposition to the war.

Among the petitions against the war, which poured in upon Congress during the month of June, were many from rural sections, especially from Vermont, New York and Pennsylvania.[91] In two instances protest appeared in the name of an entire state. The Massachusetts legislature forwarded to Congress a lengthy document condemning the war, and telling the national Congress where its duty lay. The legislature of the state of Rhode Island, instructed its senators and representatives to work for the removal of restrictions on commerce, against the imposition of direct taxes, and "all measures . . . tending to involve the country in war."[92]

A few addresses, however, commended the action of the government and promised support. The sections of the country most remote from the ocean, and the least connected with commerce were the most forward in urging war. In Kentucky, the whole male population clamored to serve in the army—for a period, however, strictly limited to six months.[93] "Except beyond the mountains," says Henry Adams, "the war party was everywhere a social minority."[94]

---

[90] Bentley, 4, pp. 100–102.
[91] *Annals 12, Cong.*, 1–2, pp. 1478–1570 passim.
[92] *Ibid.*, p. 1481.
[93] H. Adams, *Hist. of U. S.*, 6, p. 390.
[94] *Ibid.*, p. 409.

Conclusion

Thoughtful Americans looking back to the crisis of 1812, will probably agree that in the main the arguments of Pickering and Quincy and the New England Federalists were correct. The interests of the American democracy, lay rather on the side of England, the leader in civil liberty and constitutional government, than on that of Napoleon, the foe of free institutions. Yet at a time when England stood almost alone against the universal conqueror and tyrant our country ranged herself among the foes of the champion of liberty.

The explanation of this anomaly lies partly in the fact of the traditional friendship of the Republican party for France, and their distrust of England. Partly it lies in the fact that American leaders like Pickering and Cabot, who saw the European struggle in its true light, seemed entirely devoid of patriotism and loyalty to their own country. In their eagerness to see England's side they leaned backward. Partisan advantage rather than the welfare of their country, appeared to be their aim.

But the blame for failure to avoid war was by no means all on the American side. England's treatment of her daughter commonwealth aroused natural resentment. After Trafalgar, with the overwhelming preponderance of the British navy, and the offer of the American government to prevent the enrollment of Englishmen the determination to insist upon the right of search appears far fetched.

To statesmen of the school of "real politik," we had abundant justification for going to war with either of the belligerents from 1793 onward. The wonder is that after so many crises had been passed, at just the moment when Great Britain had yielded to us, and when the decline of the continental system was impending, we should have felt called upon to begin hostilities.

Modern historians, with no responsibility for their decisions, and writing long after the event, are inclined to censure our government for lack of spirit before the declaration of war. Jefferson's notes and protests have been held up in his day and ever since as the height of futility. His policy of trying to win over the belligerents, "by every act of friendship and innocent kindness" has been unfavorably contrasted with the determination to resent and resist manifested by the war hawks. But since 1914, these things look different to us. If civilization is ever to rid itself of the war system, it will have to be by just such a method—a statesman persuading a whole people rather to suffer wrong patiently, trusting to the opponent's sense of justice, to cure the wrong, rather than to bring on the greater evil of war.

In our drum and trumpet histories of the war of 1812, we hear much of the success of the Yankee seamen, and of the victories of Lawrence and Perry. The seizure of the national capital by the enemy, the poor showing of our officers and militia on the battle fields, and the enormous losses of our merchant marine, are glossed over.

In Great Britain, interest in the contest was completely overshadowed by the struggle on the continent. The long conflict against the disturber of the peace of Europe was hastening toward its victorious close. If Great Britain had put all her strength and energy into the war with America, the conflict would have been far more grim and bloody than it actually was.

The two and a half years of fruitless fighting, as we know, secured none of the objects for which the war was ostensibly fought. Suddenly the American people perceived the futility of the struggle and demanded peace.

As John Quincy Adams had declared in 1811, time was fighting on the side of the Americans. The Orders in Council were then bearing so hard upon the British people that they were bound in the end to defeat themselves. The growing strength of the United States would soon have secured the abrogation of impressments by our mere declaration.[95] So, too, the respect and consideration which our country gained as the result of her "second war of independence" would have been our portion in any case, as the result of our increase in wealth and population in the first half of the nineteenth century. The deeply rooted jealousy of our prosperity which Clay and his followers professed to see in England's actions toward us proved to be a figment of the imagination of the war hawks. After 1815, our trade with England grew to proportions which made the figures of the early nineteenth century seem small indeed.

---

[95] Adams, *Writings*, IV, p. 262.

BIBLIOGRAPHY

Manuscript Sources

In the Manuscripts Division, Library of Congress.
>Ellis and Allan Papers. Allan was an Ayrshire Scotsman and the foster father of Edgar Allan Poe. The collection comprises business correspondence and records, and some personal letters. 1795–1856. The firm did a general mercantile business in Richmond, Va., buying and exporting tobacco to England and importing and selling British goods. Sheds light on the indirect trade through Madeira and Spanish ports during the time when the American non-intercourse law was in force.
>
>Taylor-Bourne Papers, 1794–1834. Letters to and from Wm. Taylor of Baltimore who was engaged in extensive foreign and domestic commerce, during the period, largely through the firm of Sylvanus Bourne and Company of Amsterdam. Many letters to and from Bourne as Consul in Amsterdam are included. Good for trade to north of Europe 1807–1812.
>
>Collins Collection. The correspondence of Stephen and Zaccheus Collins, general merchants of Philadelphia covers the early part of the period, before the restrictions of the belligerents had become burdensome. Of slight value for the purpose of this study.
>
>The Madison Papers. One volume of these contains letters of John Armstrong, minister to France, 1804–1810.

In the Manuscript Division, New York Public Library.
>Jumel and Desobrey Letter Book, 1806–10. Stephen Jumel was a Frenchman by birth, a prosperous merchant of New York City, who married the widow of Aaron Burr. He carried on commerce with France, the West Indies and New Orleans. Some of the letters are in French, some in English. Those describing the method of procuring French goods through Spanish ports, during the non-intercourse period, are of especial interest.
>
>LeRoy, Bayard and McEwen Papers, 1751–1832. New York merchants engaged in commerce with England and France.
>
>Lawarson and Fowle Correspondence. Merchants of Alexandria interested in the grain and flour trade to Spain and Portugal, 1808–1812.
>
>Scoville Papers, Letters, accounts and prices current of Captain Noah Scoville, a merchant of Saybrook, Conn. and New York, 1794–1825.

In the Library of the Newport, R. I., Historical Society. Gibbs and Channing Papers. Four Letter Books of this firm, 1797–1811. General merchants of Newport, engaged in coastwise trade and foreign trade to East and West Indies, England and the north of Europe. The firm were large importers of Swedish iron.

The Champlin Papers. An extensive commercial correspondence involving several different firms, beginning early in the eighteenth century and through four decades of the nineteenth. For the period 1805–1812 the papers are concerned with the trade of Champlin and Robinson, shippers of Newport. The entire collection unfortunately has been divided and is now deposited in four different libraries. In Newport are to be found the *Letter Books* of the firm for the period. (See the two following entries.)

In the Library of the Rhode Island Historical Society, Providence, Champlin Papers, including correspondence, bills of lading, printed commercial forms, etc.

In Massachusetts Historical Society, Wetmore Collection, comprising additional Champlin correspondence; this collection is especially valuable as illustrating the carrying trade, 1796 to 1802.

In the Library of the Essex Institute, Salem, Mass.
Derby Family Mss. Commercial Papers, 1804–1815.

In the Library of the Historical Society of Pennsylvania.
Custom Records of Port of Philadelphia, comprising manifests of outward cargoes to foreign ports from 1789 onward, invoices of entering cargoes for the period and foreign port certificates for drawbacks from 1791 to 1800, which shed light on the carrying trade for those years.

In the Library of the University of Pennsylvania, a mass of customs records for Philadelphia, not yet catalogued. Among these is a Letter Book, 1808-1818, which contains letters from Albert Gallatin, concerning enforcement of embargo and non-intercourse.

In the State Department, Washington.
Consular Letters.—The most insignificant of these are the letters after the restrictive system of the belligerents had begun to function in 1806, to the breakdown of the continental system and the beginning of the war with England, 1812. The following were the correspondents from the more important European centers: John Forbes and Joseph Pitcairn, Hamburg; Sylvanus Bourne, Amsterdam. (See also the letters of Bourne in the Taylor-Bourne Collection, Mss. Division Library of Congress); Wichelhausen, Bremen; Lawson Alexander, Rotterdam; Wm. Lee, Bordeaux; Thomas Appleton, Leghorn.

In Record Office—London—High Court of Admiralty. Admiralty Court, Miscellanea, Bundles 465,473. Notes of cases appealed to court, 1803–1807, involving blockades and Rule of 1756.

Printed Sources.
States Papers and other Official Publications.
American State Papers.
Foreign Relations, Vols. I, II and III.
Commerce Vol. I contains annual reports of exports and imports 1790–1814; also petitions of merchants of cities chiefly against embargo and non-intercourse.
Finance Vol. I and II contains list of fines, penalties and forfeitures under embargo and non-intercourse laws.
Statutes at Large of the United States, Vol. I and II. Richard Peters, ed. Boston, 1845.
Diplomatic correspondence, 1783–1789, Washington, 1837 contains letters of Jefferson, Lafayette, 1837, Vergennes and others in regard to trade with France after 1783.
Annals of Congress, 1789–1824.
J. D. Richardson—Compilation of Messages and Papers of the Presidents, 1789-1897, Vol. I, House Miscellaneous Documents, 53 Cong. 1893-94, Vol. 37, Washington, 1896—Gov't. Printing Office.
Wm. M. Malloy—Treaties, Conventions, etc., between the United States and other powers. 61st Congress, 2nd Session Senate Document 357. Gov't. Printing Office, Washington, 1910. Treaties of United States in force 1873 (in Revised Statutes Relating to District of Columbia and Public Treaties, ed. 1889.
French Spoliation Claims, Report of Secy. of State—Papers on file in Dept. of State touching the unsettled claims of citizens of United States vs. France for spoliations prior to July 31, 1801, Washington, 1884 Gov't. Printing Office, 48th Congress, 1st Session, Senate Document 205.
De Martens, G. F., Recuiél des principaux traites d'alliance, de paix, etc., 1761–1808, 8 vols. Gottingen, 1791–1835.
Hansard, T. C., Parliamentary Debates, London, 1803–1815, good for discussion over Repeal of Orders in Council; contains petitions from manufacturing cities in favor of repeal.
Jourdan, Isambert, Decrusy eds. Recueil General des anciennes Lois Françaises, 420–1789. Paris, 1827; gives laws affecting American trade before 1789.
Duvergier, J. B. Collection Complet des Lois, Decrets, etc., 1788–1824, Paris, 1824.
Aulard, Recuéil des Actes du Comité de Salut Public, 1792–1795, 26 volumes, Paris, 1889–1913.
Archives Parlementaire, Paris, 1860. (Still incomplete) Series I (to 1794) gives debates in Assembly over commercial regulations with America.

Publications of Historical Societies.
> Historical Collections of Essex Institute, Vols. 1–61. Salem, 1859–1925 contains accounts of the early voyages from Salem to the northwestern coast of America and the far east. A rich quarry from which material for many secondary works has been hewn.
>
> Massachusetts Historical Society 7th Series, Vols. 10 and 11, Boston, 1915. Commerce of Rhode Island, 1726–1800, Worthington C. Ford ed. Vol. II, 1775-1800, is valuable for trade to England, France and Russia for the period.

Reports of Legal cases from British Courts.
> Robinson, Christopher, Decisions in High Court of Admiralty, 1798–1808, 8 Vols. London; Vol. 7, Edwards; Vol. 8, Dodson; gives judgment of Sir Wm. Scott, Judge of High Court of Admiralty on "the largest and most varied series of maritime cases that has ever occurred." Scott's decisions were later accepted by American courts as authoritative.
>
> Acton, T. H. Reports of cases argued and determined before the Lords Commissioners of Appeals in prize cases, also on appeal to the King's most excellent Majesty in Council, London, 1811.
>
> Great Britain, High Court of Admiralty, Prize Causes, 1803–1811, 3 vols. Vols. 1 and 2 Philadelphia Ships, Vol. 3, New York Ships, London, 1803–1811. Printed copies of documents pertaining to each case submitted to the Lords Commissioners of Appeal in Causes—ships' registers, depositions, letters, briefs of council, examinations in preparatory, etc. New York Library.
>
> Gaskoin, C. B. J., Prize Case Notes in the days of Stowell, Br. Year Book of International Law, Vol. 21, 1923, pp. 78–89. Account of fifteen bundles of miscellaneous documents of the High Court of Admiralty in the Record Office in London, entitled, Notes of Cases circa, 1790–1803, gives quotations from the notes.

Reports from American Courts.
> Cranch, Wm. Reports of cases argued and adjudged in Supreme Court of United States, 9 Vols. Washington, 1817, notes on cases involving embargo and non-intercourse laws.
>
> Peters, Richard, Admiralty Decisions in District Court of United States for Pennsylvania District, 2 Vols. Philadelphia, 1807.
>
> Brockenbrough, J. W. report of cases decided by Hon. John Marshall in Circuit Court of United States for district of Virginia and North Carolina, 1802–1833, 2 Vols. Phila., 1837.
>
> Report of cases adjudged in Supreme Court of Pennsylvania, Yates, Jasper, 1791-1808, 4 Vols. Philadelphia, 1889. Binney, Horace, 1791–1814, Philadelphia, 1809–16. Rawle and Sergeant, Philadelphia, 1844.

These three series include many volumes; they report cases affecting questions of insurance, barratry, salvage and rescue, but they shed much light on conditions of American commerce, 1793–1814. (The same comment applies to the two series following.)
Report of cases argued and determined in Supreme judicial court of Massachusetts. Williams, E.—Boston, 1866. Tying, D. H.—Boston, 1845.
Report of cases submitted to Supreme Court of New York. Johnson, Wm. Albany, 1808.
Scott, James Brown—The Controversy over Neutral Rights between United States and France, 1797–1800. Carnegie Endowment for International Peace, New York, 1917. A collection of American State papers on the subject and a number of decisions from Supreme Court of United States and Court of Claims connected therewith.

Correspondence and Related Documents.

Adams, C. F., ed. *Memoirs of John Quincy Adams*, comprising portions of his diary, 12 Vols., Phila., 1874–1877; supplements the writings of Adams.

Adams, Henry, ed. *Writings of Albert Gallatin*, Philadelphia, 1879. Documents relating to New England Federalism, Boston, 1877, contains J. Q. Adams' Reply to Appeal of Massachusetts Federalists, 1829, giving an account of the separatist movement of the New England Federalists in 1804 and 1808–15. Appendix contains correspondence of Pickering and Rose.

Anderson, D. R. *Wm. Branch Giles, a Study in Politics of Virginia and the Nation*, 1790-1830. Menasha, Wis., 1914. Giles was a supporter of Jefferson, and made a vigorous speech in Congress December, 1808, against the repeal of the embargo.

Austin, J. T. *Life of Elbridge Gerry, with Contemporary Letters*, Boston, 1928; contains extracts from Pickering's Review, criticising Gerry's conduct as member of Mission to France, 1797–98; justifies Gerry's course.

Bentley, Wm. *Diary*, 1784–1819, Published by Essex Institute, 1911, Vols. 3 and 4 cover period. Bentley was pastor of the East Church in Salem; he was sympathetic to Jefferson and the embargo.

Beveridge, Albert J. *Life of John Marshall, Boston*, 1916, gives full detail of Marshall's mission to France in 1797–98. Emphasizes the leadership of Marshall in the mission.

Bond, *Letters of Phineas Bond;* letters to the British Foreign Office, 1787-89. Report of Amer. Hist. Assn., 1896, Vol. I. Bond was consul general for Great Britain in America, 1787–1812.

Bruce, W. C. *John Randolph of Roanoke*, New York, 1922. Randolph was the brilliant opponent of non-intercourse, and the War of 1812. Bruce fails to explain his inconsistencies and contradictions as due to pathologcal conditions, according to the newer knowledge of disease.

Donnan, Elizabeth, ed. *Papers of James A. Bayard, 1796-1815*. American Hist. Assn. Report 1913, Washington, 1915. Bayard was senator from Delaware.

Dodd, Wm. E., *Life of Nathaniel Macon, Raleigh*, 1903, contains a few letters. Macon, a southern agriculturist of the Jeffersonian type, favored the embargo and opposed the building of a navy.

Ford, P. L., ed. *Writings of Thomas Jefferson*, 10 vols., New York, 1892-99.

Ford, W. C., ed. *Writings of John Quincy Adams*, 7 vols., New York, 1912. Adams was senator from Massachusetts in 1807, and although a Federalist, supported Jefferson's embargo policy; his letters from St. Petersburg in 1811 and 1812 show keen insight into the relations of the belligerents towards each other, and of each to the United States.

Hamilton, S. M., ed. *Writings of James Monroe*, 7 vols., New York, 1897. Monroe figures prominently throughout the period; as minister to France, after the fall of Robespierre; as minister to England at the time of the Essex Decision; and as secretary of state at the time of the break with England.

Howe, John, Secret Reports of. *Amer. Hist. Review*, Vol. 17, 1 and 2 letters of John Howe to Sir George Prevost, Lieut. Gov. at Halifax, from Colonial Office Records, Public Record Office, London. Howe was a Boston Tory who lived in Halifax after the Revolution. He made two trips to New England in 1808 and 1809, sent by Prevost to find out the strength of the federal and democratic parties, extent of military preparations, etc.

Hunt, Gaillard, ed. *Writings of James Madison*, 9 vols., New York, 1900-1910.

Jefferson Papers. *Collections of Massachusetts Historical Society*, 7th Series, Vol. I, Boston, 1900 contains a few letters referring to embargo.

Johnston, H. P. *Correspondence and Published Papers of John Jay*, 1763, New York, 1890.

King, Chas. R., ed. *Life and Correspondence of Rufus King*, 6 vols., New York, 1896.

Lodge, H. C. *Life and Letters of Geoge Cabot*, Boston, 1878. Cabot saw the danger of the Federalists' getting the name of the British party. More moderate and clear sighted than Pickering, he tried to keep the latter from seeming to play Canning's game.

McMaster, J. B. *Life and Times of Stephen Girard*, 2 vols., Philadelphia, 1918. Contains extracts from many letters of Girard, who was one of the wealthiest merchants of the period, carrying on commerce with West Indies, Isle of France, Europe and Asia.

Meigs, Wm.   *The Life of John Caldwell Calhoun*, 2 vols., New York; able, complete, and impartial.

Morse, E. L. C. ed.   *Letters and Journals of Samuel F. B. Morse*, 2 vols, Boston, 1914. Morse's letters from England in 1811 and 1812, show the serious effect which non-intercourse with America was causing on business conditions in that country.

Pickering, O.   *Life of Timothy Pickering*, 4 vols., Boston, 1867-73, biassed in favor of Pickering, who was a leader of the New England Federalists strongly pro-British in sympathies. He accused Jefferson and his followers of devotion to Napoleon.

Quincy, Edmund.   *Life of Josiah Quincy*, Boston, 1867. Quincy was leader of the Federalists in the House, 1807-1812. He denied the right of the President to lay an embargo.

Randolph, T. J., ed.   *Writings of Thomas Jefferson*, 4 vols., Boston, 1830, Contains letters in regard to commerce with France, 1784-8 not found in Ford collection.

Rives, G. L   *Correspondence of Thomas Barclay*, New York, 1894, Barclay was a Revolutionary Tory, American born. He was consul general for Great Britain in New York, 1799-1812.

Story, W. W.   *Life and Letters of Joseph Story*, 2 vols, Boston, 1851. Story was a Republican member of Congress from Massachusetts who voted for the repeal of the embargo. Later as associate justice of the Supreme Court of the United States, he rendered many decisions upholding the law.

Todd, C. B.   *Life and Letters of Joel Barlow*, New York, 1886, gives Barlow's account of his fruitless journey to Vilna in 1811; does not attempt a careful study of his mission to France; unsatisfactory.

Turner, F. J., ed.   *Correspondence of French Ministers to the United States, 1791-1797. Annual Report of Amer. Hist. Assn.*, 1903, Vol. II contains all important letters of Genet, Fauchet and Adet for period, from official records in France.

Wheaton, H.   *Life of Wm. Pinkney*, Philadelphia, 1826. Pinkney was commissioner with Christopher Gore under Jay Treaty to determine losses of American merchants and negotiate with England for settlement; minister to England, 1807-11.

Correspondence of the British:

The Correspondence of the British political leaders of the period is largely occupied with parties and politics. There is almost no mention of relations with the United States. I have examined the following:

Fitzpatrick, W., ed.   *Historical Mss. Commission Report on Mss. of J. B. Fortescue*, preserved at Dropmore House, Vols. 7 and 9, contain correspondence of Earl of Grenville, 1801-1809.

Jackson, Lady, ed. *Letters of Sir George Jackson. The Bath Archives*, 2 vols., London, 1873, contains letters of Francis James Jackson, describing his cordial reception by the "respectability" from Baltimore to Boston, after his break with the government at Washington in 1809.

Pellew, G. *Life and Correspondence of Lord Sidmouth*, London, 1847. Sidmouth joined the ministry shortly before the death of Perceval in the spring of 1812, with the understanding that the repeal of the Orders in Council would be pushed.

Ross, Sir John, ed. *Memoirs and Correspondence of Admiral Saumerez*, London, 1838, contains references to movements of American vessels in the Baltic 1810-12.

Vane, Chas. E., ed. *Correspondence, dispatches and other papers of Viscount Castlereagh*, 12 vols, London, 1848-54.

Correspondence of Napoleon:

Correspondence de Napoleon 1er *publicé per ordre del 'Emperor Napoleon*, III, 32 vols, Paris, 1858-1870.

Lecestre, Leon, ed. *Letters inedités de Napoleon*, 2 vols., Paris, 1897, contains letters omitted from the official collection of the correspondence.

Tatischeff, S. *Alexander, 1er et Napoleon d'après leur correspondance inédite*, 1801-1812, Paris, 1891.

Contemporary Books and Pamphlets.

Atchison, N. *American Encroachments on British Rights*, London, 1808 holds that British North American colonies should be given greater encouragement in British markets; laments that navigation acts have been relaxed in this direction.

Carey, Matthew. *The Olive Branch or Faults on Both Sides, Federal and Democratic*, Philadelphia, 1815.

Chaptal, J. A. C. *De l'Industrie francoise*, 2 vols., Paris, 1819 shows the wonderful stimulus felt in all branches of French industry, as a result of Napoleon's system; its benefit however were not permanent.

Coxe, Tench. *View of the United States in 1794*, Philadelphia, 1794; contains statements relative to agriculture, manufactures and commerce of United States in 1791, which show Earl of Sheffield to have been a false prophet.

Goldsmith, L. *Exposition of the conduct of France toward America*, New York, 1810. Goldsmith was an Englishman long resident in Paris; he attempts to show that the agression of France toward Americans were more serious than those of Great Britain.

Morris, Gouverneur. *An answer to War in Disguise*, New York, 1805; holds American expansion of trade on outbreak of war in Europe, was not owing to England's generosity, but was strictly legal, according to law of nations.

Nolte, Vincent. *Fifty Years in Both Hemispheres or Reminiscences of the Life of a Former Merchant*, translated from the German, New York, 1854. Nolte had many adventures and enjoys telling a good story; some of his incidents are open to question.

Seybert, Adam. *Statistical Annals*, Philadelphia, 1818; based on official sources, broader in scope than Pitkin, but not so useful for purposes of this study.

Shaw, Samuel. *Journals of, with life of author by Josiah Quincy*, Boston, 1847. Shaw was supercargo on the first American vessel to visit China. Later he was made the first American consul to that country, by commission from the Continental Congress.

Sheffield, Earl, of, *Observations on the Commerce of the American States*, Philadelphia edition, 1783, argues that the newly liberated states must still purchase their manufactures from Great Britain and sell their products there. Urges no tender consideration from the new states. By 1791 this pamphlet had gone through six large editions; its arguments influenced the thinking of Englishmen in re economic position of the United States for more than a generation.

Idem. *Strictures on the Necessity of Inviolably Maintaining the Navigation and Colonial System of Great Britain*, London, 1804. Regards the relaxation of the navigation system admitting American ships to British West Indies after 1803 as dangerous to British interests.

Stephen, James. *War in Disguise or the Fraud of the Neutral Flags*, London, 1805, blames England for generosity toward neutrals, chiefly the United States; led to passage of Orders in Council of 1807.

Talleyrand, Perigord. *Memoir concerning the commercial relations of the United States with England* (translation London, 1806) shows why America's trans-Atlantic trade is destined to continue to be largely with England rather than with France.

Pitkin, Timothy. *Statistical View of Commerce of the United States of America, 1789–1835*. New Haven, 1833 (first edition, 1818) invaluable; based on official reports. Pitkin's statistics are presented more compactly and intelligibly than those in A. S. P. Commerce Vol. I. He was a member of Congress from Connecticut, 1811–12.

Anon. *Thoughts upon the Conduct of our Administration in Relation to both Great Britain and France by a Friend of Peace*, Boston, 1808; charges Jefferson with being pro-French and anti-English.

Newspapers and Magazines.

Philadelphia; *American Daily Advertiser.*

Dunlap and Claypoole, eds. after 1800, Z. Poulson. Good for domestic

and foreign news, quotations from other newspapers and private letters, ships' sailings and arrivals, advertisements of goods for sale.
Pennsylvania Packet.
New York Evening Post.
Boston-Columbian Centinel; violently Federalist.
Washington-National Intelligencer; reflects the views of the government during Jefferson and Madison's administrations.
Niles Register, Vol. I, Baltimore, Sept. 1811–1812.
Paris-Moniteur Universal; official organ of Napoleon's government, 1799–1815.
London Times, contains little of interest for the purposes of this study.

Secondary Writings:

Adams, Henry. *History of the United States during the Administrations of Jefferson and Madison*, New York, 1889–91, severe on American foreign policy during the period; the standard history based on original sources.

Adams, James Truslow. *New England in the Republic, 1776–1850*, Boston, 1926. Chapters 8–11 covers period; shows that New England declined relatively in importance in the Union after 1790. Gives a good account of struggle between Federalists and Republicans.

Allen, G. W. *Our Naval War with France*, Boston, 1909; contains a good brief account of the claims on foreign nations for damages during the whole period, and their settlement, especially the French spoliation claims.

Bassett, J. S. *The Federalist System.* (Amer. Nation Series), New York, 1906.

Bates, Wm. W. *American Navigation*, Boston, 1902; shows that the American navigation system was not a copy of the British; colonial regulation started almost as early as the British Acts; gives a good account of navigation laws passed by the colonies before the Revolution.

Baty, Thomas. *Britain and Sea Power*, London, 1911; points out that American government in 1861–1865 reversed its position in regard to effective blockade taken during Napoleonic wars.

Bayley and Jones. *History of Marine Society of Newburyport from Its Incorporation in 1772 to 1906*, Newburyport, 1906; a few incidents in lives of captains of the period are of interest.

Bemis, S. F. *The London Mission of Thomas Pinckney, 1792–96, Amer. Hist. Review*, Vol. 28, No. 2.

Idem. *The Jay Treaty.* A study in Commerce and Diplomacy, New York, 1923. Knights of Columbus Award. Has good account of American trade relations with Great Britain from 1783 to the time of the treaty, 1794.

Bond, B. W., Jr. *Monroe's Mission to France*, 1794–96. John Hopkins University Studies in History and Political Science, Vol. 25. Points out the real services accomplished by Monroe's mission.

Bridges, Geo. Wilson. *Annals of Jamaica*, 2 vols. London, 1828. Gives a few facts in regard to the effect of the Continental System and the British revenue system of Jamaica.

Cambridge Modern History, Vol. VIII. *French Revolution*, Cambridge, 1904; sheds no light on commerce of neutrals. Vol. IX, *Napoleon* (1906) Chapter 13 by J. Holland Rose on Continental System has little to say of American trade. Argues that pressure of the continental system was largely the cause of the war of liberation.

Channing, Edward. *History of the United States*, 6 vols., New York, 1905–1925. Vol. IV, *Federalists and Republicans*, 1917, covers the period; emphasizes effect of embargo in stimulating manufactures in New England.

Idem. *The Jeffersonian System* (Amer. Nation Series), New York, 1906.

Cleveland, W. S. *Voyages of a Merchant Navigator of the days that are past*, composed from the journals and letters of the late R. J. Cleveland, New York, 1886.

Consett, M. W. W. P. *The Triumph of Unarmed Forces*, 1914–18, London, 1923; opening chapter gives interesting contrast between conditions of contraband blockade and military operations in Napoleonic Wars and the World War.

Daniels, G. W. American Cotton Trade with Liverpool under the Embargo and Non-Intercourse Acts. *Amer. Hist. Review*, Vol. 21. Based on reports of a Liverpool cotton broker to Manchester cotton spinners.

Edwards, Bryan. *History, Civil and Commercial of the British West Indies*, 5th ed. London, 1819. Shows commercial relations between Jamaica and the United States, from colonial period onward. Holds that the cutting off of American trade after 1783 was the chief cause of Jamaica's decline.

Fogdoll, Soren, J. M. P. *Danish American Diplomacy*, 1776–1920. A monograph based on printed American sources and Danish official sources. Chapers 2 and 3 cover the period of the Danish seizures and the settlement of the claims growing out of them.

Fournier, August. *Napoleon I, a Biography*, 2 vols. tr. by Annie Elizabeth Adams, London, 1912; shows how France was expected to profit by continental system.

Galpin, W. F. *Grain Supply of England during Napoleonic Period*, Philadelphia, 1925. Holds that desire to check neutral carrying trade to the enemy was more potent cause for orders of November, 1807, than idea of combatting French decrees. Chapter 8 discusses Anglo-American grain trade, 1800–1813.

Idem. The American Grain Trade to the Spanish Peninsula, 1810-14, *Amer. Hist. Review*, Vol. 28, Oct. 1922; an interesting account of the American trade to supply the British commissary for more than a year after war had been declared.

Gray, E. *Wm. Gray of Salem*, Merchant, Boston, 1914. Gray was one of the wealthiest and most prominent merchants of the period. He favored the embargo.

Hazen, Charles Downer. *Contemporary American Opinion of the French Revolution*, Baltimore, 1897, the Johns Hopkins Press; a compact statement of the impressions of Jefferson, Gouverneur Morris and Monroe.

Heckscher, Eli F. *The Continental System*. An Economic Interpretation, Oxford, 1922. Pub. by Carnegie Foundation for International Peace. Division of Economics and History. Relies principally on printed sources. Traces movement to middle of 17th century; emphasizes specially the practical working out of the system of the economic life of France and the satellite and allied states; concludes that its results were ephemeral. Has a brief chapter of comparison with situation in World War.

Hill, C. S. *History of American Shipping*, New York, 1883.

Hoeckstra, Peter. *Thirty-seven Years of Holland American Relations*, Grand Rapids, 1916; shows how Holland was gradually brought within the French political and commercial orbit after 1806.

Hunt, Freeman. *Merchants Magazine*, Vol. 32 and 36, New York, 1855 and 1857; has excellent articles on the voyages of the Derbys, Perkins, Silsbee and other pioneers in the trade to the far East.

Jennings, W. W. *The American Embargo*, 1807-1809. University of Iowa Studies, Iowa City, 1921. A study based principally on newspaper sources; gives the effects of the embargo in Great Britain and the British West Indies.

Johnson, E. R. *Domestic and Foreign Commerce of the United States*, 2 vols. Washington Carnegie Institute, Pub. 1915. Devotes little space to the early period of our national history.

Levasseur, E. *Histoire des Classes Ouvrières et de L'Industrie en France de 1789 a 1870*, Paris, 1903, 2 vols. Shows effort made to substitute French for English goods in European markets.

Idem. *Histoire du Commerce de La France*, 2 vols, Paris, 1912. Books 1 and 2 of Vol. II cover period. Of continental system declares it economically a monstrosity, as well as politically fatal.

Lingelbach, W. E. England and Neutral Trade. In *Military Historian and Economist*, Vol. II, No. 2, April, 1917, treats subject broadly from Middle Ages to World War; holds that Essex Decision cannot be considered unjust.

Idem. Saxon-American Relations. *Amer. Hist. Review*, Vol. 17, contains correspondence showing effort of Grand Duchy of Saxony to foster trade relations with United States after 1783.

Lindsay, W. S. *History of Merchant Shipping and Ancient Commerce*, 4 vols., London, 1874–76; gives a good account of commercial relations of Great Britain and United States at the close of the Revolution.

Mahan, A. T. *The Influence of Sea Power upon the French Revolution and Empire*, 1793–1812, Boston, 1894. Ignoring practical difficulties in the way, Mahon holds that the United States should have offered armed resistance earlier.

Idem. *Sea Power in Its Relation to the War of 1812*, 2 vols, Boston, 1905.

McLaughlin, A. C. *Confederation and Constitution*. (Amer. Nation Series), New York, 1905.

McMaster, J. B. *History of the United States*, 8 vols., New York, 1883–1913; gives interesting details on the embargo period.

McPherson, D. *Annals of Commerce*, London, 1805.

Melvin, F. E. *Napoleon's Navigation System*. A study of trade control during the Continental Blockade, New York, 1919. An exhaustive study; shows how the system of exclusion set up by the Berlin Decree was abandoned in favor of the Nouveau Systemè of licenses after July, 1810. Holds that the vigor of the American stand brought both belligerents to terms, although too late to prevent war. Excellent bibliography.

Morison, S. E. *Maritime History of Massachusetts*, Boston, 1922; gives good accounts of the early voyages to the far East, and the northwestern coast of America; excellent bibliography.

Nussbaum, F. L. American Tobacco and French Politics, 1783–89. *Political Science Quarterly*, Vol. XL, No. 4, December 1925; shows how the monopoly of the tobacco trade by the Farmers General in France prevented normal growth of trade between the two countries during the period.

Paine, Ralph. *Ships and Sailor of Old Salem*, New York, 1910, gives details of early voyages from that port.

Peabody, R. E. *Merchant Venturers of Old Salem*, Boston, 1910, gives particulars of the trade of the Derbys to the Orient.

Rose, H. Holland, *Life of Napoleon*, 2 vols, London, 1902, Vol. I based in part on new materials in British Official Records. Vol. II contains a chapter on Continental System; holds that the surrender of carrying trade to neutrals would have meant political extinction for England.

Idem. *Napoleonic Studies*, London, 1806; contains a chapter on Napoleon and England; holds that only from 1803 to 1812 could Britain have survived the application of the Continental System, because only at that period did the relation of industry and agriculture to her population render her at once necessary to Europe and self sufficing at home.

Sears, L. M. *Jefferson and the Embargo, Duke Univ. Publications*, Durham, N. C., 1927. An excellent monograph based largely on the Jefferson Papers. Analyzes effect of embargo in various parts of United States, in England and France. Argues that it had a serious effect on southern agriculture.

Smith, J. Russell, *The Ocean Carrier*, New York, 1908.

Sorel, Albert. *L'Europe et la Revolution Francaise*, 7 vols., Paris, 1889–1904. Part VII Blocus Continental; Le Grand Empire covers the period. Brilliant, penetrating; pronounces continental system "an immense economic and political paradox" bound in time to destroy itself.

Updyke, Frank A. *Diplomacy of the War of 1812. Albert Shaw Lecturers on Diplomatic History, 1914.* Baltimore, Johns Hopkins Press, 1915; first two chapters give a resume of the diplomatic sparring in regard to impressment and neutral trade, 1792–1812; based largely on American State Papers, Foreign Affairs.

Van Holst, H. *Constitutional and Political History of the United States*, translated by J. Lalor and A. B. Mason, Chicago, 1889.

Ward, A. and Gooch, G. P., eds. *Cambridge History of British Foreign Policy*, 1783–1919, 3 vols. Cambridge University Press, 1922–23. Vol. I, Chapters 1 and 3 cover period. Chap. 3, Contest with Napoleon by J. Holland Rose suggest that the Berlin Decree was intended by Napoleon to arouse Great Britain to reprisals and so stir up neutrals against her.

Weeden, W. B. *Economic and Social History of New England*, 2 vols., Boston, 1894, Vol. II, Chapters 22 and 23 treat of Confederation period, 1783–1789.

Wharton F. *Digest of International Law of United States*, 3 vols. Washington, Gov't. Printing Office, 1886.

Wheaton, Henry. *History of Law of Nations in Europe and America*, New York, 1845. Takes up questions of maritime law of nations during the wars of the French Revolution.

INDEX

A

Abemma, General, 112
Adams, John, 44
Adams, Henry, 204, 211, 242
Adams, John Quincy, 168, 169, 188, 218, 223, 224, 244
Adelaide, ship, 192
Admiralty Courts, vice, 32, 36, 49, 51, 59, 115
  High Court, in London, 53, 54, 55, 76, 78, 81
Africa, 20
Alexander I of Russia, 217, 218, 220, 222
Alexandria, Va., 227
Allan, John, 153, 183, 227
Ambition, ship, 88
America (U. S.), 16, 20
America, ship, 64
Amiable Matilda, ship, 120
Amiens, peace of, 47, 51
Amity, ship, 143
Amsterdam, 68, 85, 101, 125
Amelia Island, 176
Anna, ship, 162
Andrew, ship, 176
Angerona, ship, 224
Ant, schooner, 143
Antwerp, 67, 71, 113
Appleton, Thomas, 115, 133, 137
Archangel, 166, 217, 219, 222
Arabia, 17
Armed Neutrality, 35
Armstrong, Samuel, 65, 93, 96, 98, 102, 107, 113, 114, 130, 144, 145, 179, 184, 186, 188
Astraea, 21
Aux Cayes, 32, 43

B

Backer, T. H., 100, 154
Baltic, 142, 165, 166, 188, 195, 220
Baltimore, 61, 137, 151
Barbadoes, 230, 231
Barlow, Joel, 204, 207, 209, 210, 225
Barracoa, 61
Bassano, 198, 207, 209, 210
Batavia, 85
Baudin, 145
Bavaria, 188, 224
Bayonne, 213
Belts of Baltic, 165, 193, 224

Bemis, Samuel, 34
Benares, 67
Benevento, Count of, see Talleyrand
Bengal goods, 68
Bentley, Wm., 241
Berbice, 43
Bernon, ship, 48
Betsy, brig, 63
Betsy, schooner, 45
Bigelow, Abijah, 203
Blockade of Cadiz, 50, 55
  Curaçao, Elbe and Weser, 57, Elbe, 107; Elbe to Brest (Fox Blockade), 58, 90, 91, 238
  Fécamp to Ostende, 57
  Guadeloupe and Martinique, 51; Havre, 54; Holland, 50
Bonaparte, Louis, King of Holland, 99, 100
Bordeaux, 38, 68, 144, 173, 195, 213
Bordeaux Packet ship, 95
Boston, 162, 179, 190, 212, 236
Bourbon, Isle of, 28, 233
Bourrienne, 104, 105, 106
Bourne, Sylvanus, 101, 102
Brandy, 20, 23
Breadstuffs, 21
Bremen, 23, 57, 111–112, 158, 165
Brody, 224
Brougham, Henry, 214, 215
Brune, Marshell, 106
Bynkershock, 32

C

Cabot, George, 243
Cadiz, 170, 228
Cadore, 180
  letter of August 5, 1810, 184, 185, 211
Caicos Passage, 63
Calcutta, 21, 68
Calhoun, John C., 236, 239
Camelia, ship, 174
Campeachy, 68, 232
Campenhausen, 219
Canada, 239
Canning, George, 146, 147
Cape Francois (Haiti), 42
Cape of Good Hope, 20, 21
Carlskrona, 226
Caribbean, 44
Carrying trade, 67, 91

Castlereagh, Viscount, 237
Catherine, brig, 192
Cattegat, 225
Certificates of Origin, 66, 107, 108, 110, 116, 161
Champagny, 97, 98, 113, 130, 144
Champlin and Robinson, 71
Charleston, 241
Charleston Packet, ship, 128
Cheeves, Langdon, 234
China, 17, 133
Chinaware, 21, 23
Christiansand, 166
Cincinnatus, ship, 143
Circuit Court, 138
Claims, French Spoliation, 47
Clay, Henry, 233, 234, 237, 244
Cleveland, Richard, 156, 157
Cocoa, 73, 132, 195
Coasting trade, 135
Coffee, 20, 65, 73, 75, 132, 161, 192
Coke, 118
Collingwood, Admiral, 55
Colonial goods, 31, 58, 123, 132, 205, 208
Commissary, British in Spain, 227, 229
  in West Indies, 231
Commerce, 234
Commerce, ship, 43
Commission (under Jay Treaty), 36–38, 49
Confederation, Articles of, 18
Congress, 62, 63, 87, 134, 136, 148, 149, 182, 212, 232, 240, 242
Connecticut, ship, 64
Constitution, 18
Continental Congress, 27
Continental System, 188, 194, 196
Cope and Thomas, 68
Copenhagan, 71, 163
Convention (of 1793 in France), 39
Cotton, 20, 122, 133, 141, 151, 155, 156, 159, 161, 168, 222
Council of Prizes, 94, 114, 130, 156
Cremer, ship, 190
Crowninshield, Benjamin, 20
Cronstadt, 190, 217, 222
Culaincourt, 221
Curaçao, 23, 25, 45, 52

D

Danzig, 110, 234
DeBlome, Baron, 169
Declaration of War (1812), 238, 239
Decree, of Bayonne, 143, 145, 158;
  of Berlin, 46, 56, 92, 93, 94, 95, 99;
  enforcement in Hamburg, 103–111;
  in Bremen, 111–112; 134, 144, 184, 196, 209, 210; of Fontainebleau, 205; of Holland, 99, 101, 123; of Milan, 46, 110, 120, 127, 184, 196, 209, 210; of Rambouillet, 175, 178, 180; repealing decrees of Berlin and Milan, 210, 211; Trianon, 185
Decrès, 94
Degas, 115
De laCroix, 45

Demerara, 43
Denmark, 22, 108, 162, 169
Derby, Elias Haskett, 17
Derby, Elias Haskett, Jr., 18
Dessalines, 64
Directory, 42, 43, 46
District Court of New York, 138
Dolly, ship, 210
Duck, 20
Duckworth, Admiral, 52
Dumonceau, 111
Dyewoods, 223

E

Eagle, ship, decision, 83, 87
Earthenware, 22
East Indies, 28
Eckenforde, 94
Elbe, 104, 161
Eliza, ship, (1) 45; (2) 143; (3) 172
Ellis, Charles, 151, 153
Ellis and Allan, 100, 141, 172, 176
Elsinore, 166, 225
Embargo, in American ports, March, 1794, 36; December, 1807, 134, 135, 145, 147; April, 1812, 235, 236
Emmott, James, 201
Enemy goods, 30, 37
England, 16, 22, 69, 149
Enoch, ship, decision, 81
Enterprise, 20, 21
Eppes, John W., 202
Eppes Bill, 202, 203, 210, 213, 215
Erskine, 92, 149
Erskine, Lord, 118
Essequibo, 43
Essex Decision, 55, 79, 81, 83, 132
Esterbrook, David, 19, 228
Eudel, 107
Experiment, sloop, 19
Exports, from U. S., 89, 133, 233, 235
Express, ship, 235
Eyder, 159

F

Fabrics, 22
Fair American, ship, 115
Fame, ship, 86
Ferrand, General, 61, 64
Fauchet, 39
Favourite, brig, 59
Fayal, 176
Federalists, 215, 218, 239, 240, 243
Fenwick, 38
Fish, salt, 21, 22
Fitz William, brig, 95
Flour, 139, 152, 171, 226, 228, 231
Forbes, John, 57, 58, 103, 104, 107, 109, 158–159, 162, 164, 226
Foster, Augustus, 204, 205, 216, 234
Force law, for embargo, 148
Ft. Tameny, ship, 174
Fox, Charles James, 90, 238
France, 16, 22, 27, 28, 38
France, decrees of, 28, 39, 41, 46, 66
Frederick William of Prussia, 57
Franklin, ship, 179
Friendship, ship, 196
Fruits, 23

G

Gadsden, ship, 50
Gallatin, Albert, 136, 186
Galicia, 224
Gallipoli, 115
Gardiner, 200
General Court of Mass., 148
Genet, 28
George Washington, brig, 98
Gerry, Elbridge, 46
Gibbs and Channing, 43, 70
Gibraltar, 119, 121
Gilmore and Sons, 228
Girard, Stephen, 27, 32, 49, 70, 168, 225
Glückstadt, 104, 161
Goatskins, 20
Gogol, 100, 101
Good Friends, ship, 168
Gothenburg, 168, 190, 195, 220
Governor Gilman, ship, 160
Grace, ship, 131
Grace Ann Green, ship, 196, 206
Grain, 28
Grand Turk, ship, 19
Grant, Sir William, 81, 83
Gray, William, 20
Great Britain, 22, 31, 89, 214, 236
Great Britain Orders of November 6, 1793, 31, 36; January 18, 1794, 31, 34, 36; April, 1795, 37; January, 1798, 49; January, 1807, 114; November, 1807, 110, 115, 118–127, 146, 151, 184, 212, 214, 216, 233, 238, 240, 244; opening ports of West Indies, 230
Grenville, Lord, 70
Grotius, 38
Guadeloupe, 23, 32, 42, 62, 94
Gum arabic, 20
Gurieff, 224

H

Haiti, 23, 231, see also Santo Domingo
Hale, Matthew, 118
Hamburg, 16, 23, 57, 58, 68, 103–111, 158, 161, 163
Hamilton, Alexander, 18
Hamlet, ship, 123
Hammond, George, 35
Hardware, 153
Hart, Robert, 151, 152
Harriet, ship, 55
Harris, Levett, 219, 224
Harrowby, Lord, 57
Havana, 25, 63, 67, 177, 230
Havre, 54
Hawkesbury, Lord, 78
Helvetius, ship, 68, 225
Hemp, 224
Hero, ship, 119, 120
Hesper, ship, 234
Hibernia, ship, 94
Hicks, Jenkins and Co., 95
Hispaniola, See Haiti
Holland, 20, 22, 23, 59, 66
Honor, ship, 44
Holstein, 161, 218
Hood, Commodore, 51
Hope and Co. 168
Hopewell, ship, 61
Horizon, ship decision, 97, 98
Hovering of British cruisers, 238
Husum, 165, 194

I

Immanuel, ship, 76
Imports to U. S., 81, 89, 126, 133
Impressment, of seamen, 36, 238
India, 17, 18, 20
Indigo, 20, 223
Indostan, ship, 64
Industry, ship, 121
Insurance, 53, 61, 94, 120, 134, 161, 172, 175, 183, 190

Ironmongery, 22
Isaacson, Peter, 167
Isle of France, 20, 28, 55, 68, 233
Italy, 68

J

Jackson, George, 153
Jahde, 161
Jamaica, 23, 230
James, ship, (1) 44; (2) 234
James Wells, ship, 136
Jane, brig, 63
Java, 63
Jay, John, 36
 treaty, 36, 45, 47
Jefferson, Thomas, 35, 36, 62, 115, 134, 229, 234
Jeremie, 43
Joanna, brig, 61; ship, 137
John Bulkley, ship, 85
Joy, George, 163
Julian, brig, 234
Julius, ship, 107, 109
Jumel and Desobrey, 154, 160, 172, 173, 230

K

Kellerman, Marshall, 106
Kentucky, 242
Kiel, 161, 165, 194
King, Rufus, 78
Köingsburg, 110, 192

L

Lady Walterdorf, brig, 45
La Guaira, 59, 137
Lapwing, brig, 53
L'Archaye, 43
Leather goods, 22
Lee, William, 95, 131, 142, 143, 179
Leeward Islands, 25, 230
Leghorn, 14, 94, 115, 119, 137
Leogane, 42
Leopard, brigantine, 77
Le Roy, ship, 111
Le Roy Bayard and McEwers, 227
Les Cayes, 61
Lewis and Lee, 231
Licenses, of Great Britain, 117, 125, 193, 229; of France, See permits
Liverpool, 146, 151, 215
Lisbon, 171, 227, 228, 229
Little Cornelia, ship, 86
Lloyds, 172
Logwood, 192, 232
London, 146

Louis Bonaparte, King of Holland, 154, 155
Louisiana, brig, 59
Lucy, ship, 109
Lumber, 21

M

Macon, Nathaniel, 182
Macon Bill, 182, 183, 199
Madeira, 17, 68, 176
Madison, James, 64, 76, 92, 113, 144, 150, 166, 186, 204, 212, 235, 237
Mahogany, 68
Manufactures, of America, 237
Maret, 130
Maria, ship, decision, 81
Mariner, schooner, 52
Marshall, John, 46, 138
Marseilles, 27
Martinique, 42, 43, 86
Mary, ship, (1) 402; (2) 197
Massa, 196
Massachusetts, 242
Matchless, ship, 192
Mauritius, 17
May and Eliza, schooner, 51
McMaster, John Bach, 134, 135
Meade, R. W., 171
Mecklenburg, 188
Mediterranean, 94, 115, 119, 120
Mercury, ship, decision, 70
Meridian, ship, 192
Merry, Anthony, 52
Minturn and Champlin, 226
Missouri, ship, 150
Mitchill, Samuel, 234
Mocha, 18, 20, 67
Moniteur, 221
Monroe, James, 39, 41, 45, 57, 58, 79, 81, 90, 115, 204, 238
Montalivet, 181
More, Clement, 88
Mortier, Marshall, 103
Morris, Gouverneur, 38
Morris, Robert, 17
Mosquito, Coast, 63
Mulgrave, Lord, 81, 90

N

Nankeens, 21, 23
Napoleon, 58, 66, 92, 93, 96, 97, 105, 108, 113, 114, 145, 164, 177, 184, 187, 200, 220, 237
Naples, 95
National Convention, 28, 29, 30
Naval stores, 139, 141

Neptune, ship, (1) 37; (2) 122
brig, 61
Neutrals, 29, 30, 77, 114, 116, 127, 147, 209
New England, 148
New Orleans, 52, 135, 228
New Orleans Packet, ship, 195, 199, 206
Newport, 70, 71
New Providence, 23
New York (City), 59, 61, 66, 67, 135, 155, 160, 226, 236, 241
New York (State), 242
Nicholl, John, Advocate General, 78
Non-importation Act, 90, 134
Non-intercourse with France, 1798, 72
Non-intercourse law, March, 1909, 149, 156, 182
Northern Liberties, ship, 174
Norway, 168, 169
Nouveau Système, 187, 188
Nymph, ship, 115

O

Oporto, 227
Orizimbo, 19, 228

P

Palinurus, ship, 85
Parker, Daniel, 17
Parliament, 118, 146, 214, 216
Patterson, George, 49
Peace and Plenty, ship, 129
Pearl ash, 21, 22
Peggy, schooner, 61
Pennsylvania, 242
Pepper, 20, 74, 75
Peries, Joseph, 59
Permits, of France, 180, 181, 185, 198
Perry, John, 173
Perseverance, ship,
Petitions, American, 34, 87, 88, 169, 236
Petty, Lord Henry, 118
Philadelphia, 59, 85, 135, 194
Philadelphia Packet, 224
Phillimore, Joseph, 214
Pichon, 61
Pickering, Timothy, 43, 44, 45, 147
Pinckney, Charles Coteworth, 46
Pinckney, Thomas, 35, 36, 70
Pinkney, William, 88, 115, 146, 186, 196, 197
Pitcairn, Joseph, 163, 225
Platte, River, 68

Plutarch, 38
Point à Pitre, Guadeloupe, 59
Polly, ship, (1) 32; (2) 76; (3) 197
Pomerania, 208
Popham, Sir Home, 53
Port au Prince, 43
Portugal, 22, 23
Potash, 21, 22, 154
Privateers, 94, 165, 167, 191
Privy Council, 15
Proclamation of Madison, November, 1810, 150, 171, 182, 196, 199
Proctor, William, 192
Prosper, schooner, 175
Prussia, 16
Purviance, John, 130

Q

Queheille, Pedro, 173
Quincy, Josiah, 201, 203, 235, 243

R

Randolph, John, 89, 200, 241
Raisins, 20
Regnier, Grand Judge, 96, 113
Resort, ship, 155
Respect, ship, 86
Rhode Island, 242
Rice, 21, 22
Richmond, Va., 227
Ridgeway, 95, 103
Riga, 192, 217, 222
Rockwell, ship, 61
Rolla, ship, 54
Romanzoff, 217, 222
Romulus, ship, 166, 176
Rose, George, 140
Rostock, 110, 161, 193, 194
Rule of 1756, 30, 33, 34, 37, 38, 69, 75, 77, 91, 125
Russell, Jonathan, 195, 196, 198, 206, 209, 217, 235
Russia, 133, 168, 217, 241

S

Saabye, 167, 168
Salem, 17, 20, 192, 241
Sallie, Brig, 32, 61
Sally, brig, 33, 34; ship, (1) 125; (2) 129; (3) 141
Samatan, 27
Sampson, ship, 6
Santo Domingo, 32, 42, 52
Santhonax, 42
Satins, 21

Saumerez, Sir James, 165, 193, 220
Savannah, 24
Schleswig, 161
Scott, Sir William, 33, 54, 76, 212
Sea letter, 162
Sea Nymph, ship, 43
Seizures by British, 32, 34, 75
Senegal, 28
Serrurier, 198, 202, 204, 205
Sheffield, Lord, 26
Shepherdess, ship (1) 54; (2) 125
Short Staple, ship, 37
Siam, 17
Sienen, von, 106
Silks, 23
Skiddy, J., 160
Skipwith, Fulwer, 41, 49
Smith, Robert, 149, 162
Spain, 22, 23, 25, 170, 226
St. Bartholomew, 136
St. Croix, 23, 25, 52, 67
St. Eustatius, 21, 23, 25
St. Jago, 61
St. Kitts, 232
St. Lucia, 43
St. Marks, 43
St. Sebastian, 172
St. Thomas, 25, 231
Stephen, James, 70, 79
Stettin, 110
Story, Joseph, 139
Sugar, 20, 23, 73, 75, 132, 161, 192, 221, 222
Sukey and Polly, ship, 52
Sumatra, 68
Supreme Court, 136, 138
Sweden, 188, 190, 194, 241
Swift, John, 192
Switzerland, 224
Sylt, 165

T

Talleyrand, Count of Benevento, 94
Tariff, of Trianon, 187, 207; of Russia, 222
Tario, ship, 129
Taylor, William, 99, 141, 152, 154
Teas, 23, 162
Telegraph, ship, 210
Three Apprentices, ship, 129
Tobacco, 21, 139, 141
Tobago, 43, 64
Tonningen, 57, 111, 159, 161, 169
Tortola, 230
Treaty, England and European Powers, 30; U. S. and England, 1783 (Versailles Treaty), 36; 1795 (Jay Treaty), 36, 45; U. S. and France, 1778, 29; 1801 (Morfontaine), 47, 112, 113; Tilsit, 59, 100, 217
Trinidad, 230, 232
Trumbull, Jonathan, 149
Tucker, Gideon, 192
Turks' Island Passage, 52
Turpentine, 154
Turreau, 64
Two Betsys, ship, 234
Two Marys, ship, 129

U

United Netherlands, see Holland
Union, ship, (1) 123; (2) 194

V

Van Ness, Justice, 120
Van Sander, 162
Varel, 161
Vattel, 38
Vera Cruz, 232
Vermont, 242
Victory, ship, 98
Vienna, 224
Voltaire, 19

W

Waln, William, 85
Walker, ship, 95
Washington, ship, 234
Watches, 23
Wagram, 164
Wellesley, Sir Arthur, 227
Wellesley, Richard Colley, Marquis, 186, 187, 197
Weser, 161
West Indies, 15, 18, 23, 31, 42, 68, 229
Whale Oil, 21
Wheat, 140, 141, 152
Wheaton, 200
Wichelhausen, 111
Willaumez, Admiral, 65
William, ship, decision, 81
William King, ship, 137
William Wilson, ship, 191
Windward Islands, 25, 230
Wine, 20, 22, 23
Wirgman, Peter, 191
Wismar, 110, 161, 194
Wood products, 22
Woolens, 152

Y

Young Eagle, ship, 67

Z

Zulema, ship, 95

Library of
Early American Business And Industry

I. John Leander Bishop, A HISTORY OF AMERICAN MANUFACTURES FROM 1608 TO 1860, with an introduction by Louis M. Hacker, 3 volumes.

II. Albert S. Bolles, THE INDUSTRIAL HISTORY OF THE UNITED STATES, Copious Illustrations, with an introduction by Louis M. Hacker.

III. Freeman Hunt, LIVES OF AMERICAN MERCHANTS, with an introduction by Louis M. Hacker, 2 volumes.

IV. George S. White, MEMOIR OF SAMUEL SLATER, Illustrated with engraving, woodcuts and folding diagram.

V. Rolla M. Tryon, HOUSEHOLD MANUFACTURES IN THE UNITED STATES, 1640-1860. A study in Industrial History.

VI. J. D. B. DeBow, THE INDUSTRIAL RESOURCES, etc. of the Southern and Western States, 3 volumes.

VII. TENCH COXE, A VIEW OF THE UNITED STATES OF AMERICA, with folding tables.

VIII. Charles F. Adams, Jr., and Henry Adams, CHAPTERS OF ERIE and other Essays.

IX. Stuart Daggett, RAILROAD REORGANIZATION.

X. Stuart Daggett, HISTORY OF THE SOUTHERN PACIFIC.

XI. Nelson Trottman, HISTORY OF THE UNION PACIFIC, a financial and economic survey.

XII. Howard D. Dozier, A HISTORY OF THE ATLANTIC COAST LINE RAILROAD.

XIII.   Timothy Pitkin, A STATISTICAL VIEW OF THE COM-
        MERCE OF THE UNITED STATES OF AMERICA.

XIV.   Katherine Coman, ECONOMIC BEGINNINGS OF THE
        FAR WEST, 2 volumes.

XV.   William R. Bagnall, THE TEXTILE INDUSTRIES OF
        THE UNITED STATES.

XVI.   Witt Bowden, THE INDUSTRIAL HISTORY OF THE
        UNITED STATES.

XVII.   Melvin T. Copeland, THE COTTON MANUFACTURING
        INDUSTRY OF THE UNITED STATES.

XVIII. Blanche E. Hazard, THE ORGANIZATION OF THE BOOT
        AND SHOE INDUSTRY IN MASSACHUSETTS BE-
        FORE 1875.

XIX.   Albert Gallatin, REPORT OF THE SECRETARY OF THE
        TREASURY ON THE SUBJECT OF ROADS AND
        CANALS, 1807.

XX.   Henry S. Tanner, A DESCRIPTION OF THE CANALS
        AND RAILROADS OF THE UNITED STATES.

XXI.   J. Warren Stehman, THE FINANCIAL HISTORY OF
        THE AMERICAN TELEPHONE AND TELEGRAPH
        COMPANY.

XXII.   Kathleen Bruce, VIRGINIA IRON MANUFACTURE IN
        THE SLAVE ERA.

XXIII. Abraham Gesner, A PRACTICAL TREATISE ON COAL,
        PETROLEUM AND OTHER DISTILLED OILS, revised
        and enlarged by George W. Gesner.

XXIV.   Alexander Hamilton, INDUSTRIAL AND COMMERCIAL
        CORRESPONDENCE OF ALEXANDER HAMILTON
        ANTICIPATING HIS REPORT ON MANUFACTURES,
        edited by Arthur H. Cole. With a Preface by Prof. Edwin
        F. Gay.

XXV.   Lewis Henry Haney, A CONGRESSIONAL HISTORY OF RAILWAYS IN THE UNITED STATES, 2 volumes in one.

XXVI.   Adam Seybert, STATISTICAL ANNALS. Quarto.

XXVII.   Samuel Batchelder, INTRODUCTION AND EARLY PROGRESS OF THE COTTON MANUFACTURE IN THE UNITED STATES.

XXVIII.   Tench Coxe, A STATEMENT OF THE ARTS AND MANUFACTURES OF THE UNITED STATES OF AMERICA FOR THE YEAR 1810.

XXIX.   (Louis McLane), DOCUMENTS RELATIVE TO THE MANUFACTURES IN THE UNITED STATES (Executive Document No. 308, 1st Session, 22nd Congress.

XXX.   B. F. French, THE HISTORY OF THE RISE AND PROGRESS OF THE IRON TRADE OF THE UNITED STATES.

XXXI.   Frederick L. Hoffman, HISTORY OF THE PRUDENTIAL INSURANCE COMPANY OF AMERICA, 1875-1900.

XXXII.   Charles B. Kuhlman, DEVELOPMENT OF THE FLOUR MILLING INDUSTRY IN THE UNITED STATES.

XXXIII.   James Montgomery, A PRACTICAL DETAIL OF THE COTTON MANUFACTURE OF THE UNITED STATES OF AMERICA.

XXXIV.   Henry Varnum Poor, HISTORY OF THE RAILROADS AND CANALS OF THE UNITED STATES.

XXXV.   Henry Kirke White, HISTORY OF THE UNION PACIFIC RAILWAY.

XXXVI.   Frank B. Copley, FREDERICK W. TAYLOR, FATHER OF SCIENTIFIC MANAGEMENT, 2 volumes.

XXXVII.   Edward Winslow Martin, HISTORY OF THE GRANGE MOVEMENT: or, The Farmer's War Against Monopolies.

XXXVIII. J. T. Henry, THE EARLY AND LATER HISTORY OF PETROLEUM.

XXXIX. Arthur Cecil Bining, PENNSYLVANIA IRON MANUFACTURE IN THE EIGHTEENTH CENTURY.

XL.   Thomas F. DeVoe, THE MARKET BOOK.

XLI.   Obed Macy THE HISTORY OF NANTUCKET.